Khmer Sculpture
and the Angkor Civilization

Khmer Sculpture

and the Angkor Civilization

Madeleine Giteau

Harry N. Abrams, Inc.,
Publishers, New York

Translated by Diana Imber
Photographs by Hans Hinz

Library of Congress Catalog Card Number: 66-10991

Harry N. Abrams, Incorporated, New York
Printed in Switzerland. Bound in the Netherlands

TABLE OF CONTENTS

LIST OF PLATES

COLOUR PLATES

BLACK-AND-WHITE PLATES

INTRODUCTION

Pl. 1 Head of a woman in limestone mortar. Pagoda of Kom Nur, Angkor Borei (Ta Keo). National Museum of Phnom-Penh. Height: 24 cm. 6th / 7th century.

The early sculptors of Cambodia made use of stone, bronze and wood – the raw materials of their country – and from these fashioned idealized heads, poignantly realistic portraits, majestic and impassive divinities, and benign, smiling gods. Embroidering and embellishing their legends into a complex mythology, they could yet fit them easily into the simple framework of daily life. These incomparable artists expressed the bond between the human and the divine in stone. Cambodia's calm skies, her swift-rising storms and exuberant forests, generating vitality, nurtured the Khmer artists. Gentle, peaceful men, they were nevertheless easily stirred to fierce passion and deep emotion. The art of the Khmer – subtle, gay and measured – is a reflection of every aspect of life, and a true image of the country and its people. Moreover, of all the arts of the Far East few are as readily understood by the western mind. Its profound beauty can be easily appreciated without previous knowledge of the country's history. The universal value of an art at once so moderate, restrained, and so harmoniously balanced is unquestioned.

THE RELIGIOUS BACKGROUND

Khmer art spread beyond the limits of the Angkor Empire, from south of Laos to the ancient Cham kingdom and as far as the river Menam; but the earliest pre-Angkor masterpieces date back to the sixth century A. D., three centuries before the foundation of Angkor. Nor was art simply abandoned after the great flowering at Angkor, as is often thought, for the sixteenth and seventeenth centuries still produced works of great beauty. Khmer art has kept its religious character throughout its long years of evolution because the artists, in their buildings, bas-reliefs, statues and bronzes, were paying tribute to their gods or divine princes. Buddhism and Hinduism, the two great religions of India, which reached Cambodia soon after the beginning of the Christian era are the dominant influences and few traces remain of any earlier religious beliefs, although these undoubtedly survived among the people. Khmer art was preeminently aristocratic, dedicated to the service of the Indian religions which were sustained by the kings and high officials, who were the patrons of the religious foundations.

Buddhism and Hinduism had been introduced by Indian travellers seeking fortune or refuge in South East Asia, and Brahman priests, who alone were capable of celebrating the rites, were not slow to follow. The Brahmans were very powerful; counsellors, spiritual advisers to the kings, guardians and tutors of the young princes in close contact with the royal family, they encouraged art, and some of the finest works resulted from their patronage. Until the end of the twelfth century temples were nearly all Hindu; either small, simple, village chapels or immense buildings containing temples with many sanctuaries enclosing the Holy of Holies, where the divine image could be dimly perceived in the shadows. The god was usually Śiva, sometimes Viṣṇu. This supreme being was accompanied by lesser deities enshrined and venerated in the corners of the temple. Within the sanctuary Śiva resided in his phallic symbol, the *linga*, which was usually preferred to an anthropomorphic likeness. Whether it is worshipped as Śiva, the propitiator, Hara, the god who inspires, Ugra, the violent, Śambhu, the peacemaker, or the very ancient Rudra, god of terror, it is always Iśvara, god of the sanctuary, benign guardian of his flock. In Cambodia little is made of the fearsome aspect. When Śiva is pictured as king of the dance it is in a hieratic, harmonious choreography with none of the frenzy presaging world annihilation. They loved to fashion him in an idyllic pose, seated on the bull, Nandin, embracing his wife, Umā, a gentle reassuring image which was repeated again and again.

Legends of Śiva were the inspiration for many of the bas-reliefs, but the artists more often found subjects for their decorations in the stirring tales of Viṣṇu. Epic poems and popular belief have woven a rich fabric of the Viṣṇu legends. Sunk in cosmic sleep he creates a new world, or appears on earth to support and succour with his flail all those in danger. Wearing the aspect of an animal-deity, he defeats the intrigues of the *asuras;* incarnate hero of myth, he is the witness of the tribal warfare which formerly racked the Indian kingdoms; reared by shepherds, he becomes Krishna, whose deeds are recounted in the long poem, *Mahābhārata*. In the form of a simple mortal magnified to cosmic proportions, he conquers the universe to become the Universal Ruler, an ideal which earthly kings also strove to attain. He is called by many names: Bhagavant, the blessed; Hari, the wild; Acyuta, the constant; but to his own disciples he is the quintessence of the divine and to this extent Hinduism is monotheistic. Viṣṇu and Śiva have sometimes even been combined to make a conglomerate portrait of Harihara. The god is not simply a divine principle; he descends also to earth and it is he who governs the mind of the ruler.

Royal temples were dedicated to the divinity residing in the sanctuary idol and partly incarnate in the king. Thus every ruler had to raise his own temple where he was still worshipped after reunion in death with the god whose incarnation he had been. Princes and officials, too, wanted to make sure of survival by union with a god, so sanctuaries and idols multiplied and a whole world of statues arose beneath the chisels of the sculptors. The developing spirit of Khmer art was a response to such personal cults. For a long period the idol had been an idealized and impersonal representation, but gradually, as art became more realistic, the principle was embodied in a man-deity. This apotheosis was probably only accessible to a small number of the privileged and it is likely that the great mass of simple people was only admitted to the temple to contemplate and adore the pictured mythology of the gods. The lintel and pediment at the entrance would be sparsely decorated, but the legendary epics gradually increased in richness, filling the walls of the galleries so as to excite the imagination and devotion of the faithful by reiteration of the age-old stories.

The advent of Buddhism did not efface all traces of Hinduism. The two schools of Buddhism, Hīnayāna and Mahāyāna – the Small and the Great Vehicle (on the Way to Salvation) – came early to Cambodia, but Hīnayāna, while not disappearing altogether, quickly gave place to Mahāyāna. Mahāyāna lends itself to philosophical speculation and great heights of piety. Apart from Śākyamuni, the revealed Buddha and Law-giver, it provides its devotees with many forms of Buddha and Bodhisattva. Compassionate beings who delayed their own certain salvation to help others, the Bodhisattva were images of hope and fervour in the breasts of the pious. Their images multiplied and their protection was invoked by believers hoping to rejoin them in paradise. The lightning-bearer, Vajrapāṇi, and Maitreya, the future Buddha, were part of the Khmer iconography, but Avalokiteśvara was by far the most popular. A merciful god, watching over the unfortunate and answering their prayers, he is sometimes called Lokeśvara – the Lord of the world – as an alternative to Avalokiteśvara – the Lord who looks down from above. The Khmer people created sanctuaries and statues in which his miracles were recalled and where prayers to his image could be repeated.

The cult of Avalokiteśvara was practised in the pre-Angkor period and continued with a strong following up to the end of the twelfth and the beginning of the thirteenth century when Mahāyāna influence was strongest. It was during the thirteenth century that a school of Buddhism which had originated in Ceylon came to Cambodia. Theravāda or Hīnayāna, was the doctrine of the *Thera*, the Elders of the monastic order of the southern school of Buddhism. Disciples clung strictly to the teachings of Buddha, accepting only one path to salvation: *the Three Jewels* – Buddha, his Law and his Community. In the sanctuaries Buddha alone is represented, accompanied sometimes by *arhats* in prayer. This doctrine allows no royal cult, therefore Buddhist monarchs had perforce to bring the Brahmans from India to conduct their court ritual. Temples with many courtyards were no longer constructed of stone and no attempt was made to build lasting sanctuaries to house the god. Buildings were intended as a meeting-place where the faithful could hear the word of the law and pray together. A wooden or brick-built chamber was all that was needed for the new cult, a vast sanctuary where the devoted could kneel before the Buddhas on the altar.

Of all the monasteries built between the fourteenth and the seventeenth century very little remains; only a few statues far from their original site and, here and there, traces of carved wood panels; a brief reference in the chronicles of Cambodia, or, even more rarely, an inscription commemorating the founding of a temple.

Lolei. Devatā

THE HISTORICAL BACKGROUND

The early history of Cambodia is legendary. Chinese annals relate that the country was formerly ruled by a queen called Liu-yeh, but that she and her people were conquered by a foreigner from the land of Chi. His name was Hun-t'ien and he dreamed that he was given a magic bow by a spirit who told him to sail his junk towards the land of Fu-nan. He shot an arrow from afar which pierced the wall of Liu-yeh's ship, so that she was afraid and submitted. Hun-t'ien married the queen. Cambodian records and a Cham inscription tell of a hero called Kauṇḍinya who was given a javelin by a Brahman, with instructions to build a new city where the cast spear struck the ground. This he did and founded the capital of Fu-nan, marrying Soma, daughter of the snake-king, who enlarged his son-in-law's domain by drinking all the water. This country was given the name Fu-nan by the Chinese. It is likely that it spread more widely along the coast with far less penetration into the interior than present-day Cambodia, but the story of the snake-king is undoubtedly an allusion to the draining of the swamps and the reclaiming of the marshland, which is recorded in an old inscription. The people of Fu-nan, who were sailors and traders, soon extended their power over the basin of the lower Mekong and seem to have been at the height of their power under Kauṇḍinya-Jayavarman in the early sixth century. It is recorded in an Imperial edict that an exchange of ambassadors took place between this king and the emperor of China: "Kauṇḍinya-Jayavarman, king of Fu-nan, lives beyond the bounds of the ocean. From generation to generation his family has governed the southern land." At his death Kauṇḍinya-Jayavarman was succeeded by an usurper, Rudra-

Pl. 2 Bust of a Bodhisattva (?). Angkor Borei (Ta Keo). National Museum of Phnom-Penh. Height: 71 cm. 6th / 7th century.

varman, his bastard son, who assassinated the legitimate heir and seized the throne. The troubles which followed so weakened Fu-nan that it was overthrown by Ch'en-la, a vassal state.

The state of Ch'en-la probably developed to the south of modern Laos in the region of Vat Ph'u, traditionally the cradle of the Khmer royal line. Linked to the Fu-nan dynasty by family ties, the people of Ch'en-la rose against its usurper-king. Bhavavarman, a Fu-nan prince, who was married to a princess of Ch'en-la, pressed his claim on Fu-nan during the unrest at the close of the sixth century. The power of Ch'en-la extended up the Mekong river to the north of the Dangrek mountains and west towards Battambang, enclosing the region of the Great Lakes. The conquest was completed by the early seventh century when the aggrandisement of Ch'en-la was at its height. Īśānavarman founded a new capital at Sambor Prei Kuk in the plain of the Great Lakes and this was to become the heart of the kingdom of Angkor.

Until the early eighth century the finest masterpieces of pre-Angkor art were created in the region of Sambor Prei Kuk and the Mekong river. Jayavarman I, however, removed the capital to the south and almost certainly to Angkor Borei. The death of Jayavarman I without an heir in 681 was the cause of renewed unrest. The conquest had been achieved too rapidly and the vassal states stirred rebelliously, while the rich, divided country attracted the ambitions of her neighbours. Java, expanding quickly, took advantage of the situation and annexed part of Ch'en-la. The old dynasties of Fu-nan and Ch'en-la seemed to have died out. Nevertheless one prince did survive – the future Jayavarman II – who was probably exiled to Java. About 802 he returned to his country where he not only repudiated the Javanese conquerors but united the Khmer under his own leadership. Leaving the Mekong behind, he settled to the north of the Great Lakes, where his descendants lived continuously until the end of the fifteenth century. The positions of Jayavarman's successive capitals mark the stages of his conquest. The summit of his career was reached at his coronation which was celebrated about twenty years after his accession on Mount Mahendraparvata, now called Phnom Kulen. An inscription on the stele of Sdok Kak Thom throws some light on the ninth and tenth centuries; it reveals that a Brahman who "was skilled in the magic arts" was invited to carry out a ceremonial ritual to ensure that "the land of the Cambodians was not dependent on Java and had only one king, whose sway was universal". Java was very weak at that time and made no move to quell this flouting of her authority, although it must in any case have been almost negligible. It is scarcely likely that all the other Cambodian princes would have recognized the new king, but Jayavarman II had achieved a position which he was to spend the rest of his life defending, but which was established permanently by Indravarman who was anointed king in 877. Before this event, however, he had already effectively regrouped the states lying to the west. He completed the unification of Cambodia when he inherited the land of the Great Lakes from Jayavarman II's son. The inscriptions ring with his praise, boasting of his constancy, courage and magnanimity.

Hariharālaya (present-day Roluoh) was his capital and there he built beautiful temples, draining and irrigating the surrounding region. He founded a temple at Preah Ko in memory of his ancestors and a sanctuary at Bakong in 881 to house the royal *linga*, Indreśvara. He died in 889 leaving the throne secure for his son Yaśovarman, founder of Angkor.

The young king's future was full of promise. "When he came to the throne the lotus flowers opened as to the rising sun... the light of the other stars grew pale." He had been educated in a manner befitting the heir to the throne and inscriptions describe him as "beautiful enough to fill the god of love himself with envy". Very gifted and an enthusiastic patron of all the arts, he was an untiring warrior "whose ardour reduces the strength of his enemies to nothing". When he became king, Yaśovarman lived for a time at Hariharālaya, where he founded the temple of Lolei in the centre of an artificial lake to the glory of his ancestors. This pious duty completed, he applied his mind to greater projects. He left Hariharālaya to found a new city about eight miles away on the site of Angkor. It was called Yaśodharapura; a capital which was intended to be the earthly model of the heavenly city. He built a mountain temple with five towers reminiscent of Mount Meru on the hill of Phnom Bakheng. This temple was to house the royal *linga*, source of the nation's power.

Later the centre of the city was moved but Yaśodharapura remained the capital of the Khmer kingdom except for short intervals until the fifteenth century. Yaśovarman constructed an artificial lake to irrigate the country which was known as the Eastern Barai and extended his power to the west by the peaceful method of reclaiming land, at the same time defeating the Cham and Indonesian raiders in a victory over "a thousand white-sailed junks". Yaśovarman died about 900. The sons who succeeded him were far less powerful and in 921 Jayavarman IV, brother-in-law of the late Yaśovarman, rebelled against his nephews and established a government at Koh Ker, about fifty miles to the northeast of Angkor. After seven years he became the legitimate ruler, probably on the death of Yaśovarman's last child. Jayavarman IV erected huge buildings in the new capital.

Behind Prasat Thom, the royal temple, on a pyramid one hundred and fifteen feet high he erected an immensely heavy *linga* dedicated to Ugra, "rejoicing the hearts of men of feeling and annihilating the pride of the stiff-necked". The city of Koh Ker created by Jayavarman IV barely survived him. After the very short reign of his son who died in 944, the life of the temple continued but the city itself began to crumble away.

Yaśovarman's nephew, Rājendravarman, became king in 944 and moved his capital back to Angkor thus linking up again with the legitimate line. He made new sanctuaries: the Eastern Mebon, to honour his ancestors in the centre of the Eastern Barai, and the temple of Pre Rup near the shore of the lake. During the second half of the tenth century the government was in the hands of high dignitaries of the Brahman caste and the Brahman Yajñavarāha acted as regent during Jayavarman's minority. He was a man who "had seen beyond the farther reaches of knowledge" and when Jayavarman V came of age Yajñavarāha was not displaced because the young king "was under the influence of his *guru* and always disposed in his favour". He therefore usually subscribed to the laws which were suggested to him. Nowadays Yajñavarāha's greatest claim to fame is that he founded a beautiful building of pink sandstone near Angkor, the temple of Banteai Srei. But Jayavarman V, while retaining the capital at Yaśodharapura, built his own palace near the city. The centre of his new residence was "The Mountain of the Golden Horn", which may have been the temple which we call Ta Keo.

Jayavarman died in 1001 without issue. The lack of a direct successor and the very brief reign of the dead king's nephew resulted in a period of crisis. There followed a war of nearly ten years' duration, at the end of which a new dynasty emerged in the person of Sūryavarman I. He is described in a fulsome eulogy as "a god of wealth and freedom, deep as the ocean, splendid as the sun, brave as a lion and beautiful as the moon", which list concludes with the more practical addition "a master of knowledge". Sūryavarman probably came from the Malay peninsula, but his ambitions were directed westward towards the Menam river. His greatest achievement was to restore the country's stability after the years of war. Pacification in his reign was so complete "that men could sleep alone in the jungle without fear of attack". He probably continued the work at Ta Keo, but the royal palace at Angkor gained most from his attention. He completed the temple of Phimeanakas in the centre and enlarged it by construction of the precincts and an entrance pavilion.

Sūryavarman I died about 1050, leaving two sons who succeeded him in turn. Their reigns were disturbed by rebellions, but these were apparently easily suppressed. The kingdom continued to develop. In the capital a new Barai was constructed to irrigate the land to the west of Angkor and buildings were erected: a Mebon in the centre of the Western Barai, and the royal temple of the Baphuon apart from provincial sanctuaries. The influence of the spiritual mentors of the kings probably encouraged the interest in building. One of the king's Brahmans, Divākarapaṇḍita, was at that time on the threshold of a brilliant career. His political skill, perhaps also his manipulative intrigues, enabled him to control the kingdom for about thirty years.

He transferred his allegiance from Sūryavarman's son to the usurper, Jayavarman VI, and personally officiated at the anointing of the new king, a devout person who could not do enough for the ambitious Brahman. When Jayavarman VI died in 1107, leaving no children, the kingdom went to his brother, Dharaṇīndravarman I, a heavy burden for a prince who had no wish to rule. His was a short and tragic reign. In 1113 one of his great-nephews, the future Sūryavarman II, was overwhelmed by a desire to wield the royal power. Dharaṇīndravarman wavered, whereupon Divākarapaṇḍita, abandoning the master whom he had but lately crowned, hitched his fortunes to those of the young prince whose future seemed so bright. A duel of dramatic proportions was fought between uncle and nephew. "At the end of a battle lasting all day the young pretender let loose upon the field all the hordes of his army. Leaping on to the head of the enemy's elephant he killed the king just as Garuḍa slew the serpent on the mountain top." Soon afterwards Sūryavarman II was anointed king by Divākarapaṇḍita.

Sūryavarman increased his attacks on the Cham and the Mons of Burma, and fought against the growing power of the Dai Viet, the future Vietnam, which was gradually extending its territory southwards from the plain of Tonkin. He was the recognized ruler over all the territory extending from the Champa to the Pagan kingdom and from south of Laos to the Gulf of Siam. He sent an ambassador to the emperor of China who favoured him with titles and recognition, but he is remembered today as the founder of Angkor Vat rather than for his prowess as a ruler. He erected a temple, considered to be the most beautiful of all Khmer art, where he could be worshipped as Paramavisṇuloka after his death, when he would be reunited with Visṇu. He is idealistically represented on one of the bas-reliefs at Angkor Vat, a majestic and supremely elegant figure. Strangely enough there is no information about the

Pl. 3 Krishna "Lord of Mount Govardhana". Vat Koh (Ta Keo). National Museum of Phnom-Penh. Height: 161 cm. 6th century.

end of his reign. Probably there were defeats and setbacks in the last years, but these seem insignificant today beside the dazzling artistic achievement of the temples of Banteai Samre, Beng Mealea, Thommanon, Chau Say, Tevoda, Vat Ph'u, Preah Khan and Kompong Svay.

Sūryavarman II died in the middle of the twelfth century and Cambodia entered a troubled period. In 1165 one of the mandarins killed the reigning sovereign and occupied the throne. The usurper was not, however, to enjoy his power in peace. "Jaya Īndravarman, king of the Cham, presumptuous as Rāvana, transported his army in chariots to fight the land of Kambu, equal to heaven." The first campaign brought no decisive result, but in 1177 a Cham fleet led by a Chinese castaway appeared before the capital, which was plundered. The usurper king disappeared and the situation seemed hopeless when the seventh prince of this name, Jayavarman VII, arose from the shadows.

Jayavarman VII was a descendant of the pre-Angkor dynasties; his father had become king after the death of Sūryavarman II. He had not succeeded to the throne when his father died because he was fighting in the Champa country when the usurper seized power. Nevertheless he returned to Cambodia and awaited his hour. When the capital was taken in 1177 he proclaimed his rights to the crown and began to restore the power of the Khmer. The Cham were finally repelled by a naval victory which is commemorated by bas-reliefs in the temple of the Bayon on Banteai Chmar. But this success was not enough to appease Jayavarman VII, who "had sworn a fearful vengeance on his enemies". He organized the kingdom and was anointed king in 1181. A second Yaśodharapura was built and this is present-day Angkor Thom, centred on the temple of the Bayon and surrounded by fortifications. Bridges were built over the rivers and roads driven through the jungle to connect Angkor with the great cities of the kingdom. Jayavarman VII, a pious Buddhist, built many temples: Ta Prohm, Preah Khan, Neak Pean, Banteai Kdei and Banteai Chmar, to mention only the most important. These were sanctuaries founded to honour dead ancestors and were consecrated to Buddha or the Bodhisattva. The Buddhist faith caused Jayavarman to be merciful to his subjects and an inscription on a stele tells that "he suffered more from the troubles of his people than from his own". He undertook many social schemes for their welfare, building roadside inns for the shelter of travellers and constructing one hundred and two hospitals throughout the kingdom for the treatment of the sick.

Although he came late to the throne, Jayavarman VII reigned for nearly forty years and was almost a hundred when he died. He left his son an empire which stretched from the coast of Annam to the banks of the Menam, embracing the whole of south Laos. Some of the states, united by force under Jayavarman VII, broke away immediately from the domination of his son and in 1220 the Khmer withdrew from Champa without hostilities. At the same time the Thai of the Menam basin declared themselves independent and founded the kingdom of Sukhodaya, but the Khmer still remained powerful. The reign of Jayavarman VIII, a follower of Śiva, saw the last foundations of the Brahmans. In 1295 Ch'ou Ta-k'uan, a Chinese emissary, visited Cambodia and was amazed by the luxury of the court and the fertility of the kingdom. After the middle of the fourteenth century the inscriptions tell us no more about the history of the kings, though the annals relate the story of a sovereign whose father acquired the kingdom in strange circumstances. Neang-Trasac Paem was called the "King of the delicious cucumbers", a reference to his lowly origin as a royal gardener. As such he grew cucumbers of so fine a flavour that the king reserved the whole crop for himself giving Trasac-Paem a javelin to ward off potential thieves. However, one night the king, driven either by greed or by the desire to put Trasac-Paem's vigilance to the test, stole into the garden. Taking him for a thief, the gardener killed him. Later when the question of a successor arose, the white elephant chose Trasac-Paem.

To legalize his seizure of power the new king married his predecessor's daughter. It is recorded that the sons of this legendary king reigned in succession. They had to repel the first Thai invasions, and after the foundation of the Siamese kingdom of Ayudhyā in 1347 Cambodia was in grave danger. Angkor was attacked several times by Siamese raiders and in 1430 the Thai beleaguered the city once again. The siege lasted seven months, but then the city surrendered and the king was killed. Master now of Angkor, the king of Siam put his own son on the Khmer throne. The legitimate heir, Chau Ponhea yat, had been able to escape, and although only eighteen years old, he organized resistance from the Mekong. Rather than run the risks of war he caused the usurper to be assassinated and marched on Angkor, where the people opened the gates to receive him. Now that he was king, Chau Ponhea yat decided to move the capital, because the eastern Khmer provinces had fallen into the hands of the Thai and Angkor lay in a dangerous position on the perimeter of the state. Such a rich and famous city was bound to excite the passions of ambitious neighbours. Chau Ponhea yat left Angkor and settled at Phnom-Penh. But although Angkor was no longer the capital of the kingdom, it remained the most illustrious city. Kings still went there on pilgrimage and its renown waned only as the jungle encroached, leaving at last only the temple of Angkor Vat, which had been transformed into a Buddhist sanctuary.

The history of the last decades of the fifteenth century is very confused. In 1473, when the Siamese invaded the country again, the king was taken prisoner; he seems to have died in captivity, but not before the birth of his son whom the Siamese held as a hostage. Subsequently kings of Siam educated Cambodian princes at the Siamese court to make sure that pretenders were under their own control.

Cambodia was just recovering from the devastation caused by the Siamese invasions when a new crisis arose in the shape of an usurper called Neang Khan. The king was assassinated and rebellion spread throughout the kingdom. However, a relative of the dead king, called Ang Chan, who enjoyed a certain prestige and had the support of the monks, organized resistance at Pursat. After a successful naval battle during which Neang Khan was killed, Ang Chan was anointed king at Lovek. He and his son, Barom Reachea, saved Cambodia from total obliteration at the hands of the Thai. It is true that the Siamese continued their attacks; their aim was to put Prince Ong, their own claimant, on the throne of Lovek, but Ong was killed while riding on his elephant and the Siamese had to retreat. Cambodia began to rebuild. She claimed new lands from the jungle and discovered and exploited seams of iron ore. Monasteries decorated by skilled wood-carvers were built as a thanksgiving.

Barom Reachea's son unfortunately stifled this renaissance irrevocably by failing to profit by the attacks made on the

Siamese by the king of Pegou. He even went so far as to take their part and send support. The Thai invaded Cambodia twice more and in 1594 captured Lovek. The fall of Lovek is the most serious event in the later history of Cambodia. It was not the first time that the Siamese had captured the capital, nor the first time that the king and his heir had been defeated; nevertheless the taking of Lovek marks a turning-point. It was the end of the independent state of the Khmer.

After the fall of Lovek the country was ruled by a series of usurpers, and this weakened the monarchy. Life in the palace was dramatic and bloody. A short reign and a violent end were the lot of eighteenth-century Khmer rulers, who were nearly all assassinated or killed in battle. Kings abdicated, willingly or unwillingly, to return to the throne when the moment was propitious, and the situation of the country grew more and more disquieting. Harassed already in the west by the Siamese, Cambodia was now attacked from the east by the young and vigorous Vietnam. While Siam imposed her dominion on Cambodia, Vietnam gnawed away at the eastern provinces and after Preah Outey II had used the power of Vietnam to seize the throne their demands became ever more exigent.

These troubles reached their peak in the late eighteenth century. In 1779 three powerful and rebellious mandarins assassinated the king, but they soon quarrelled among themselves. The sole survivor fled to Siam, dragging in his train the young king who was to be crowned at Bangkok in 1794. He died shortly afterwards. His eldest son, Ang Chan II, sought the support of Vietnam, while the younger son preferred to side with Siam. He returned to Cambodia at the head of a Siamese army to reclaim the throne which the Vietnamese had occupied since the death of Ang Chan. In 1842 he settled at the new capital of Oudong as king. The Vietnamese were virtually dislodged from Cambodia by 1846 and therefore came to terms.

Ang Duong proved to be a good governor, fair and benevolent towards the people, firm with prevaricating officials and merciful to the poor and enslaved. He was well-versed in the Buddhist texts, reading both Pāli and Sanskrit with ease, and he loved to join the monks in learned discourse. He died in 1859, whereupon the succession was immediately disputed by his sons. The eldest was chosen and given the name Norodom. Order was established but the king, in an attempt to escape from the powerful ambitions of his Thai and Vietnamese neighbours, signed a treaty of protection with France.

The country's recovery, set in train under Ang Duong, went ahead with the reigns of Norodom and Sisowath. Art of the period was greatly influenced by Siam but it is not entirely derivative. Travellers in the late nineteenth century stumbled in amazement upon the ruins of the Angkor period and when the province of Angkor was given back by Siam the *École Française d'Extrême-Orient* undertook to look after the monuments. Cambodia gradually took her place in international affairs and after the Second World War the king, Norodom Sihanouk, claimed independence from France and this was granted in 1953. Prince Sihanouk abdicated in favour of his father, King Suramanit, and himself led the movement for reform and renovation. Cambodia, awake at last to the greatness of her past, has taken her rightful place in South East Asia.

THE SOCIAL LIFE OF THE KHMER

The sculpture of Angkor tells us a great deal about the life of the Khmer in the Angkor period. Chinese texts and Khmer inscriptions supply much information and picturesque narrative, but the bas-reliefs depict the palaces and houses, describing the lives of both rulers and people.

The society which emerges from these different descriptions was strongly hierarchic. It was divided into castes in the Indian manner, but the nobility held all the positions of power and authority and the people were subservient and needy.

The king occupied the summit of the social edifice. The omnipotent monarch had to ensure the security of the kingdom and with it the prosperity and peace of his people. A king endowed with such power and with such obligations to his people was divine; he became the incarnate god by anointment on his accession and was worshipped throughout his life. After death he was venerated as a god. When king Indravarman died he became the god Īśvaraloka — he who enters the kingdom of the master, in other words, Śiva; and king Sūryavarman II became Paramaviṣṇuloka – he who enters the world of Viṣṇu. The king inherited his rights to the throne through the royal line. If a son or nephew of the late king was not available someone related to the family had to be found and usurpers did not rest until they had legitimized their accession to power by marriage with a daughter, or even the widow, of their predecessor.

Ch'ou Ta-k'uan, an enthusiastic witness, described the life of a Khmer king in the thirteenth century. The sovereign wore his hair dressed in a chignon and crowned with a diadem or simply decorated with a garland of flowers; his shoulders were uncovered and his hips draped with a closely printed floral material which was very precious, worth two or three gold ounces, and which was made for the king alone. "Almost three pounds of large pearls" hung round his neck and wrists, while his fingers and ankles were loaded with jewels. The Chinese ambassador saw the king emerging from his palace on several occasions. "I remained more than a year in that country and I saw him four or five times as he left the palace. When the prince leaves, the soldiers march at the head of his escort; then come the standards, the pennants and the band. Palace girls, perhaps three hundred or more, wearing flowery costumes, their chignons garlanded, hold long lighted candles in their hand, even in broad daylight. Then follow more girls carrying the gold and silver vessels, the spear and the shield. These are the private guardians of the palace... ministers and princes all ride on elephants and you can see their innumerable red sunshades from a long way off. Behind them come the wives and concubines of the king and last of all the king himself, standing on an elephant, holding the sacred sword."

Ch'ou Ta-k'uan was fascinated by the palace. "The royal palace, official buildings and the noblemen's houses all face east. The roofs are imposing, while the long verandahs and open corridors weave and wind prettily. I have been told that there are many marvellous places within the palace, but it is strongly guarded and I have not been able to get inside." The ceremonial audience made a deep impression on the Chinese envoy: "Music is heard from far off within the palace and this is answered by a long blast on the conches outside to herald the arrival of the king... a moment or two later two of the palace girls raise the curtain with their tapering fingers and the king, carrying the sword, appears at the

Pl. I   Musicians.   Detail of a lintel of the Vat Eng Khna (Kompong Thom). National Museum of Phnom-Penh. Height of the lintel: 54 cm. Prei Kmeng style. Late 7th century.

golden window. The whole crowd, ministers and people, join hands and touch the ground with their forehead; they are allowed to raise their heads only when the music of the conches has ceased. Thereupon the king takes his seat. On the throne is a lion-skin which is one of the hereditary royal treasures. As soon as the business of the audience is accomplished the king withdraws; the two girls let the curtain fall across the window and everyone stands up."

Court scenes were the inspiration of many of the bas-reliefs decorating the temple walls. Here the king receives the homage of his subjects, or rides to war on his elephant; in others he sets off on a voyage, perhaps a pilgrimage.

Richly-apparelled ladies and gentlemen sit in airy pavilions watching the dancing. Ch'ou Ta-k'uan remarked ruefully that every time he went to the palace "to see the sovereign, the king came out with his first wife and sat down in the [frame of the] golden window in the main chamber. The palace ladies were all standing in rows on both sides of the verandah below the window but they moved and leaned against [the window] to catch a glimpse of the king and his escort."

The heaviest duties were laid on the princes and the priests. As tutors to the young prince, advisers to the king, priests and servants of the cult of *devarāja*, and often linked by matrimonial ties with the royal family, the Brahmans played a far from negligible role in the political life of the country. The support of one priestly family had brought a whole province under the sway of Jayavarman II; we have already seen how in the tenth century the Brahman, Yajñavarāha, who was related to the royal family, became regent during the minority of Jayavarman V and how, at the end of the eleventh century until the accession of Sūryavarman II in 1113, Divākarapaṇḍita arranged the successive accessions to the throne of several kings. In the thirteenth century the Brahman family of Mangalārtha was still playing an important role. While these powerful ministers surrounded the monarch, important administrative posts were divided between the great nobles.

"Generally", Ta-k'uan relates, "they choose princes for these posts, but on occasion a commoner will offer his daughter as a bribe. When the officials go out, the size and insignia of their train are fixed by protocol. The highest dignitaries have a palanquin with gold stretchers and four parasols with gold handles."

The king's ministers were themselves responsible for the recruitment of their staff. They were all bound to the king by a solemn oath. One such oath of allegiance used by civil servants has been found inscribed on the royal palace of Angkor. It reads: "We swear, each and every one without exception... offering our lives and grateful devotion without blemish to His Majesty, Sri Sūryavarmadeva. We shall adore no other king, we shall never be traitors. We shall do no harm in any way. We shall force ourselves to carry out all the actions which are the consequence of our devotion to the king Sri Sūryavarmadeva. If war breaks out we shall fight with all our strength, scorning death in our devotion. Should anyone of us here break this oath made to His Majesty – may he reign for many years – we demand that the king will punish us with every kind of royal torture. If we hide so as to avoid fulfilment of this promise may we be reborn in the thirty-two hells so long as the sun and moon shall rise. If we fulfil our promise without fail... may we reap the reward of those who are devoted to their masters, now and for ever." This formula or something very like it had to be repeated by all civil servants, and the functionaries and ministers of the royal palace at Phnom-Penh repeat a similar pledge today.

The life of the sovereign's important dignitaries and more generally of the nobility was comfortable if not luxurious. "The houses of the princes and high officials differ from those of the people. All the houses on the outskirts of the city are thatched, only the family temples and the principal apartments being roofed with tiles, and a man's official rank determines the size of his dwelling. The noble and rich houses use domestic vessels of silver and sometimes even gold. There are mats of plaited straw on the ground, but some houses have tiger-skin rugs, or panther, stag and chamois skins... recently tables about a foot high have been introduced. At night they sleep on bamboo mats on the floor, but some people are beginning to use low beds."

The bas-reliefs tell a great deal, unfortunately in a fragmentary way, about the aristocracy and the great state functions. Apparently important men, generals, administrators and so on, whether as a reward from the king for meritorious service or because they wanted to acquire religious merit, were permitted to erect their own religious statues and steles within the precincts of the royal sanctuaries. These steles commemorated the largesse of the rich benefactors who inscribed a list of the slaves whom they owned in the temple. The names of some very lowly servants have been recorded which are quite pejorative, such as "Detestable", "Stinker" or "Dog". But these unfortunate names were only applied to the most servile of categories. Musicians and dancers who were at the disposal of the temple were given more agreeable names. The treatment meted out to slaves depended probably on their origin and ability, but it seems never to have been unduly harsh.

Between noblemen and slaves there were the free men of small or medium fortune. The Chinese have described them, and the bas-reliefs depict a few episodes, but the inscriptions say nothing about them at all. They were not rich enough to be able to afford their own inscriptions and their existence is not recorded on the monuments. But they were the people who lived in the towns, supplied the army with its commissariat and the public services with foremen and workers. They brought new land under cultivation and our Chinese informant thought them very skilled: "The farmers calculate the moment when the rice will ripen, when the river will rise and by how much, and then they sow the land at their disposal." These were the boat-builders, the makers of palanquins and all manner of objects used in everyday life. From scenes drawn on the temple bas-reliefs and the descriptions of Ch'ou Ta-k'uan it appears that they led a simple life. "The ordinary people only roof their houses with thatch and have no idea how to make use of tiles. The size of a house depends on the fortunes of its owner but the people would never dare to imitate the design of a nobleman's house. People of this class have a house but it lacks everything: table, bench, bowl or bucket. They have an earthenware stewpot for cooking the rice and a cooking pot in which they make the sauce. They build their fire over three stones in the ground and use a coconut shell as a spoon."

It can be seen from the bas-reliefs that the villagers lived in houses unprotected from the public gaze and almost without furniture. Large baskets hang from the beams. The life of the village is concentrated on the market place. People buy and sell and gossip. Sometimes discussion degenerates into argument. All legal questions were settled by the king, though sometimes by "Trial by god". Ch'ou Ta-k'uan describes the scene: "There are twelve small towers in front of the palace and the two men to be tried are seated in a separate tower watched over by relatives. They remain there for one or two days, perhaps more, at the end of which time they are released. It will be found that the one who was in the wrong has invariably become ill, while the righteous man is healthy. This is known as the judgement of heaven."

Studying the Khmer of the Angkor period as they go about their family business, gossiping round a market-stall or betting at a cock-fight, we can recognize the simple pleasures and unhurried life enjoyed by the Cambodian villagers of today.

ARTISTIC INFLUENCES IN SOUTH EAST ASIA

Within a primarily Hindu or Buddhist religious framework it is natural that the first temples, the first images of the gods in Cambodia should have been inspired by Indian models. In pre-Angkor sculpture Indian influence is seen in the composition of bas-reliefs, the type of foliage, costumes and attitudes and even the physiognomy of the statues. The characteristics of Amarāvatī art of the second and third centuries A. D. can be seen on the Buddhist images of Cambodia but the real relationship should be sought in post-Gupta art. Similarities with the sculpture of Elephanta and Ellora are to be found in scattered Brahman divinities or Khmer Bodhisattvas. Much has been made of the resemblance between Pallava and Khmer art and the kingdom of Pallava is indeed contemporary with Fu-nan and Ch'en-la; the Indian artists carved out the rocks of Māmallapuram when Īśānavarman was building Sambor Prei Kuk. There is undoubtedly a relationship between the two sculptures, not only similarities of costume, coiffure and iconography, but a common aesthetic. On the Coromandel coast and in the Mekong valley beauty was seen in simplified form, dignity of gesture and elegance of attitude; naturalism was tempered by an inborn concern for aesthetic value.

The dominance of Indian art over Khmer sculpture in the early period receded quickly once the artist's individuality asserted itself. The sculptors still drew their inspiration from Indian myth and legend but their execution was fresh and imaginative. Although the religious ideas of the Brahmans were enriched and regenerated by the philosophical schools of India in the centuries that followed, the art of Cambodia was untouched. During this period the Khmer artists looked, not to the faraway land of India, but towards their near neighbours, Java and Champa, and to the royal kingdoms which succeeded one another in the plain of the Menam.

Probably Java and Ch'en-la were already in contact before the Indonesian kingdom of Srivijaya gained the upper hand over part of the country. The influence of Java – say, in a headdress or the attitude of a bronze – can occasionally be seen in art of the pre-Angkor period, and some of the ornate statues wear jewels cut in the Javanese style. Java's influence which was already noticeable in the Angkor period grew stronger in the early ninth century, for at this time Khmer art, freed from the yoke of the Śailendra, gradually assimilated the decorative *motifs* of its former overlords. Indonesian ornament was still being copied in the tenth century. Gradually Java's influence over the Khmer shrank and only slight traces of Indonesian culture remained in the art of Angkor and modern Cambodia.

Champa, which was much nearer to Cambodia, seems to have exercised a stronger ascendancy over Khmer sculpture, but all the same it can only be seen in isolated pieces, strange images, which often fall between the two styles. It is certain that Khmer sculpture was of less interest to the Champa than to their western neighbours.

Artistic exchanges multiplied between Cambodia and the successive states of the plain of Menam – the Mon kingdom of Dvāravatī and the Thai of Sukhodaya, Ayudhyā and Bangkok. Dvāravatī was closely connected with Ch'en-la. Some of the statues found in Cambodia show features characteristic of the art of Dvāravatī, although it was not until after the eleventh-century conquest over part of the Mon state that Dvāravatī exercised a real influence on Khmer art. In the thirteenth century when Cambodia adopted Theravādic Buddhism the image of Buddha grew sober and restrained, a figure with half-shut eyes, standing and wearing a long robe.

The Siamese art of Sukhodaya was developing at the same time and Khmer and Thai influenced one another so that it is often difficult to determine which was responsible for the changes. All the sixteenth-century work reveals the anxiety of the Khmer artists to remain faithful to their traditions, and the simultaneous attraction exercised by the art of Ayudhyā, which was even more tempting since its original inspiration frequently came from Cambodia. At this period the two arts were still evolving separately, but gradually coming closer and closer together. After the eighteenth century we shall see their total fusion.

During the whole of its history Khmer art has assimilated foreign influences. The artists of Fu-nan and Ch'en-la, when first confronted with Indian models, transformed them to accord with their own inspiration. Unimportant figures are still Indian in appearance, but the large idols rapidly adopt the Khmer physical type, expression and technique; foreign influence is only discernible in the detail. The sculptors were looking for material to embellish, not for inspiration. They well knew the firm foundation of their own artistic tradition, the balance, moderation and beauty of its line.

I. STONE

Abbreviations:

Pl. I to XVI: Colour Plates
Pl. I to 100: Black and white illustrations in the text
Cat. I to 135: Black and white illustrations in the catalogue
*: An asterisk before a number refers to a textual reference in the outer column of the page

The discovery of Angkor by the west brought to Khmer architecture a prestige which was much enhanced by its dramatic forest setting; the sculpture, however, did not receive such immediate acclaim. But in due course, as the monuments were freed of the encroaching jungle and the débris which had buried them, more and more bas-reliefs were revealed; a whole pantheon of gods appeared lying among the ruins, as well as idols which had been placed in the sanctuaries to receive the prayers of the faithful. Seated in meditation, or standing with their distinguishing attributes, the divinities are nearly all carved in rigid attitudes. This is because representation of the gods was subject to fixed rules laid down in the Śilpasastra, treatises on works of art which had to be scrupulously obeyed. Such statues must have tended to produce an effect of monotony, and indeed this is true of the second-rate works; but the really fine pieces pulse with life, their immobility notwithstanding. Bas-reliefs, on the other hand, allowed the artists greater liberty to follow their own creative ideas. Whilst the statues were actual representations of the gods or divine princes, the bas-reliefs glorified their exploits. Legends were depicted on the pediments and lintels, and more freely on the walls of temples for the edification of the faithful who passed under the arches of the outer walls to walk through the galleries. To this day broken and decapitated statues are found lying on the ground beneath the ruins, their limbs shattered, their heads defaced. Sometimes they were cast down and broken when a town was sacked because it was thought
*Pl. 3 that mutilated statues were shorn of their magic power and unable to protect the enemy; but more often they were overthrown by robbers hoping to find gold or precious stones concealed in the base.

TECHNIQUE

Until the close of the Angkor period sculptors preferred to work in sandstone, very occasionally using brick, stucco and earthenware. Shale was only used as a background for inscriptions or pedestals, because its composition made it unsuitable material for statuary. Cambodia is rich in sandstone deposits. The quarries supply different qualities and colours, pink, purplish, yellow and greenish, and many shades of grey. The quarries used during the Angkor period are situated in the foothills of Phnom Kulen and in the early days of Khmer art especially the stone chosen was a very fine-grained grey sandstone, which would take a high polish and which acquires a dark patina with age. Some of the unfinished figures and reliefs that have been found show the sculptor's methods. The statues were carved direct from the block; having no previous model, the artist naturally made mistakes and unfinished statues are usually ill-proportioned pieces which have been discarded. Nevertheless this method of working produced a spontaneity which is sometimes lacking in more painstaking techniques. The sculptures vary in height from a foot or two to more than six feet, but whatever their size the problem of support always arose. The Khmer artists tried to make free-standing figures from the outset, seeking to escape the bondage of their Indian models which were always carved in high-relief, supported by a stele or in some other way. These limitations put a brake on the development of the sculptor's technique. One of the oldest images of the sixth century, the Krishna Govardhanasvamin (Lord of Mount Govardhana) of Vat Koh is in high-relief. The position of the god, with his hand outstretched to support Mount Govardhana, made it impossible to balance him if resting on the feet alone. So he was placed against a stele. The Krishna Govardhanasvamin in the Lyon Stoclet Collection (Brussels), is also carved on a stele, but the torso is entirely unsupported. Other pre-Angkor statues are carved in the round, although they are all supported in some way to ensure balance. Gods with two hands outstretched have a stay beneath each hand; an attribute, or a fold of the drapery falling to the ground were later used as supports. Statues with many arms presented more difficulty. The artist had recourse to arcs which gave support to the upper arms in the form of a halo. The arc on the four-armed Viṣṇu was discarded quite soon, while the lower hands rested on a club or stay; but the upper arms, free and unsupported above the head of the god, were too fragile and so a portion of the arc was retained between the upper hands and the head. This device, which first appeared in the seventh century, was still in use a hundred years later. Buddhas in monks' clothes were not supported; their feet, however, were carved in high-relief, the hands remaining free.

During the ninth century supporting stays and buttresses disappeared but the figures themselves became heavier in consequence. These massive images were made until almost the end of the tenth century; in the eleventh, however, when elegance of line was fashionable once again, the limbs grew finer, but a supporting stay was fitted behind the heel giving a firm base. Towards the end of the twelfth century, when carved images were multiplying with the result that quarries of fine sandstone became depleted, the limbs and feet grew heavy again because the artists could not trust the coarse and more fragile sandstone. Statues at that period were composed of several pieces, an example being the Lokeśvara of the Gate of the Dead, whose arms were fitted on and held by pinning. The thirteenth-century method of making large standing Buddhas was taken from the art of Dvāravatī, and only the arms were separately fitted.

Many of the Khmer statues are figures standing in a frontal position, but until the ninth century idols were often carved in a less rigid pose. On the oldest pieces the movement of the body seems to have been very precisely modelled from life. There are some very rare statues which apparently follow the rhythms of the Hellenistic tradition in which the body is supported by an outstretched limb. In the greater number, however, the torso is made to lean over the bent leg in the position known as *tribhanga*,[1] – the Indian triple flexion. Usually the oblique movement is barely noticeable but it is accentuated sometimes by a gesture as in the supple flexing of Krishna Govardhanasvamin, or the violent movement of the Durga (?) of Sambor Prei Kuk. During the seventh century this attitude grew stiff and less naturalistic. By the end of the eighth century the flexing of the hips borders on deformity, and is scarcely explained by the position of the limbs and torso. In the art of Angkor the idols are absolutely straight and only one exception – a Lakṣmī, found at Prasat Trapeang Totung Thngai – is slightly oblique. The expression of a movement in a three-dimensional plane, rare in the Angkor period, hardly makes an appearance before the art of Koh Ker in the tenth century. There the figures stride forward, ride or fight among themselves; but the representation of movement was soon abandoned because it is far more suitable to bas-reliefs. Although the reliefs offered the artists a wider field, they posed quite different problems. In relief-carving the artists were freed of all anxieties about stability and could allow the imagination free play. Different stages of their work can

Pl. II Dancer and musicians. Banteai Srei (Siem Reap). Second half of the 10th century.

be seen on unfinished bas-reliefs. They first engraved the outline and cut out the ground, finally chiselling the details of face, body and ornament. Composition and the way to render perspective were the artist's two main problems. When they first began to carve the surface of sandstone on pediments, lintels or walls they either adopted a harsh clear-cut relief reminiscent of three-dimensional sculpture, or a true bas-relief in which the figures were only lightly cut away. Some lintels at Banteai Srei are rather deeply carved, and although the first scenic murals towards the end of the eleventh century seem to waver between the two techniques, after the Angkor Vat period the bas-relief can be seen to have won the day. Thus sharp, vigorous reliefs generally cover the smaller surfaces and the bas-reliefs unfold along the walls. In the thirteenth century the characters are arranged in rows on the lintels in conditions where the problems of perspective can almost be ignored. It is a different matter, however, in large mural reliefs, where the scene is set in a palace, a forest, house or boat and where it is necessary to indicate seven or eight different planes in depth. The artists of Angkor Vat achieved this effect by staggering the outlines in relation to one another; they painstakingly carved the faces of people seen through gaps in a building or behind the wheels of a chariot. Palaces or houses are seen from the front thus avoiding the difficulty of lines of perspective.

The passing years have affected the sandstone according to its composition. Occasionally damp has formed a kind of skin on the surface which rises and bursts. Some statues are literally flayed on the torso and back, sometimes even on the face, but this does not happen on the polished pieces. Polished sandstone generally takes on a fine dark patina of a darkly golden hue, but why these early statues exhibit this

Pl. 4 Hand of Viṣṇu from the Phnom Da (Ta Keo). National Museum of Phnom-Penh. Height of the statue: 270 cm. 6th century (cf. Cat. 46).

brilliant polished surface resembling bronze is not known. It has been called "waxed sandstone", and at Angkor Vat where certain parts of the bas-reliefs seem particularly highly polished, it is thought that this could have been the result of the visitors touching the reliefs as they passed. But this picturesque explanation only applies to a small proportion of the idols. At Angkor Vat and on the greater number of all polished statues it seems more likely that a priming coat was applied which may well have been the foundation for gilding. After the Angkor period the statues were generally given three coats of lacquer – black, red and gold – in the manner of wooden sculpture. Early idols, which are still venerated today, receive the same treatment; they are lacquered, covered with gesso and even re-carved with the no doubt pious but philistine intention of adapting them to the taste and manners of our time. Nevertheless Khmer sculpture, eroded by tropical rains, mutilated during the destruction of the temples by iconoclasts and robbers, degraded even more by modern piety, still reveals the hand of the artist, his sureness of technique and his desire to create the finest possible work of art.

THE PRE-ANGKOR PERIOD

ARCHITECTURE

In Cambodia the earliest known art, that of Fu-nan, developed in the south. No pieces have been definitely attributed to the period, but a group of statues of the sixth century, probably Funanese, has been discovered in caves on the site of Phnom Da at Angkor Borei. These caves are simple fissures in the rock carved out and then closed in front with

Pl. 5 Paraśūrāma (?). Phnom Da (Ta Keo). National Museum of Phnom-Penh. Height: 157 cm. 6th century.

a brick wall. The earliest known architectural buildings are the brick constructions of Ch'en-la dating from the seventh century. A vigorous art developed, reaching its height in the temple of Īśavarapura at Sambor Prei Kuk. The artists built the sanctuary in three groups developing a new type of architecture based on rectangular and octagonal shapes, with buildings of a size and scope never achieved before or since. Subtle and rich decoration reinforced the lines of the buildings. Sandstone lintels were filled with foliage, fabulous beasts and mythological scenes, while heavenly palaces rose out of the brick walls. Unfortunately the tribulations of Ch'en-la which followed the death of Jayavarman I saw the decline of architecture also. The formulae used at Sambor were abandoned and by the eighth century nothing more was built except small sanctuaries with impoverished decoration.

DEVELOPMENT OF STYLES

The statues discovered near Angkor Borei and particularly those at the Phnom Da seem to be the oldest known works of Cambodian art. Brahman or Buddhist, these idols were all the product of a well-developed aesthetic sense. It is almost certain that stone-sculpture was preceded by work in wood, bronze and terra-cotta. Archaeologists' excavations in the Fu-nan port of Oc Eo in the Cochin Chinese delta have uncovered several images of Buddha, one of which may even be as early as the fourth century, but is certainly not later than the early fifth.

The statues in the Phnom Da style are considerably later, indeed they could not have been carved before the sixth

Pl. 6 Head of Buddha. Tuol Chan, Angkor Borei (Ta Keo). National Museum of Phnom-Penh. Height: 15 cm. 7th century.

century. Bas-relief appears early in the seventh century simultaneously with the style of Sambor Prei Kuk, and the gods become more naturalistic, carved with muscular male and opulent female bodies. In the late seventh century the style of Prei Kmeng retained the naturalistic flavour which the art of Prasat Andet refined and idealized. The Kompong Preah School still continued to produce fine work although the political crises which arose in Ch'en-la were impoverishing architecture; but during the eighth century artistic skill began to falter, sensitivity failed and convention displaced naturalism.

BRAHMAN ART OF PHNOM DA

The practice of the Brahman religion in Cambodia stems from the rise of Hinduism. Chinese annals reiterate that the people of Fu-nan worshipped "heavenly spirits", in other words, Brahman deities. They also describe a type of sculpture which must have been contemporary with the first Brahman idols of India. The statues discovered at Angkor Borei, and more especially at Phnom Da, cannot be earlier than the sixth century. They are very fine works. Primitive art with its touching lack of sophistication has vanished from Cambodia without trace.

Pl. 3 The Krishna "Lord of Mount Govardhana" of Vat Koh, thought to be one of the oldest pieces, is a masterpiece. The artist must have been inspired by the poetic myth which relates how Krishna protected his companions against the fury of the storm unleashed by Indra: "All the domestic animals, shivering beneath the lashing rain and wind, and the shepherds huddled together against the cold, ran to Govinda for protection, and then Hari, the Blessed One, said: this unseasonable tempest, this wind and sandstorm are sent by Indra to destroy us... because the world sees me as its refuge and protector I will save it. Thus spoke Krishna and with one

Pl. 7 Standing Buddha. Pagoda of Tuol Lean, Angkor Borei region (Ta Keo). National Museum of Phnom-Penh. Height: 56 cm. 7th century.

hand lifted Mount Govardhana by the base, holding it high in the air as easily as a child lifts a mushroom" (*Bhagavata Purāṇa*). On the bas-relief of Vat Koh, Krishna raises his left arm to hold up the mountain, which is suggested by an overhang on the stele. It is an effortless movement; the god leans carelessly over his right leg, his body tilted slightly backwards. His robe is just a simple piece of cloth draped over the hips; while a supple train falls to the ground on his left, a belt, bias-folded, is attached by a large knot to his side. This is the kind of clothing which the Chinese attribute to the rich young men of Fu-nan. Curly hair knotted in three small chignons on the top of the head was the style of the adolescent. The curving line of the left hand, the raised arm and the sweep of the thigh are beautifully composed.

The Vat Koh Krishna is an exceptional work. The modelling, movement and style of the drapery lead to an attribution to the earliest Phnom Da period. This group is an example of a school of sculpture at Phnom Da in which all the statues are closely related. The method of draping is like the modern Cambodian dress known as the sampot. The cloth, wrapped round the body, is tied in front. The panels are lightly twisted to form the "tail" which is passed between the legs and fastened at the back. In the Phnom Da style the upper part of the material falls again to the front and is folded like a fan. The hair is generally dressed in plaits, covering the nape of the neck. However it is the physical characteristics rather than the costume and coiffure which reveal the close relationship between the early statues of Phnom Da. The sculptors drew the elongated, almond-shaped eyes in full, oval faces beneath finely-arched eyebrows with great care, and painstakingly hollowed the eye-sockets, iris and lids. The nose is aquiline with narrow,

Pl. III Rāma and Lakṣmaṇa. Detail of a façade of the Banteai Srei (Siem Reap). National Museum of Phnom-Penh. Second half of the 10th century.

sensitive nostrils while the muscles on the narrow-hipped body are only suggested.

The pieces at Phnom Da represent for the most part images of Viṣṇu and his *avatars* but one statue over nine feet high is iconographically surprising (Pl. 4). The god wears the cylindrical mitre on his curling hair while his eight arms are supported by an iron arc. It appears that this is a statue of Viṣṇu although the attributes which have been identified – fire, baton, antelope skin and bottle – are not those usually carried by this god. The hands are carefully modelled, although the palms are too short and the movement of the wrists is ungainly, but the long tapered fingers and delicate nails are of extreme elegance. Like two other images of Rāma and Balarāma which obviously come from the same workshop, the Viṣṇu is carved in dark stone with a soft velvety patina. One or two pieces in the same style have been discovered converted into the Buddha with stucco and lacquer by pious monks from a Vietnamese monastery in Phnom Da. The stucco can be removed, but a layer of dark lacquer spoils the plaited coiffure of a beautiful deity whose face still bears traces of a putty-coloured coating. This image is one of the most attractive in the Phnom Da style (Pl. 5). It has a finely smiling face, an easy posture and supple elegance of body with a light fold in the robe and long pleated train which, though broken now, formerly reached the ground. Less vigorously youthful, the Harihara of Asram Mahā Rosei is nevertheless a fine piece. This is the earliest representation of a god "who united in his own body the god of good fortune (Viṣṇu) and the god who supports the moon (Śiva)." The headdress clearly shows the two aspects of the god: on the left the polished mitre of Viṣṇu and on the right the *jatā*, the high chignon of an ascetic worn by Śiva. Traces of

Pl. 8 Standing Buddha. Vat Romlok, Angkor Borei region (Ta Keo). National Museum of Phnom-Penh. Height: 125 cm. Early 7th century.

Pl. 9 Buddha seated in meditation. Phum Thmei, Kong Pisei (Kompong Speu). National Museum of Phnom-Penh. Height: 90 cm. 7th century.
Pl. 10 Reclining Nandin. Basak, Romduol (Prei Veng). National Museum of Phnom-Penh. Height: 56 cm. 7th century.

gold give the face a strange and rich appearance. The long panel attached to the belt in front of the robe presages an evolution in style. Subsequently the marvellous suppleness of the early Phnom Da period changed. The type of face altered, becoming more oval, the almond-eyes more slanting, the smile impenetrable. Pl. 5

A small and very damaged female statue probably belongs to this first period of Cambodian sculpture. The head Cat. 22 is dressed with a high chignon widening at the top and growing narrower with a twist at the base. The breasts are heavy and the hips broad. The long robe is pleated in front and held on the hips by a twisted scarf. Although this statue was found in one of the Phnom Da caves it is really a precursor of the style which follows. For, while the style of Sambor Prei Kuk was spreading and developing from the early seventh century, the art of Phnom Da suffered a gradual decline over the next hundred years.

BUDDHIST ART OF ANGKOR BOREI

Towards the end of the seventh century the Chinese pilgrim I-ch'ing, commenting upon the religious beliefs of Funan, made the following observation: "People there used to worship many gods and later the law of Buddha prospered and spread, but all this has been destroyed by an evil king." The sixth and seventh centuries have bequeathed us a Buddhist art of great beauty but we can scarcely recognize any Buddhist piece dating from the centuries immediately following with confidence. Did Buddhism suffer from persecution such as I-ch'ing describes? Statues of Buddha of the sixth and seventh centuries were created almost entirely outside the Brahman schools of sculpture, whereas images of the Bodhisattva came from these schools. The most important group of statues of Buddha was found in the monastery of Vat Romlok of Angkor Borei, where they

had been placed long ago by the faithful. We do not know their exact provenance. Undoubtedly the earliest piece is a head of Buddha now in the National Museum of Phnom-Penh, which Pierre Dupont attributed to the end of the fifth century. It is in dark sandstone with a full, slightly smiling face. The lowered gaze filtering through fringed, slanting eyelids, and the long, lobed ears give this face an Asiatic look which is belied by the rest of the physiognomy, for the fine nose and sensitive nostrils, narrow mouth and fleshy lips and the small jutting chin do not correspond to the Khmer physical type. Indeed they are far less Indian than Hellenistic.

The two Buddhas of Vat Romlok in the same museum emanate great charm yet the two pieces are quite different. One is a small statue of extreme elegance in which the Buddha, standing on two opening lotus flowers, makes the gesture of reassurance. His shoulders are covered with a monk's cloak in post-Gupta tradition, clinging closely to the figure. The body is slightly inclined over the bent leg in the graceful Indian position. The larger of the two wears a monastic cloak which leaves his right shoulder uncovered. The torso leans towards the outstretched leg in the Hellenistic manner as the Buddha bends forward in a gesture of reassurance to his followers. The stance of these two Buddhas is discreetly naturalistic: suppleness in the Indian movement combined with balance and freedom in the Hellenistic pose. The faces, beneath the curls, have been damaged but they are full of charm. The sculpture of Vat Romlok introduced Buddhist fervour into pre-Angkor art. The same expression of compassion reappears later at the end of the classic period on the statues of the Bayon.

SAMBOR PREI KUK

The art of Phnom Da is known to us through its statues alone; at Sambor Prei Kuk, however, the artists also carved rich decoration and legendary scenes, covering the walls with friezes, scrolls and bas-reliefs. A new spirit was abroad. The statuary of Phnom Da represents gods in the guise of idealized humans; Sambor, while not denying an ideal of beauty, preferred to treat the images with vigorous naturalism. A new vitality creeps into the bas-reliefs and the legendary scenes become humanized.

At Sambor Prei Kuk light falls sharp and clear on the carved golden brick. It outlines the foliate scrolls on a pillar, shows up the lotus flower on a frieze and illumines two figures leaning from an opening far above. On the walls of the pediments scenes unfold in palaces, supported by friezes of *haṃsas*, winged horses, and small *garuḍas* which are reminiscent of cherubim. The ceilings above the windows and in

*Pl. 8

Lolei, decoration on a false door

Pl. IV Temple guardian. Banteai Srei (Siem Reap). Second half of the 10th century.

Pl. 11 Śiva dancing. Detail of a lintel at Sambor Prei Kuk (Kompong Thom). National Museum of Phnom-Penh. Height of the lintel: 89 cm. 7th century.

the gables are crowded with figures, probably representing gods surrounded by their court. The bas-reliefs are in a very poor state of preservation and it would be vain to try to identify the characters: the most one can discern is a mitred figure or a well-rounded female form. A servant walks in front of the palace bearing a pitcher; more frequently a guard is watching the entrance.

On the southern boundary-wall work was begun on the

Pl. 12 Head of Viṣṇu. Unknown provenance. National Museum of Phnom-Penh. Height: 18 cm. 7th century.
Pl. 13 Torso of Durgā. Sambor Prei Kuk (Kompong Thom). National Museum of Phnom-Penh. Height: 59 cm. 7th century.

carving of medallions, but only three are finished and they are very worn. One of them shows a lion about to attack a man who tries to escape while attempting to kill the wild beast with a dagger. Another man lies dead on the ground. The struggle of the half-naked man against the beast is moving and pathetic. A second medallion depicts two animals fighting a buffalo and another scarcely identifiable beast. Only the twisting movement of the two bodies is discernible, the thrashing of hooves and the charge of the buffalo with lowered head. The third scene is in better condition and depicts a woman at her toilet. She stands, hips aslant, doing her hair; in her hand is a glass, while at her feet a hunch-backed ape-like creature offers her a kind of tray. Languidly elegant, she is exquisitely feminine; the movement of her hand as she holds the beribboned glass to her face is full of grace. The contrast between this charming figure and the grotesquely crouching acolyte is sharp. Could she be Sītā hearing news of Rāma from Hanuman? Or perhaps the unfortunate creature is human? In that case the scene probably represents the scene from the Rāmāyaṇa in which Manthūra, the hunch-backed servant, persuades the queen Kaikeyī to demand from her husband the exile of Rāma her stepson. In any case this mural bas-relief, one of the earliest in Cambodia, has a free composition which well transmits the rather sensual atmosphere inherited from India.

Carved sandstone bas-reliefs can be seen on the broad lintels of Sambor. Above the eastern door of the central sanctuary in the southern group Indra, holding the *vajra*, symbol of lightning, fills the whole of the lintel. On another lintel Śiva is dancing, his head dressed with a high chignon of curls and a snake twined across his neck and shoulder. The dance is accompanied by musicians led by a cymbal-player. At each end of the lintel a *garuḍa* struggles with a *nāga*-king. The iconography of the humanized *nāga*-kings, their heads crowned with snakes and with prominent nose, large beard and moustache, is Indian in origin.

Considering that such an enormous quantity of architectural decoration has survived it is surprising that there are so few statues in the Sambor style. The central sanctuary of the southern group enclosed a gold statue of "Śiva smiling".

Pl. 14 The Lady of Koh Krieng. Koh Krieng (Kratie). National Museum of Phnom-Penh. Height of the statue: 127 cm. 7th century (cf. Cat. 4, 10, 40).

Unfortunately the greater number of Sambor statues vanished long ago. No trace has been found of the gold *linga* nor the "Śiva with limbs hidden in the darkness of night", nor "Śiva dancing".

In many ways the Avalokiteśvara of Rach-gia, now in the Didelot Collection in Paris, is reminiscent of the art of Phnom Da. The Bodhisattva stands, smiling distantly, with a lotus beneath each foot, his curling hair surmounted by a tiara. The robe is a *dhoti*, an undergarment worn by Indians, while a jewelled belt encircles the hips. Viṣṇu appears most frequently in seventh-century statues, Śiva only rarely because he was generally worshipped under the phallic aspect of the *linga*. Viṣṇu always wears the cylindrical mitre and in the seventh century at any rate the fine curling hair disappears. The statues of Viṣṇu usually wear a *dhoti* which is draped in front with pleats falling to the ground, and held on the hips by a belt which is later discarded.

In the Viṣṇu of Kompong Cham Kau all traces of hip-movement have disappeared. Among all the statues of the mitred Viṣṇu very few achieve the quality of this unfinished piece. The god stands upright leaning slightly back. The mitre, still similar to those of Phnom Da, covers his short hair, while the square face and aquiline nose are of a type which is rarely seen among the Khmer people. Whilst it is a pity that it remained unfinished, the work gains strength from the uncut stone, a simplicity which accentuates the dignity of expression and attitude.

If the Viṣṇu of Kompong Cham Kau seems curious in shape, a similar accusation can be made about a Śiva of the same provenance. Śiva is figured here in an aspect peculiar to him, that of Yogin, the ascetic. An attempt to simplify the work has clearly been made. The muscular construction of the body is not even suggested. The arms are stiff and thin, while the long legs are left unmodelled.

Although the images of Śiva mentioned in Sambor Prei Kuk inscriptions have never been found, one may still try to picture their appearance by referring to the Śiva side of the Sambor Harihara. His costume is a short sampot, the front piece folded back to form a pocket, its ends falling in an outspread anchor-like shape. The headdress differs sharply from that of Phnom Da. On the Śiva side the god wears a high chignon of an ascetic, the coils of which have been lifted over the top of his head and fall behind the chignon in large loops. The Viṣṇu side of the mitre is the same size as the Śiva side. On examination of the face and the lines of the body one can see how far the aesthetic has advanced since the Phnom Da period. The smiling face has fine lines, the almond-shaped eyes are lightly cut, while a small dimple hollows out the chin. The artist has been at pains to show the muscles and the legs are fine and well-bred. Although it is much broken, this image of Harihara still retains great charm and elegance.

In contrast to the style of Phnom Da, Sambor Prei Kuk gives female figures a prominent position. The torso of a Pl. 13
female deity with four arms and firm hip-movement was found in the northern group at Sambor. This figure follows all the Indian canons of beauty: rounded, slightly separated breasts, broad hips and delicate carving. The swaying movement, which is very pronounced, denotes Indian influence. The shoulders held well back and turned slightly to the right, the left thigh advanced and a slight twist of the figure all suggest a strong movement. This is the attitude which is normally associated with the goddess Durgā in her aspect of Mahiṣāsuramardinī – the slayer of the buffalo-*asura*.

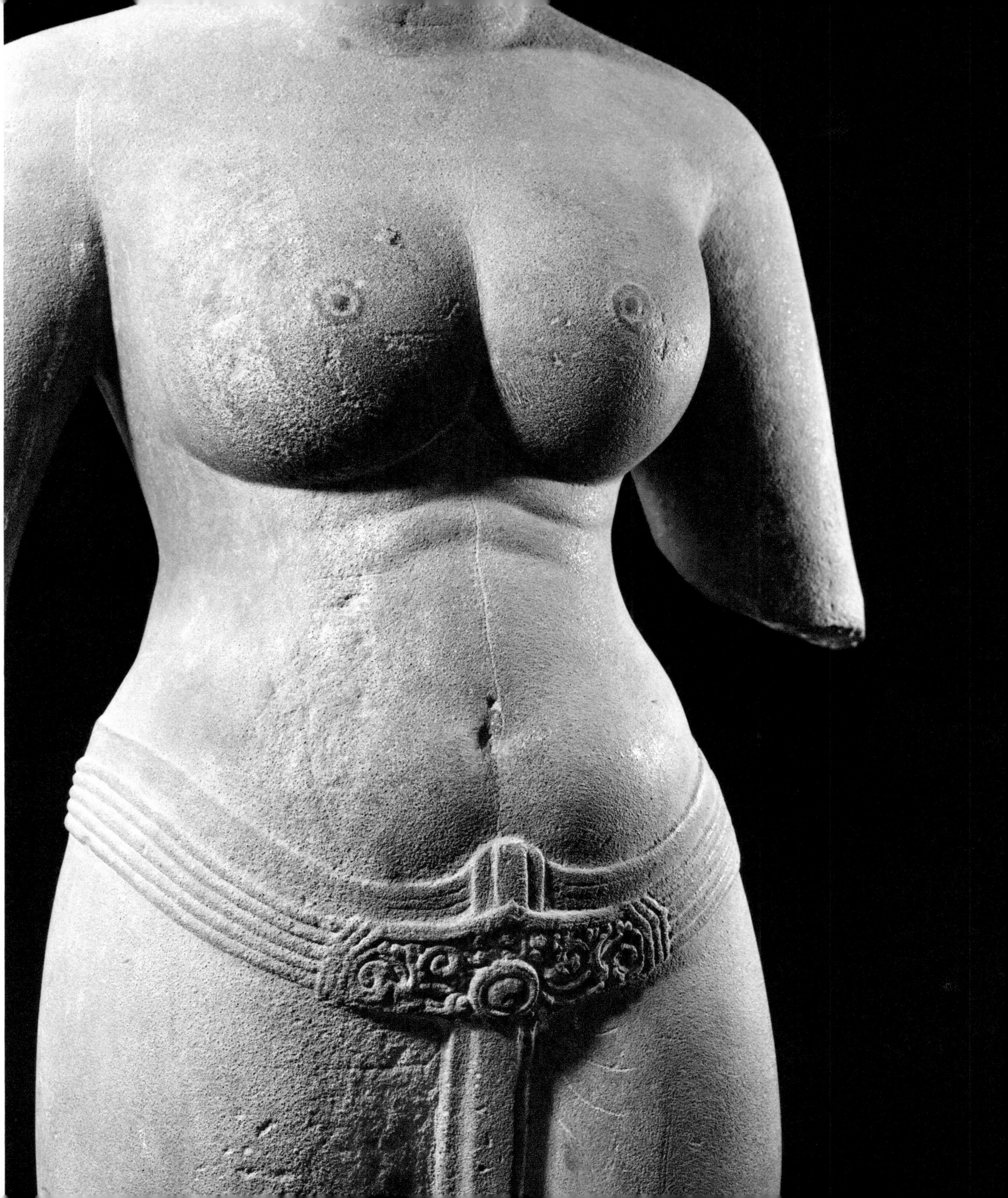

Pl. 15 Reclining Viṣṇu. Lintel of the Tuol Baset (Battambang). Museum of Vat Po Veal at Battambang. Height: 63 cm. Length: 158 cm. End of the 7th century.

Although she also belongs to the early part of the seventh century, the Lady of Koh Krieng in the Museum of Phnom-Penh was carved in a very different spirit. She was found near Sambor on the Mekong with arms and feet broken; she wears the high chignon decorated with falling loops seen on the Śiva side of the Harihara of Sambor Prei Kuk. Her clothing covers the lower part of her body and is draped in pleats in front. The delicate material, falling in folds down her side, scarcely hides the body. Her skirt is *Pl. 14 held by a finely-worked belt fastened by a broad clasp. There is a real relationship between the scroll decoration of this clasp and the strapwork on a chiselled gold belt recently found at Oudong. The realism of this image is startling. It owes almost nothing to India. The artist has used a living

model, no Indian woman, such as the statue of Sambor, but a woman of Cambodia past her first youth and portrayed in the guise of a divinity. The mature body is modelled with rare verisimilitude. The folds beneath the breasts and spreading hips suggest a figure running slightly to fat. The belly, constricted by the belt, is a remarkable piece of observation and the lines of the limbs beneath her sarong are suggested with great subtlety. The flat back and carriage of the head are typical of Cambodian women. The face, too, is intensely alive. Her eyes, wide open under high arched eyebrows, slightly aquiline nose and firm, compressed mouth all combine to give this face an expression of dominance. She gives the impression of a great lady. Are we then faced with a portrait? It is tempting to think so. Be that as it may, it must be conceded that the artist was inspired by his observations of Cambodian women to produce one of the finest pieces of the pre-Angkor period, and the most moving female statue in Khmer art.

PREI KMENG

In the early stages at least, the style of Prei Kmeng developed on lines parallel to those of Sambor Prei Kuk and its finest period was probably about the middle of the seventh century. The school of Prasat Andet, which was the child of Sambor and Prei Kmeng, can be recognized only by some free-standing sculpture. In this period there are no large compositions such as we find at Sambor Prei Kuk, nevertheless certain isolated monuments still show fine architectural decoration. In this respect the temple on the summit of Phnom Bayong is one of the most interesting, although the bas-reliefs are unfortunately in very poor condition. Scenes of celestial palaces unfold along the walls in the same way as those of Sambor Prei Kuk. Fortunately the frieze at the base of the superstructure, one of the finest of the Angkor period, has been preserved. It is decorated with a row of

Koh Ker, triangular façade

Pl.V Devatā. Angkor Vat. First half of the 12th century.

Pre Rup, decoration on a lintel representing Indra on his elephant

haṃsas. The bird of Brahma is shown here as a swan with outstretched wings, its long neck curving gracefully. The elegant line and close observation of the bird's anatomy and movement bear witness to the interest already shown by artists of the seventh century in the representation of animals. The bas-reliefs which decorate the lintels are the only examples from the period which are intelligible. On the lintel of Tuol Ang, Viṣṇu lies on a coiled snake whose seven heads form a halo round the god. The charm of this archaic image lies in its naiveté, for how could artists of a country, where every pool of water is full of fish, have failed to see that the cosmic ocean would also be populated? The lintel at Tuol Baset is in better condition. It is conserved in the monastery of Po Veal in Battambang and has a very interesting composition and technique showing strong Cham influence. Viṣṇu lies beneath the flattened arch characteristic of the Prei Kmeng style. The cylindrical mitre fits close to the god's forehead, finishing in a tiered crown. His costume is similar to the long frontal panel seen at Phnom Da, though in this case the panel has been folded back into a loop held by a jewelled belt. Viṣṇu's headdress, which is foreign to Khmer, is similar to that of the god on the pediment of Mi Son E_1. *Arhats* praying on the corbels are typical of Cham art. The faces, too, are surprising; thick arched eyebrows, sinuous and joined, large nose and heavy moustache covering the upper lip are all features which can be found on Cham statues. This lintel is carved in a purplish sandstone and must surely have been made in the Battambang region where the material is found.

A lintel from Vat Eng Khna is carved with an unusual bas-relief depicting two scenes: under the arch, the divine anointing of a king, and the procession to the king's private baptism. At either end of the lintel behind the officials stands a group of people, a dancer and musicians, drummers, Pl. 1
flautists and cymbal-players. The group has been rather carelessly carved, but it is full of life. The arch is flanked by three medallions, the central one of which has a *mukhalinga*, that is a *linga* with the head of Śiva. Of the others the one on the left has a portrait of Viṣṇu, the one on the right of Brahma. The sculptor clearly tried to show Śiva revealed in the *linga* proving his power over Viṣṇu and Brahma.

Figures on the Vat Eng Khna lintel show the male costume of the Prei Kmeng period in detail. It consisted of a length of cloth wound round the hips and knotted, sometimes with a folded panel in front. One of the sanctuaries of Sambor Prei *Pl. 15
Kuk has a Brahma with just this roll of material and no draping, but although the modelling of this figure is still fairly good it lacks the naturalism associated with works of the Sambor period.

Pl. 16 Female divinity. Prasat Thleay (Ta Keo). National Museum of Phnom-Penh. Height: 48 cm. End of the 7th century (cf. Cat. 23, 132).

Pl. 16 A new ideal of feminine beauty now manifests itself in elegant heads, softer bodies and slanting shoulders. The female figure of Prasat Thleay follows the new rules, likewise
Cat. 5 the portrait of Umā from Kompong Kleang, which remains graceful in its long robe despite the erosions of time. The costume of the Prasat Thleay statue is more sophisticated; although the fullness still comes to the front, the incised pleats are embellished with a soft loop in relief. The lower part of this figure is broken but one can still discern the twisting movement of the body. The model, with its sloping shoulders, high breasts and slim frame is young and graceful and the oval face has great purity, while the gaze of her almond-shaped eyes seems to follow a half-smiling dream. The Lady of Koh Krieng is full of dignity and verisimilitude, whereas the statue of Prasat Thleay possesses a subtle, langorous charm.

THE SCHOOL OF PRASAT ANDET

Prasat Andet is a small building constructed in the style of Prei Kmeng; in this humble sanctuary was concealed the
Pl. 17 Harihara, the most remarkable male statue in all pre-Angkor art. This is the best example of the school of sculpture which originated at the end of the seventh century and appears to have lasted into the early eighth. The two statues of Viṣṇu, in the Cleveland Museum of Art, foreshadow the Harihara of Prasat Andet with their high mitre, covering the crown of the head and sampot fastened on the hip and draped in front to form a pocket, but the muscular frame is still that of Sambor Prei Kuk.

The Harihara of Prasat Andet exhibits all the characteristics of the school which bears its name, and seems to be al-

Pl. 17 Harihara. Prasat Andet (Kompong Thom). National Museum of Phnom-Penh. Height: 194 cm. End of the 7th/early 8th century (cf. Pl. 18; Cat. 16, 34).

most a pattern for the aesthetic ideal of the period. The unsophisticated costume was handled with a patent desire to render the fall of the material exactly, showing the supple drapery of the pocket and rigidity of the tailpiece. A fine jewelled belt in the form of a simple chain adorned with a scrolled clasp holds the sampot; the slim figure has a slight twist to the right. Originally a supporting arch strengthened the figure so that the artist was free to fine down the legs. The torso is modelled less vigorously than is the case with the two Viṣṇus of the Cleveland Museum, but the carving of the muscles is at once less obvious and more exact. The artist faced a difficult problem when he came to model the back because he had to make double shoulders to bear the weight of the four arms; therefore the arch of the loins was accentuated to avoid too great a disproportion. The modelling of the legs where the muscles are no more than suggested is particularly fine, and the tensed ankles are well observed. The curling headdress of Śiva is united with the cylindrical mitre of Viṣṇu and a small flat ribbon with a denticulate edge borders the face, herald of the diadems to come. The face has Cambodian features: straight eyes, high cheek bones and clear-cut lips. Although the nobility of the pose and grave mien are hieratic, the Harihara of Prasat Andet still has an expressively human face. The two are hardly comparable, but the proportions and handling of a Harihara found recently at Ta Keo could well be an imitation of the figure from Prasat Andet. In the museum of Vat Po Veal at Battambang there is a head of Viṣṇu with arched, joined brows and a thick mouth under a clear-cut polished moustache, showing the smug self-satisfaction which was to reappear with even more assurance on the Viṣṇu in the style of Kulen at the beginning of the following century.

Pl. 18 Head of Harihara from Prasat Andet (cf. Pl. 17).
Pl. 19 Head of Viṣṇu. Unknown provenance. Michel Beurdeley Collection, Paris. Height: 17,5 cm. 8th century.

In contrast with the serious mien of the masculine divinities, female goddesses of the Prasat Andet school are nearly always smiling. They wear a long skirt draped in pleats with a soft bow. This robe clings to the hips then flows gently outwards in a bell shape. The pleats are indicated by incised lines, with a bow carved in relief. Undoubtedly the most attractive of these elegant statues is the image of Lakṣmī (?) from Popeal. As in most other female statues of the period the relaxed position of the hips is rather clumsily achieved. Although she has an almost childish face, her figure is very well-developed. Nevertheless, she seems to be a young girl because the full cheeks, smiling mouth, slightly parted lips and bright eyes express the friendly confidence of youth.

Pl. 20 Head of Harihara. Prasat Phum Prasat (Kompong Thom). National Museum of Phnom-Penh. Height: 21 cm. Early 8th century.
Pl. 21 Male head. Thma Dap, Phnom Kulen (Siem Reap). National Museum of Phnom-Penh. Height: 25 cm. First half of the 9th century (cf. Cat. 17).

THE STYLE OF KOMPONG PREAH AND THE END OF THE ART OF CH'EN-LA

The style of Kompong Preah arose during the troubles which disturbed the eighth century. Decoration weakened on the monuments as they degenerated into insignificant sanctuaries. After the fantastic animals people and flower garlands had been abandoned, imaginative decoration disappeared altogether. There is great variety in costume, technique and conformation of the statues. The art of Kompong Preah was inspired by the styles which preceded it and the handling of certain elements is the direct result of de-

Pl. 22 Female figure. Angkor region. Dépôt archéologique de la Conservation d'Angkor. Height: 91 cm. Second half of the 10th century.

velopments originating in the middle of the seventh century. Thus, the coiffure, mitre or *jatā-mukuṭa*, is contained within a cylinder which narrows slightly from the top of the head to the chignon. The many statues of Harihara had contributed to the standardization of the two aspects of the divided headdress.

The variety of costume is less the result of evolution than a return to earlier styles, though a Harihara found at Trapeang Phong wears a robe pleated at one side and folded over the belt, foreshadowing the art of the ninth century. It is possible that this Harihara was made a few years after the turn of the century. The physical types are, however, very varied. Some more or less successful attempts were made to copy the Harihara of Prasat Andet. The pieces from Trapeang Phong, both Śiva and Harihara, have the heavy lines associated with the ninth century, while the tendencies noticeable in the Prasat Andet school are confirmed in the female figures; the hip position is exaggerated to the point of deformity. Faces on the early examples of the style are still smiling, but this expression gradually fades in the course of the eighth century.

Pl. 20 There are still some finely-carved pieces. A head of Harihara has recently been found at Prasat Phum. The body, which has been preserved in Angkor for a long time, is rather worn, though the head is in good condition. The full face has delicately moulded features: a fine nose, sensitively carved, and almond-shaped eyes modelled close to the head with finely arched eyebrows. The parted lips, with only the shadow of a smile, give the face an attentive expression. The young-faced Harihara must be regarded as one of the first examples of the style of Prasat Andet. Female statues of the school show an early example of this youthful ideal,

Pl. 23 Female torso. Bakong (Siem Reap). Dépôt archéologique de la Conservation d'Angkor. Height: 40 cm. Second half of the 9th century.

Pl. 24 Apsaras. Bakong (Siem Reap). Second half of the 9th century.

Pl. 25 Wrestlers. Prasat Thom, Koh Ker (Siem Reap). National Museum of Phnom-Penh. Height: 80 cm. Second quarter of the 10th century.

coming rather close to the goddesses of the Kompong Preah style. A statue of Durgā Mahiṣāsuramardinī, found near Kompong Trabek, exemplifies the transition between the styles. The resting position is depicted by a thickening of the left hip but it implies no movement, only a deformity. The eyes are carved within the profile, but the fleshy mouth has been drawn with care and the face is animated by an expression at once sulky and astonished. A female statue more typical of the style of Kompong Preah was discovered at Koh Krieng. It has only two arms and wears a high chignon just like the "Lady of Koh Krieng". These two pieces, so similar in iconography, are enormously different in their technique and expression. The face is still expressive but the body has lost much of its suppleness. The mouth, in a somewhat flattened face, no longer smiles and the lower lip can hardly be said to give the face a comely appearance. The whole of this rather robust figure reveals a definite sense of authority with more strength and youth, but far less nobility than the "Lady of Koh Krieng" possesses. Apart from these two pieces the eighth century has left us some more or less mediocre statues and after the first resistance to the political crisis of Ch'en-la this style in turn begins to degenerate.

Pl. 26 Decorative lintel. Phum Or Taki (Battambang). Museum of Vat Po Veal at Battambang. Height: 43 cm. First half of the 10th century.
Pl. 27 Viṣṇu rides on Garuḍa. Bas-relief of the Prasat Kravan, Angkor. First half of the 10th century.

THE DEVELOPMENT OF ANGKOR

In Cambodia the end of the eighth century was a critical period. Art was sadly impoverished after the crumbling of the Ch'en-la empire, but the reconstruction which took place under Jayavarman II infused new life. The traditions of pre-Angkor art were exhausted and it was necessary to interpret fresh ideas in a new way. The artists of the early ninth century appear to have been unprejudiced, and to have looked everywhere for inspiration in an attempt to create a powerful and fecund art.

The style of Kulen, which begins after Jayavarman's capture of Cambodia, developed and spread, although it was still contained within the framework of the sanctuary. At Prasat Damrei Krap the construction is purely Cham: at Rong Chen the greater depth of the foundation is the first timid step towards the temple built on an artificial mound which was to make its appearance in the style introduced at the end of the century. The towers of Preah Ko are grouped on a common pedestal; the temple mountain of Bakong stands on a high sandstone pyramid. Sculptors were now faced with the decoration, not only of lintels and pediments, but also of the facings of the terraces and the blocks of sandstone which were embedded in the brick walls.

Pl. 28 Śiva and Umā. Banteai Srei (Siem Reap). National Museum of Pnom-Penh. Height: 60 cm. Second half of the 10th century.
Pl. 29 Head of Śiva. Banteai Srei (Siem Reap). National Museum of Phnom-Penh. Height: 32 cm. Second half of the 10th century.

THE STYLE OF KULEN

The only Kulen-style bas-reliefs to have been preserved are the lintels. Surrounded by foliage, figures leap or pray; sea monsters – *makaras* – rear their horns, huge heads of *kālas*, inspired by Java, bare their teeth, supporting a divinity attended by women. Up till now we have found only images of Viṣṇu in the sanctuaries and an abstract conception, of course, of the *linga*, the phallic emblem of Śiva. Viṣṇu is always represented with four arms and the tall, mitred headdress covering the entire head. The sampot is draped into a pocket in a more or less naturalistic way and the upper part of the folded material falls to the right.

Undoubtedly the finest Viṣṇu images come from Rup Arak and the central sanctuary of Prasat Damrei Krap. Of course the extreme elegance of line of the Prasat Andet school has gone, but in the Kulen period the ideal was neither distinction nor finesse. The artists sought to exalt the power of the god, who therefore appeared as a muscular young man in the flower of his strength. The smiling face beneath the tall mitre is self-confident, even a little smug.

The last images in the Kulen style which come from this sanctuary of Thma Dap, are rather worn but they have a more amiable expression; it is possible that the sweetness of their faces comes from wear on the stone.
Pl. 21 Another carved male head is adorned now for the first time with a diadem and a jewelled cap for the chignon,
Cat. 106 and a rather surprising piece is a *garuḍa*-head whose round little eyes seem to twinkle with mischief.

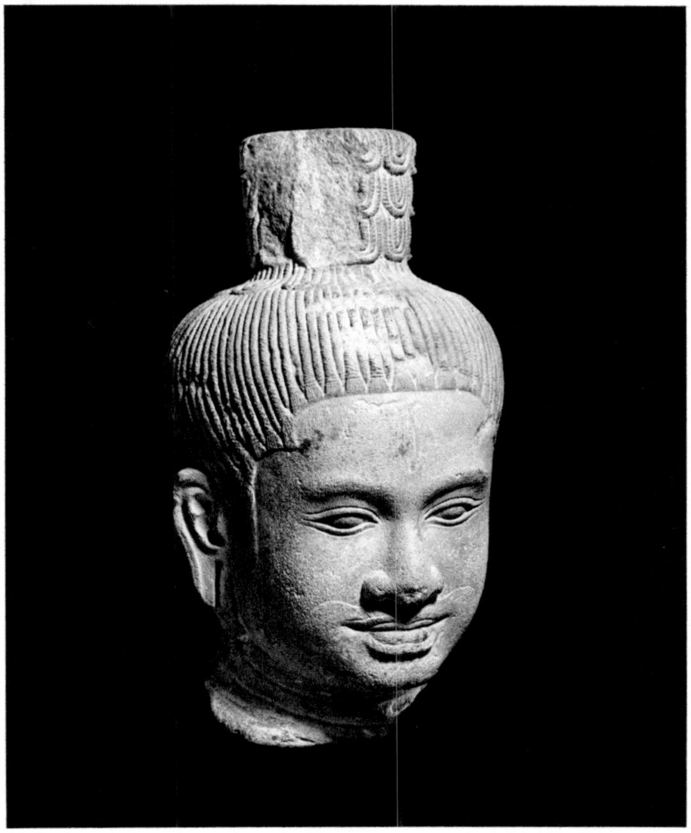

THE STYLE OF PREAH KO

By the end of the ninth century the statues were carved freely in the round without support, but the outline became clumsier in consequence and crudely-modelled legs supported the heavy-chested and broad-hipped divinities. Of all the varied male costumes of the Kulen school the sculptors chose the polished sampot, folded with a pocket on the left thigh and a broad pleated panel in front. Since no female statues have been found at Phnom Kulen we are completely in the dark about the evolution of the bell-skirt of the eighth

Pl. VI Devatā. Angkor Vat. First half of the 12th century.

century which resulted in the costume of the Preah Ko style, where the skirt has a pleat folded over at the top and a small triangular panel, also pleated and draped over the left hip. The diadem which appeared at Thma Dap is worn on the forehead in the form of a jewelled crown fastened by a ribbon at the nape of the neck. Viṣṇu wears a carved headdress over the chignon, narrow at the base like the crest of a helmet. The *jatā* worn by Śiva is now rigidly cylindrical and entirely covered with rows of small looped fillets. A jewelled tapering headdress covers the chignon on the female figure. The line of the eyebrows, thick and unbroken, gives the faces an almost rectangular look. The mouth is half-smiling and clearly outlined, and the eyes, with the iris deeply engraved, have a far-away gaze. The masculine figures have a closely-shaven beard covering the chin and cheeks.

The Śiva of Bakong stands slightly oblique, a massive and noble figure, but the female figures are more naturalistic, albeit still hieratic in feeling. The museum of Angkor possesses a fine female torso of generous proportions and an Pl. 23
even larger one in the National Museum of Phnom-Penh has been identified, by its inscription, with the divine image of Queen Rājendradevī. In the sanctuary at Bakong three finely-carved statues stand together upon one pedestal. This is a representation of Śiva "with his loins embraced by the arms of Umā and Gangā". The *devatās* and *dvāra-* Cat. 35
pālas, sculptured in high relief in the blocks of sandstone attached to the walls of the sanctuaries of Preah Ko, have the

Ta Keo, drawing of the elevation reconstructed from incomplete documents

Pl. 30 Devatā. Banteai Srei (Siem Reap). Second half of the 10th century.

Pl. 31 Krishna and Balarāma. Detail of a façade at Banteai Srei (Siem Reap). National Museum of Phnom-Penh. Height of the façade: 189 cm. Second half of the 10th century (cf. Cat. 119).

*Pl. 24 same features as the statues and wear similar clothes. They are adorned with necklaces, bracelets and many belts.

In contrast to the fixed gravity of the gods, the bas-reliefs are remarkable for their fantasy and animation. Small creatures run about in foliage on the lintels, riding on fabulous and sometimes grotesque animals, or they gather in groups on the friezes. The whole of the front of the wall of the final level at Bakong was covered with bas-reliefs. Usually they are split and broken; only an occasional fragment preserves

Cat. 118 the fierce mien and savage gesture of the *asuras* fighting. The broken scenes leave us only to guess at the elegance of line and beautiful balance of the composition. Here and there flying figures survive, full of life, while their pleated draperies float around them. The frenzy of the dance inhabits the carved figures.

The divine images of the ninth century are remarkable for their heavy bodies and frigid hieratical expression, and it must be admitted that they are a disappointment after the brilliant flowering of pre-Angkor; but the small figures dancing on the walls to the sound of distant music are proof that the artists had not lost their inherent sense of vitality.

Pl. 32 Śiva. Phum Bavel (Battambang). Museum of Vat Po Veal at Battambang. Height: 134 cm. First half of the 11th century.
Pl. 33 Female torso. Banteai Kdei, Angkor. Dépôt archéologique de la Conservation d'Angkor. Height: 140 cm. First half of the 11th century.

THE ART OF ANGKOR

PHNOM BAKHENG

Very few years divide the styles of Preah Ko and Phnom Bakheng. The reign of Yaśovarman was a continuation and development of that of Indravarman, his father; likewise the art of Phnom Bahkeng carried on and developed the style of Preah Ko. The temple of Lolei represents a transitional phase and marks the abandonment of Hariharālaya by Yaśovarman. After the king had taken up residence at Angkor a new architecture arose and flourished; brick was relegated to the secondary sanctuaries, while the pyramid of Phnom Bakheng was built in sandstone as were also the five towers which form its crown, and three sanctuaries of Trimūrti built on the two other hills of the Angkor region, Phnom Krom and Phnom Bok.

Sculpture remains faithful to the spirit of Preah Ko. The costumes of the statues change and are pleated all over on both the male and female statues. The front of the male sampot has a panel, pleated, but stiff like a double anchor. The fixed, hieratic effect of the ninth century becomes rigid in the Bakheng style. The line of the eyebrows is more decisively rectangular and the regard more distant. There is no warmth in the smile.

The bas-reliefs on Yaśovarman's buildings have suffered greatly from the ravages of time. The surface of the stone has frequently cracked and the towers at Phnom Krom, torn by the winds of the Great Lake, have seen their reliefs being gradually eaten away. The rare fragments which have survived are magnificent. The central sanctuary of Phnom Bak-

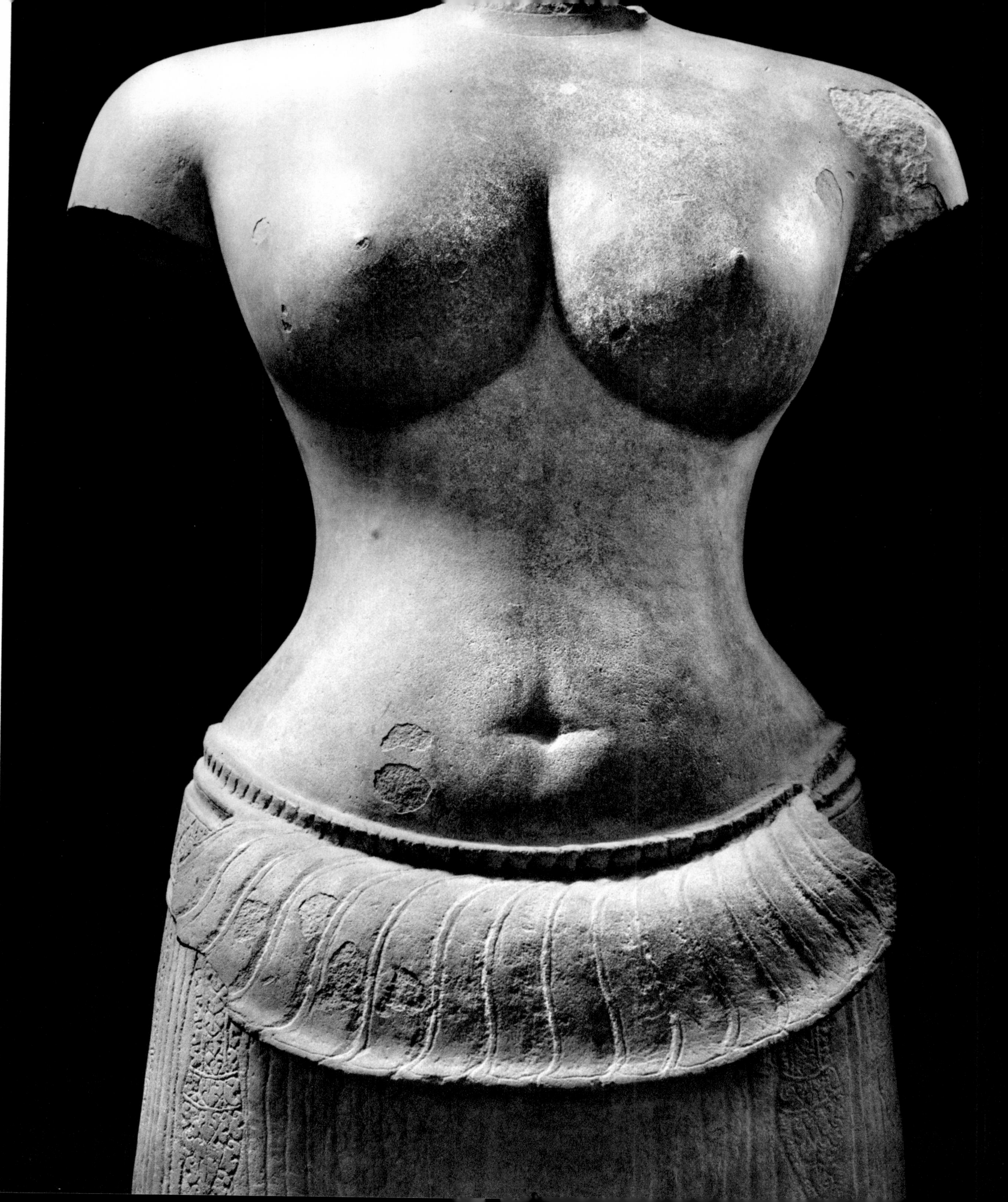

Pl. 34 Male figure. Prasat Rolom (Battambang). Museum of Vat Po Veal at Battambang. Height: 135 cm. Second half of the 11th century.

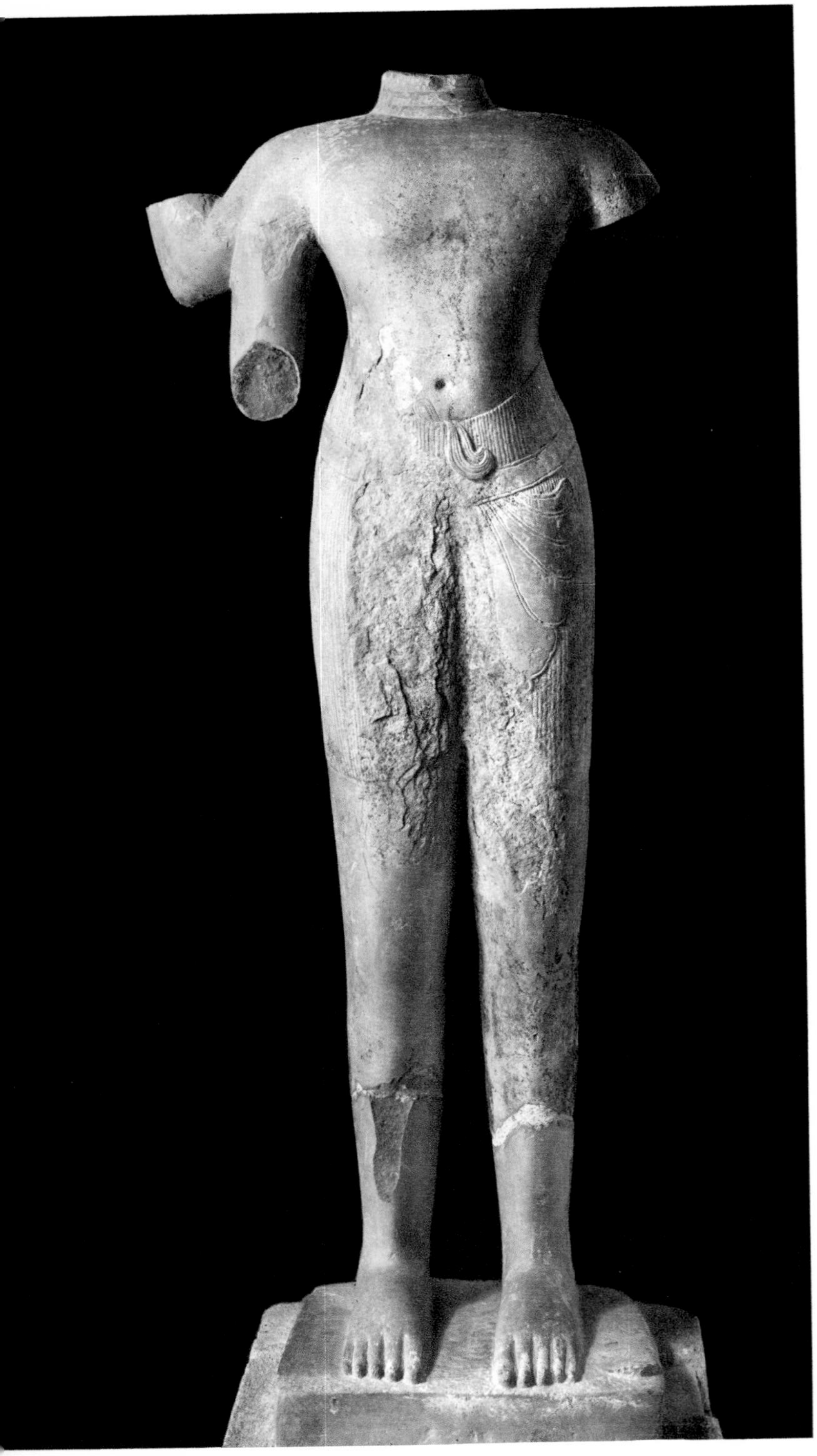

heng still guards some fine large-hipped *devatās*. These mature figures are close to smiling and their finely-carved hands hold a flower or a fly-whisk. On the lintels foliage intertwines but no longer conceals the small figures that gave Preah Ko its charm, and in this respect the Bakheng style seems the least successful in Khmer art.

INNOVATIONS IN THE STYLE OF KOH KER

Koh Ker evolved under the influence of an usurper with a fine sense of grandeur, burning with zeal for novelty, and it marks a turning-point in Khmer art. The sanctuaries of Prasat Kravan at Angkor, and Prasat Neang Khmau in the province of Yaleo, were constructed during the reign of the two sons of Yaśovarman. In the Koh Ker group the religious setting of this ephemeral capital can be seen in the vestiges of imposing buildings decorated with remarkable sophistication.

It is generally accepted that Koh Ker statuary exhibits a certain rigidity in comparison with Bakheng, because the examples best known in Europe and coming from Phnom Bok, show hard and stiff faces which were never to appear again in Khmer art. These pieces, which mark the transition between the two styles have caused a certain denigration of Koh Ker; but the examples which actually come from Koh Ker are far more interesting. It is true, however, that the torso of the idols is still stiff and the costume remains almost unaltered except for the disappearance of the draped pocket on male figures, and the pleated triangular panel on the skirt of female figures. A fine, mature, female figure was carved in Cat. 6
sandstone ranging in colour from dark green to a bronze pa-

Pl. 35 Male head. Bassac (Prei Veng). National Museum of Phnom-Penh. Height: 24 cm. Second half of the 11th century.
Pl. 36 Figures of Śiva and Umā. Prasat Don Ap (Siem Reap). Dépôt archéologique de la Conservation d'Angkor. Height: 40 cm. Second half of the 11th century.

tina. Discovered at Prasat Neang Khmau in the "Sanctuary of the Dark Lady", which gets its name from her, the figure is now in the National Museum of Phnom-Penh.

The fundamental characteristics of Khmer art are most clearly seen in the handling of the facial expressions. The lips of the gods smile once again, and the sculptors of Koh Ker made greater efforts than before to perpetuate their living models; they created isolated figures and groups. At Prasat
Pl. 25; *Pl. 26 Chen the two monkey-kings, Sugrīva and Vālin, come to blows in a sudden access of rage with cries of hatred emerging from their shattered jaws. In a broken group two wrestlers grip one another in man-to-man combat. An immense Śiva once adorned Prasat Kraham, but alas, only fragments remain. He danced, hieratic and stiff, with bent knees, his ten arms deployed round the polished torso like a fan, and his five beautiful heads smiling benevolently, for he was called "The Propitious".

The museum of Vat Po Veal at Battambang owns a lintel carved with the legend of Śiva, which is rather unusual in composition and iconography. There are three scenes side

Pl. 37 Viṣṇu. Prasat Trapeang Totung Thngay (Siem Reap). Dépôt archéologique de la Conservation d'Angkor. Height: 155 cm. Second half of the 11th century.

by side. On the right, Śiva accompanied by his two wives stands in a chariot drawn by a lion; in the centre he is with Parvatī on Mount Kailāsa which is being assailed by Rākṣasa Rāvaṇa. On the left the artist has illustrated the legend wherein the god is the conqueror of three cities which have been built by three *daityas*, enemies of the gods. The city on earth was of iron, the one in the sky of silver and the one in heaven of gold. Gaining merit through ascetism the *daityas* had Brahma's promise that the fortresses could only be conquered by a single arrow. Strong in this assurance they began to harass the gods, and Śiva agreed to attack them. Mounted in a chariot with Brahma as his charioteer he annihilated the three cities. The story is treated in a very picturesque manner here. Śiva advances triumphant on his chariot drawn by a lion led by Brahma, while the three *daityas* and their citadels fall headlong from the other end of the lintel. A similar mood inspires the central scene where the torso of Rāvaṇa with its many heads and arms appears from the front of the mountain, while the legs can be seen in the background. These unusual compositions translate the naïve fantasies of the people into stone.

Although the two scenes are of great interest they cannot be compared with those which decorate the sanctuaries of Prasat Kravan; carved in brick, these reliefs owe the restraint of their lines and the vigour of their modelling to the coarse, coloured material in which they worked. Sometimes a ray of sunlight filters through the broken vault flickering over the Viṣṇu idols of the inner sanctuary; suddenly in the shadows an eight-armed god or Viṣṇu can be discerned standing above the waters or advancing in triumph supported by Garuḍa. The interior of the sanctuary is only rarely decorated with bas-reliefs and in any case not after the Koh Ker style; likewise carving in the round was soon to be discarded for figures in movement.

Koh Ker, reduced to the rank of a provincial town in a distant corner of the realm, gradually saw its influence wane as the kings returned to Angkor. Nevertheless, smiling vitality permeated its sculpture and the more humanistic treatment of figures reappearing there was not to be abandoned again.

BANTEAI SREI

*Pl. 27

After Angkor had been restored to its position as capital the artists turned back for inspiration to the preceding century.

Pl. 38 Krishna fighting with the serpent. Bas-relief from the Baphuon. Angkor. Second half of the 11th century.
Pl. 39 Rāma consoling Sugrīva. Bas-relief from the Baphuon. Angkor. Second half of the 11th century.

Summoned to decorate the mountain temples of Pre Rup and the Eastern Mebon, they copied the lintels of Preah Ko and began to model in stucco again. This decoration of the buildings reveals a sureness of hand and rather dry handling of the material. Nevertheless the development begun at Koh Ker continued and the idols have a fragile sweetness of expression which heralds the art of Banteai Srei.

It is often said that there is nothing in Khmer art to compare with Banteai Srei. Perhaps this may seem exaggerated, but it is certainly true that Banteai Srei contrasts sharply with the buildings of other stylistic periods, especially in the vivid tones of its pink sandstone, its small proportions and the prodigious richness of delicate decoration. As one moves from the eastern door towards the central sanctuary the dimensions of the surrounding walls and of the pavilions centred on them grow smaller while the decoration on the walls becomes bolder and richer.

Magnificence and astonishing variety emerge as the dominant characteristics of the Banteai Srei style. The visitor is at once struck by the decorative plant *motifs*, the friezes, arches, and representations of humans and animals both in relief and the round. The imaginative wealth of subject and brilliant interpretation of the carved figures balance the richness of the decoration.

Never before had the artists depicted so many adventures of the gods. Seeking inspiration in legends and epics, they used the chronicles of Śiva and Viṣṇu. The iconography of the northern library is that of Viṣṇu; while the myths of Śiva covered the whole of the southern library. Occasionally one god occupies a whole pediment; Śiva, shining

Pl. 40 Horseman. Detail of a frieze on the western entrance to Angkor Vat. First half of the 12th century (cf. Cat. 92).

with nobility and grace, dances in the aureole of his ten arms. Turning back in a triumphant gesture, Durgā spears the demon-buffalo lying unconscious at her feet. Sometimes there is a crowd of figures; in the palace of Kaṃsa, smitten down by Krishna, women and slaves run about in terror; the jungle beasts spring with joy in the refreshing rain unleashed by Indra; Umā on the mountain-top, shaken by Rāvaṇa, leans against her husband. It is impossible to enumerate all the mythological stories carved on the lintels and pediments of the *gopuras,* chapels and main sanctuaries of this temple. Above the door gods and heroes danced, fought or sat enthroned in majesty, guarded by *dvārapālas* and *devatās*; within the sanctuaries the idols reigned, hidden from view and watched over by the animal-headed guardians at the gates.

The sculptors adopted a great variety of costume, jewellery and headdress for the different deities. The sampot and the female skirt were often still a simple piece of material pleated and arranged with a turned edge in front and stylized floating panels shaped like an anchor; but the polished robe knotted with a bow at the belt reappeared, in imitation of the Preah Ko style, and also the panel folded on the left hip in a pocket on male figures. The *dvārapālas* of Banteai Srei and a few three-dimensional figures, among them the Lokeśvara of Tuol Ci Tep, wear this kind of dress.

Some of the statues of Viṣṇu still have the diadem decorated with a flower on the forehead. Others have the cylindrical chignon embellished with little looped tassels, but there is a new freedom in the treatment which was not seen at Preah Ko.

One particularly graceful headdress is reserved for the *devatās.* Looking at them one can easily picture the young woman arranging the complicated chignon of her hair, threading a garland of jasmine and choosing the flowers for
her forehead. A head in the Phnom-Penh National Museum Cat. 11
has a headdress of this kind. It is an unfinished portrait, for *Cat. 61
the hair has not been carved, only the mass of hair is knotted, *Cat. 124
falling in a plait on the nape; small flowers have been carved out all round the chignon.

Surprising as it may seem, this very decorative style was sparing in its use of jewels. *Dvārapālas,* who elsewhere are weighted down with precious stones, are unadorned at Banteai Srei. The deities of the reliefs and the sanctuary idols are similar, but it is possible that the statues were be-

Pl. VII Incident in the Battle of Kurukṣetra. Angkor Vat. First half of the 12th century.

Pl. 41 Male divinity. Provenance unknown. Dépôt archéologique de la Conservation d'Angkor. Height: 109 cm. Early 12th century.

Pl. 42 Prajñāpāramitā. Vat Kompong Ampil (Battambang). Museum of Vat Po Veal at Battambang. Height: 74 cm. Middle of the 12th century.

decked with real jewels. Only the *devatās* and the figures on the high levels wear necklaces, bracelets and earrings, which hang from the elongated lobes of their ears; the belts adorned with garlands of pendant pearls in the Indo-Javanese style are reminiscent of those on the *devatās* of Phnom Bayong

*Pl. III carved almost three centuries before. The restraint shown in the handling of jewellery accords with another aspect of the art of Banteai Srei – its elegance. The slim graceful *devatās* are very different from the nobly-proportioned ladies of the Bakheng sanctuary. By tradition ample and solid, the Banteai Srei *dvārapālas* are young and slim.

The purity of line to which decoration was always subservient is the reason for the success of Banteai Srei; on the tympana of the entrance pavilions several vigorously carved figures stand out from a plain background. On the pediments where the monkey kings are locked in combat, Rāma, confident and noble stringing his bow, his brother at his feet, makes a fine contrast. Elegance of gesture is combined with a remarkable skill in composition. On the same façade the group of Rāma and Lakṣmaṇa is balanced by Vālin, dying in his mother's arms. A skilful triangular composition divides the protagonists and spectators of the battle

Pl. 43 Head of Buddha on the nāga. Banon (Battambang). Museum of Vat Po Veal at Battambang. Height: 39 cm. First half of the 12th century.

Pl. 44 Head of Lokeśvara. Beng Mealea (Siem Reap). Dépôt archéologique de la Conservation d'Angkor. Height: 56 cm. First half of the 12th century.

Pl. 45 Devatā. On the western entrance gates of Angkor Vat. First half of the 12th century.

between Bhīma and Duryodhana; on one side the four brothers of Bhīma and on the other his allies, Krishna and Balarāma, make a framework while the point of the triangle is formed by lines converging on the body of Bhīma and the chariot of Balarāma.

The art of Banteai Srei, elegant and imaginative, is vital and alive: the terrified Umā runs to Śiva for protection; Sītā cries out as she is dragged off by a grinning demon; Sugrīva and Vālin fight to the death before the eyes of the two old monkeys crying with sorrow; and Śiva with Olympian calm turns his third eye on the carefree god of love. The *Pl. 31
handling of animals is brilliant. The beasts sit solemnly on steps; horrified by Rāvaṇa's boldness they run to Kailāsa for protection and, joyful in the rain sent by Indra, they bound through the forest. Khmer art is reborn at Banteai Srei. The knowledge and artistic taste of its founder, Yajñavarāha, were partly responsible, reawakening the genius which had lain dormant since the decadence of pre-Angkor art.

Pl. 46 Devatā. Angkor Vat. First half of the 12th century.
Pl. 47 Devatā. Angkor Vat. First half of the 12th century.

ART OF THE ELEVENTH CENTURY

By the late tenth century the Khleang style had developed the classical temple-mountain. Galleries gird the building on the steps of the two pyramids, laterite at Phimeanakas and sandstone at Ta Keo. The latter lacks the greater part of its foliage decoration as it was never finished. The proportions of its five sanctuaries, the lines of the galleries and rhythm of the angular towers and pavilions on the perimeter are of classical purity. Dating from the second half of the century, the temple of the Baphuon already bears the seed which was to flower at Angkor in the addition of a long causeway passing through the perimeter walls. Although much dilapidated and restored on the western façade, the

Pl. VIII Devatā. Preah Khan, Angkor. Late 12th / early 13th century.

Baphuon's outer pavilions are decorated with small legendary scenes placed one above the other. Even though it is impossible to cite a single bas-relief in the Khleang style, the dramatic scenes in the Baphuon are equal to those of Banteai Srei.

The walls of the pavilions of Prasat Khna Sen Keo are covered with dramatic scenes, decorated lintels, and pediments reappear at Vat Ek near Battambang after the transition period between Khleang and Baphuon. Subsequently many small village sanctuaries contained a legend, nearly always about Viṣṇu. The Khleang style developed a school of statuary, though very few pieces survive. On the pleated male costume the double-anchor fold and pocket become gradually more stylized and the diadem is sometimes lacking, as at Banteai Srei. The plaited hair is held high
Pl. 33 in a horizontally constructed chignon. One very fine female figure from Banteai Kdei wears a pleated skirt held on the hips by a belt decorated with long jewelled tassels.

The style of Khleang is less tense than that of Banteai Srei, and a particular characteristic of this school of sculpture is a slightly veiled, smiling expression. It can be seen on the head of Lokeśvara in the Phnom-Penh National Museum and on the faces of three idols representing Brahma, two of which are at Vat Po Veal in the gardens of the governor of Battambang, and the third in the National Museum of Phnom-Penh. A curious fact is that Lokeśvara, who is normally rather rare, was depicted at least three times during the same period in the region of Battambang. The Baphuon style has a different fashion in costume. Pleats are extremely narrow and both male and female costumes leave the belly almost completely uncovered, but rise high at the back. The short sampot is held by a belt knotted on the right hip; the pocket fold on the left hip becomes more and more stylized until it is no more than a decoration, the origin of which has been forgotten. The tail of the sampot, folded back into the belt, spreads out into a broad butterfly bow. Female figures wear a broad piece of material reaching from hip to ankle and clinging close to the body; in the front hangs a vertical panel in the shape of a fish-tail. A jewelled belt fastened with

Pl. 48 Musicians. Detail of a façade of Banteai Samre (Siem Reap). First half of the 12th century (cf. Cat. 115).

a cord encircles the hips; towards the end of the period the belts are decorated with two rows of flat oval discs and this fashion will be seen engraved on jewelled work in the early Angkor Vat period. Simplicity in costume extended also to the headdress. Tiaras are rare. Plaited hair coiled on the top of the head forms a round chignon held in place by a gold ring or a garland of flowers while the most elegant figures have rows of pearls separating the strands of hair. The fashion for braided hair was even extended to the Buddha and may be seen on the very fine Buddha of Peam Cheang; a small jewelled border on the forehead of the god hides the roots of the hair and a conical chignon carved with denticulations covers the *uṣnīṣa*. It is the headdress of Viṣṇu, which is normally accompanied by a tiara.

The faces in Baphuon art are distinctive, with clearly drawn features, lips outlined and a cleft chin. Male figures wear a close-cut beard ending in a point on the chin. The eyes are very large, but incised not carved. Although many

Pl. 49 Warrior chief wounded and dying on his chariot. Detail of the battle of Kurukṣetra. Angkor Vat. First half of the 12th century.
Pl. 50 Devatā. Bayon. End of the 12th / early 13th century.

of the idols which have been found have a hollowed iris, they show no signs of incrustation, but this does not necessarily exclude such a possibility. A rather large head almost always surmounts a very slim body.

The adoption of a support behind the ankles allowed a fining-down of the legs. The delightful Lakṣmī of Prasat Trapeang Totung Thngai is slim as a taper; she glides forward, scarcely moving her hips, her hands held out to receive fresh-cut lotus blossom.

The spirit of the bas-reliefs was the same whether they were cut on walls or lintels. Viṣṇu legends usually graced the lintels – the cosmic sleep of the god, or his churning of the sea of milk to extract the elixir of life, or an episode taken from Rāmāyana. But the walls depict animals confronting or attacking one another; scene after scene, the marvellous history unfolds. Here are the stories of Krishna's boyhood and here Rāmā and Lakṣmaṇa, surrounded by despairing monkeys, lie bound by the coils of the snakes springing from the magic arrows of Rākṣasa Indrajit, while Garuḍa, enemy of the serpents, flies to their rescue; and finally at the top of the frieze the two princes kneel to thank their deliverer. The composition of these reliefs is simple; a few figures, a tree or two, and some animals, for the sculptors of the Baphuon were worthy successors to the Banteai Srei artists, carving fine animal-scenes. The bas-reliefs unfold a bestiary where the animals are sometimes treated naturalistically and sometimes as symbols moving in an epic story – a bird flutters up, a squirrel climbs along a branch, a rabbit crouches between the hooves of a rearing horse.

Subjects are endlessly varied. Rāvaṇa leaps into his chariot; riders move majestically forward, then turn slowly, each one forming a fine rhythmic curve, from his tilted

Pl. 51 The fruit thief. Bas-relief on the Bayon, Angkor. End of the 12th / early 13th century.
Pl. 52 Hunting-scene. Bas-relief on the Bayon, Angkor. End of the 12th / early 13th century.

head to his outstretched legs. Two *asuras* fight for the possession of the beautiful *apsaras* Tilottama, who sits between them, lost in a dream and apparently indifferent to the struggle around her. In a more serious scene the exiled Śitā mourns beneath a tree with one hand before his face, a gesture which the modern Cambodian ballet has retained as a symbol of sadness; Rāma leans down to Sugrīva touching his shoulder to ease his sorrow.

THE ART OF ANGKOR VAT

The search for formal beauty preoccupied the artists in the Angkor Vat period. The preceding centuries had left them heir to a highly developed art corresponding to their highest aspirations. They sought to bring to perfection a standard established over several centuries. The perimeter walls, causeways, galleries and sanctuary towers were already part of the Khmer temple, but there remained the task of creating rhythm and harmony, which even the temple of the Baphuon had only imperfectly realized. While the temples of Banteai Samre, Thommanon, Chau Say Tevoda and, in part, that of Preah Khan of Kompong Svay each keeps its courts independently of the others, Beng Meala, which is also constructed on the same level plan, has a cruciform court which joins the outer temples. *Pl. 39

The artists of Angkor Vat succeeded in connecting the different sections, towers and galleries of the temple

Pl. 53 Lokeśvara. Bas-relief on Banteai Chmar (Battambang). End of the 12th / early 13th century.

Pl. 54 Tower carved with four faces. Bayon, Angkor. End of the 12th / early 13th century.

in such a way as to translate into architectural terms the progress of the public towards the central sanctuary, the heart of the building, which was excluded from the gaze of the profane by its interior defences. Their fine sense of balance enabled them to endow each sanctuary, each staircase and gallery with the detailed proportions necessary to harmonize with the monumental concept of Angkor Vat.

Disciples who were allowed to worship the idol were to be imbued with a sense of the superhuman character of the god. Remembering the early Angkor idols they tried to sculpt hieratic figures, consequently the physical aspect, the ornament, even the costume, has a rigid appearance. Nothing exhibits this tendency better than the Viṣṇu of Vat Khnat with its square shoulders, muscular torso and stiff limbs. The slightest movement, the least flexing of the body is rigidly prohibited. Costume is handled in the same way. The traditional pleated sampot sometimes has a turned border; the pocket, if it is retained at all, develops into an ornament which covers almost the whole sampot, and ends in a double anchor. Female figures no longer wear the supple dress of the Baphuon. Their costume is squarely pleated and has a fishtail panel which is quite separate from the material of the skirt. Nearly all the divinities, male and female, wear a tiara, and their hair is plaited over the top of the head beneath a jewelled mitre which is much taller and thinner than in previous periods. The statues of Śiva and of certain benevolent *dvārapālas* wear their hair in a narrow, cylindrical chignon often drawn in at the base. The demon *dvārapālas* wear a helmet on a terrible crest bristling with curls. The square-jawed faces have a fixed stare with pouted under-lip, giving the mouth a hard, rather ugly expression which spoils some of the figures.

Technique in the Angkor Vat style is remarkable. The female figure of the National Museum at Phnom-Penh achieves the calm beauty which all the artists strove to attain. The body is slim and young with square but delicate shoulders and well-carved, slight breasts. The sculptor carved the beautiful, embroidered skirts and fine jewels with loving care. A splendid pectoral adorns the breast of a female

Pl. 55 Female divinity. Region of Kompong Thom. National Museum of Phnom-Penh. Height: 45 cm. End of the 12th / early 13th century.

Pl. 56 Figure of Ardhanarīśvara. Tuol Tapoun (Battambang). Museum of Vat Po Veal at Battambang. Height: 56 cm. End of the 12th / early 13th century.

Cat. 28; *Pl. 43 figure of the Phum Anlong Seng. Carved in fine sandstone, the statues took a high polish. They gleamed with the sombre patina of "polished sandstone" to be seen on the Buddha discovered in a cave near Sisophon and now in the National

*Pl. 44 Museum at Phnom-Penh. Elegant and linearly brilliant, the piece is very fine, though the face with all the characteristics of the period is far from expressing the compassion of Buddha. In this respect a head of Buddha on a *nāga* at Banon is preferable, having a solemn but gentle expression. It is true that on several pieces the typical features of the style are diminished and the face is more agreeable. The expression attains a severe grandeur in the fine head of Lokeśvara of Beng Meala. A female head at Preah Pithu is handled with greater freedom despite a pouting lower lip and square jaw;

Pl. 57 Male Head. Unknown provenance. Jean Fribourg Collection, Paris. Height: 35,5 cm. Lopburi style. End of the 12th / early 13th century.

the face is lit with a mysterious smile, but it must be noted that this is not the head of an idol but rather a *devatā* in high relief.

When the artists of Angkor Vat were not carving idols, which were subject to strict rules, they abandoned the stiff, hieratic style. This explains the presence, side by side with a cold, unemotional statuary, of the rich world of the reliefs. With the exception of Banteai Samre, temples of this type are decorated with *devatās;* but, whereas in all the other Khmer buildings these graceful female figures stand alone under an arch or with a background of foliage, in the temple

at Angkor Vat they are carved in groups, talking and strolling together. Near the western entrance the relief is very low but the figures are more strongly carved in the cruciform court. Their costume is often a pleated or flowered skirt, draped with a triangular panel on the hip and a long floating panel in front; the lace or brocade borders are minutely carved and one can recognize some of the patterns still to be seen today on the embroidered sampots worn on holidays. Sometimes the dress is very short; occasionally nothing more than a simple loin cloth with two long panels skilfully folded behind. The positions, costumes and ornament of the *devatās* are infinitely varied. One, wearing a three-point tiara, lifts her beautiful head while her hand plays with the long floating panel of her dress; another *devatā*, wearing a flowering branch in her plaited hair, puts her arm round her companion's shoulders; another looks in a glass. A solitary *devatā* with a book in her hand, a long panelled skirt, and her hair arranged in short tresses is smiling. Depicted on all the walls of the galleries and pavilions, in the central sanctuary the *devatās* become solemn and religious. Each one is set in a niche. More richly decorated than all the others, they were placed there to guard the god of the temple.

Mythological events are illustrated on the façade in more vigorous relief. One scene often covers the whole surface, but the tympanum may also be divided into horizontal registers where dozens of epic tales are unfolded, relentless combats in which gods and *asuras* struggle with monkeys and *rākṣasas*. On one tympanum at Banteai Samre Śiva dances his measured step with immense dignity and poise. His legs have been much damaged but the face, which is intact, has an almost imperceptible smile. The *apsaras* Cat. 121

Pl. IX Jayavarman VII. Preah Khan, Kompong Svay (Kompong Thom). National Museum of Phnom-Penh. Height: 41 cm. Late 12th / early 13th century (cf. Pl. 64 and 65).

Pl. 58 The Horse Balaha. Detail. Neak Pean, Angkor. End of the 12th / early 13th century.

dancing on the pediment of Chau Say Tevoda are whirled along more rapidly; although it is greatly worn and defaced, the sculpture is still vigorous enough to communicate the joy of these young divinities led on by the music, long-since silenced. The rhythm of the music is evoked on several bas-reliefs and especially in the carved orchestra of the façade of Banteai Samre. The dancers there are accompanied by a chorus of young women with hair dressed high in extravagant knots, playing on several different instruments. One is strumming a harp. On a lintel at Phimai the dancers move, not to the sound of a sophisticated court orchestra, but to the music of a conch, flute and gong. Above them a Buddha makes the gesture of reassurance and receives the gifts of the faithful. Musicians and dancers bring their art as an offering.

The storied lintels are rare in the Angkor Vat period; but sometimes a legendary event has been slipped in between the foliage and the pillars. On a lintel at the western entrance to Angkor Vat, Viṣṇu sleeps on the *nāga* surrounded by foliage. This same scene, which is rather solemnly depicted at Angkor Vat, can be seen on the base of a pillar at Banteai Samre. The divinity is of such slight stature that he scarcely seems to press upon the serpent.

The bas-reliefs of Angkor Vat are completely different from any of the other sculpture and hold a very important position in Khmer art. Immensely long compositions stretch down the galleries, sometimes to a distance of a hundred yards. The artists therefore had to solve new problems. It was not simply a question of balancing the different elements of one scene with another, but of composing the drama in the dimension of time without its becoming too monotonously long drawn-out. Of the eight half-galleries at Angkor Vat only six were constructed at first. The two galleries on the north-east quadrangle had to wait four hundred years before they received their ultimate decoration. The corner pavilions built on the west side are also covered with reliefs, scenes of more modest dimensions it is true, but of equal sculptural value nonetheless. All the murals of this *Pl. 48 third enclosure at Angkor Vat are done in real bas-relief; it is interesting to follow the planes as they succeed one another in the low carving. The two western galleries re-tell the vicissitudes of the last battle of the Rāmāyaṇa and Mahābhārata. At either end the warlike sound of trumpets announces the deployment of the armies; battle is joined. The centre of the composition holds the heart of the action; it is a fight to the death on the plain of Kurukṣetra on one side, and the final assault which delivers the armies of Rāma and Rāvaṇa into the hands of Laṅkā on the other. There is vivid contrast between the solid block of marching soldiers and the fearful seething mass of warriors in hand-to- Cat. 72 hand combat, wrestling, overthrowing and spearing one another. Despite the interest aroused by the bas-reliefs on the southern side representing the bliss of the fortunate new arrivals in heaven as well as the tortures of the damned, the Cat. 54 attention of the visitor is primarily drawn towards the Cat. 53 decorations which he will see in the gallery of history; because the Khmer sculptors recorded here for the first time a scene depicting contemporary events. The king, Sūryavarman II, riding on his elephant sets out to war with his court. The monarch, seated either on his throne or his howdah Cat. 1 turns his head to review the armies gathered in his train. The artists always seemed to enjoy stressing the dignified and haughty poise inherent in the king's person. Among the crowds pressing their gifts upon him only one figure re-

Pl. 59 Warrior overthrown by an elephant. Royal terrace, Angkor. End of the 12th / early 13th century.

mains in the memory: a beautiful woman looking back as she walks and holding a basket close against her breast, her eyes haunted by a far-away expression.

THE ART OF LOPBURI

In a study of Khmer art of the twelfth century one cannot pass over in silence a school which flourished in the district between Lopburi and K'orat, places which are now Thai, but which were dependents of the Khmer kingdom from the early eleventh to the end of the thirteenth century.

The Lopburi school must have matured about the time of Angkor Vat's most rapid growth, but it continued long after the end of Khmer domination. Its finest period corresponds with Angkor Vat and the Bayon. It is a descendant of Dvāravatī art whose traditions it combined with those of Khmer. We are only interested here in the pieces influenced by the Khmer and in this respect a head of Buddha in the collection of Jean Fribourg in Paris is important (Pl. 57). This head retains the joined, highly arched eyebrows carved in a relief which is characteristic of Dvāravatī art. The *uṣṇīṣa* with its two rows of broad lotus petals, and the hair style arranged in crescent-shaped loops, point to a certain freedom in the interpretation of Khmer *motifs*; but the meditative expression with downcast eyes connect it closely with the carving of the Bayon.

THE BAYON

The reign of Jayavarman VII at the end of the century saw a profound artistic revolution. Early in the twelfth century

Chau Say Tevoda, base of a column

buildings with fine and simple lines were erected slowly and with great care. By the end of the century a great deal was being built very fast. Finish was no longer important and the huge wall-surfaces of complex buildings were decorated with haste and little consideration. Galleries, cloisters, corridors and sanctuaries seem to intermingle without plan in the monasteries of Preah Khan, Ta Prohm, Banteai Kdei, Banteai Chmar and even in the temple-mountain of the Bayon, situated in the centre of the reconstructed Angkor Thom. At Angkor Vat the stylized, hieratic sculpture manifests a brilliant technique; but in the Bayon style, apart from one or two admirably realistic pieces, the figures are often poorly carved, though the faces seem nearly always to be portraits and sensitively done.

Reliefs cover the walls of the galleries of the Bayon and Banteai Chmar. Their affinity with the great scenes of Angkor Vat is undeniable, yet they are palpably different both in technique and inspiration. Mythological scenes are rare except in the internal galleries of the Bayon, and historical events take their place. Armies march past impatient
for the battle with the Cham invader against whom Jaya- Cat. 71
varman had mobilized the whole nation; boats ram one
another and a sea-fight takes place and at the very top of the Cat. 87
relief sits Jayavarman VII – a straightforward sketch – watching the defeat of his enemy.

These bas-reliefs are much less competent than those of Angkor Vat and errors increase in proportion to the proliferation of picturesque detail, and clumsily handled designs multiply with the failure of technique. Rare at Angkor Vat, they become commonplace in the Bayon. Behind the marching army a whole village moves along, families in a
long line of carts, the women carrying the youngest child on Cat. 78
their hip. They stop. Through the wheels of a cart a young man can be seen, his cheeks swelling as he blows hard to kindle a fire. A slim girl is gossiping in the market with a
flabby-breasted fishwife and a village-boy carrying a basket Cat. 79
stands watching a cock-fight, forgetting his errand in the
excitement of the moment; a little girl steals some fruit Pl. 51
from a snoozing old market woman. Then we enter the houses, where men sit and talk under the baskets and provisions hanging from the beams. One member of the family is sick and clutches his stomach with his hands and a mother draws her child lovingly to her side. Sometimes a

Pl. 60 Male head in the form of a gargoyle. Neak Pean, Angkor. End of the 12th / early 13th century.
Pl. 61 Head of Buddha. Collection of sculpture discovered below the pedestal of the Buddha of Tep Pranam, Angkor. National Museum of Phnom-Penh. Height: 41 cm. End of the 12th / early 13th century.

Cat. 75 mischievous element is introduced; all the soldiers are marching stiffly onwards, faces rigidly to the front, but the last man takes a swig from his bottle.

At Banteai Chmar religion dominates the bas-reliefs. Concern about an after-life haunts the scenes of hell, though
Pl. 53 the adjacent gallery has eight images of Lokeśvara with multiple arms, one succeeding another and all smiling with an expression of sweet serenity. The iconography of the interior carvings of the Bayon which were done later is primarily Brahman and although many legendary scenes have been handled in a perfunctory manner – feeble drawing, uneven relief and clumsy composition – others are not unworthy of the style which went before. Even though it does not attain the brilliance of the Angkor Vat composition, one scene, the churning of the sea of milk, ranks among the best on the Bayon. The drawing is firm, the relief sharp and the whole composition solidly balanced. These qualities are usually retained in the handling of the *devatās*. Surrounded by foliage and much less graceful than those of Angkor Vat they are dressed more uniformly; however they possess an intimate charm which seems to spring from their sweetness and their ingenuous youth.

Pl. 62 Female figure. Terrace of the Leper-king, Angkor. End of the 12th / early 13th century.
Pl. 63 The child Prajñāpāramitā. Found in the undergrowth on the north side of Angkor Thom. National Museum of Phnom-Penh. Height: 73 cm. End of the 12th / early 13th century.

The "Towers of the Four Faces" which dominate some of the temples founded in the second half of the reign of Jayavarman VII – the Bayon, Ta Prohm, Banteai Kdei and Banteai Chmar – and which also crown the five entrance-gates to the capital, are at once architectural and sculptural. The faces have a rather hypnotic effect due to the solemn handling of the stone which contrasts sharply with the rich headdress. Although they are overgrown with lichen and worn away by time, the faces of Lokeśvara, or other Bodhisattvas, which gaze outwards from every wall, meditating, and smiling, create an overpowering atmosphere which is strangely moving. *Pl. 54; Cat. 135

As the personal cults developed, the sculptors had to carry out many more commands. Such quantities of idols had never been carved before and this is why the quality is uneven. It is possible to see well-carved works in the finest sandstone side by side with crudely-hewn figures of rough stone. The artists usually needed to make a solid base to the

free-standing figures and therefore the legs were often excessively clumsy, while the torso would be well-handled in a naturalistic manner quite equal to the preceding styles. The
Cat. 3 emaciated body of Queen Jayadevī is obviously a study of a sick woman. The Prajñāpāramitā-child in the Phnom-Penh National Museum shows a little girl with a fat body and round shoulders, and the statue which is thought to be
Cat. 2 a portrait of Jayavarman VII is of exceptional beauty. The king is seated in the Yoga attitude, right leg crossed over left, his body bent slightly forward. The carving of the knees and legs is remarkable. It shows that, although much of the figure treatment of the Bayon was crude, the science of anatomy had rarely been so advanced among artists.

The costumes of the Bayon style show little variety. Male statues wear a short draped sampot with a simple anchor-shaped panel made of striped material bordered with pearls. Female statues wear a skirt of stiff material with a pattern of scattered flowers and the front is decorated with a big triangular panel. Headdresses carved in the round also lack variety. Whereas the *devatās* wear a high tiara decorated with flowers and feathers, the female goddesses arrange their plaited tresses in a chignon fixed to the top of the head; this chignon in turn is surrounded by a mitre of finely-worked lotus petals. The plaited hair is stiffly arranged in rows of small crescents separated by borders. This coiffure is also adopted for the Buddhas, although the hair-style of the masculine divinities is very different; whoever the person is intended to be, the hair is generally combed into a stylized plait which is woven on the head in a round chignon. This *jaṭā* was then marked with the sign *om* to signify Śiva or with a small *Amithābha* on the headdress of Lokeśvara.

The finest idols often lack jewellery and their costume will be fairly crudely carved. This was because the temple servants decked them with jewels and silk; the artists felt that there was little use in spending time on the parts which were to be covered. It had been a custom for many years to pierce the lobes of the ears on the statues and to thread lotus buds through them. A pectoral was hung on the neck and perhaps a diadem on the forehead. The female divinities would be adorned with the double shoulder band which the *devatās* wear across their breast. There are several references on inscriptions to offerings of cloth and jewels; a fragment of a large pectoral and an earring have come to light, both made of bronze, and they are too big to have been used for anything but large statues.

Moving figures carved in the round, which had had a very ephemeral career at Koh Ker, reappeared in the style of the Bayon. The causeways leading to the gates of Angkor Thom have the traditional *nāga*-heads supported here by rows of giant *asuras* on the right, and *devas* on the left. The head and tail of the *nāga* are supported by many-headed giants. The *nāga*, emblem of the rainbow which connects the gods with earth, is the symbolic communication between the divine king in his capital and the rest of the kingdom. Buttressed by the legs, the *devas* and *asuras* grasp the body of the *nāga* with both hands. Fifty-four powerful figures on solid foundations all repeat the same movement which could be an evocation of that cosmic rhythm known as churning the sea of milk. Another group, also in trimmed stone, was erected near the basin of Neak Pean, but unfortunately it is very worn. It tells the story of Lokeśvara who comes to the rescue of shipwrecked sailors threatened by ogresses, takes on the aspect of a magic horse and carries the poor creatures to safety. This scene shows the divine

Pl. X Buddha on a nāga. Banon (Battambang). 13th century.

horse stepping towards the sanctuary dedicated to Lokeśvara in the centre of the lake. A more dramatic, even more violent scene is carved in high relief on a corner inside the royal terrace of Angkor Thom; an elephant overturns two soldiers with its trunk. Held firmly upside down, the figures struggle in the relentless grip. A curious detail is that the artist made only three legs for these two soldiers, the leg which follows the rib of the stone can belong to either according to one's point of view.

The statuary of the Bayon shows us that the sculptors laid as much stress on faces as on movement and pose, and especially if they wanted to depict strong emotions. They were generally content to cut out only the essentials of a figure and to lavish particular care on the heads; indeed, they were such masters of physiognomy that these faces express an eloquence which is found only in portraits; the serenity of the *deva* giants, the scowling snarls of the *asuras*; the thin, wise, sometimes sardonic smile of the *devatās*. Art, developing in a Buddhist framework, learned to understand suffering and to render it with emotion. For example, one of the soldiers crushed by the elephant cries with fear and pain as he is tossed aside; on the same relief people with clearly defined faces pray to the gods and a painful solemnity marks the face of the Prajñāpāramitā-child. Such pain evokes pity–Lokeśvara with half-closed eyes gazes sadly out upon his devoted followers from the Gate of the Dead. Compassion and withdrawal soften the features of Buddha and Bodhisattvas. The "Smile of the Bayon" lights up their faces. It is almost imperceptible and points to the search for an ideal of beauty and peace.

The head of Jayavarman VII found at Preah Khan of Kompong, with lids lowered in contemplation, probably explains more than any other the richness of emotion characteristic of the art of the Bayon. The carving is exceptional giving a fine outline to the mouth and expressing the trembling cheeks and sensitive eye. The slightest inclination of the head, of the light falling upon it and the whole expression changes. If the face is clearly illuminated it becomes wilful and dominating, but under a soft light and turned to its original position it can be seen to be meditative, sweet and unworldly. But was not this the character of Jayavarman VII – a dynamic, tenacious and authoritarian monarch who yet had the Buddhist compassion for suffering, and the ability to withdraw into an interior, contemplative world? *Pl. 58 *Pl. 59

STONE-CARVING IN THE POST-BAYON PERIOD

It appears that shortly after the reign of Jayavarman VII the inspiration of Cambodian stone-carvers began to give out fast. Decadence and sterility are accepted and the carvings of this period are sparse. It seems as though stone suddenly became unpopular; only with difficulty can one find a *Cat. 126
few small buildings erected after the great king's death. After *Pl. 63
the introduction of Theravādic Buddhism no great sanctuaries were built to house the *linga* of the king. Previously the religious building had been a narrow cell for the divinity with many dependent buildings. Now the faithful were able to enter the temple and kneel before the Buddha, paying homage and receiving the wisdom of the god. Thus architectural problems were completely changed. It was necessary to build vast sanctuaries, but there was no ques- *Pl. IX

Pl. 64 Head of Jayavarman VII (Realistic left-hand profile). Preah Khan at Kompong Svay (Kompong Thom). National Museum of Phnom-Penh. Height: 41 cm. End of the 12th century.
Pl. 65 Head of Jayavarman VII (Idealized right-hand profile). Preah Khan at Kompong Svay (Kompong Thom). National Museum of Phnom-Penh. Height: 41 cm. End of the 12th century.

tion of constructing a permanent temple to perpetuate the founder's memory; it was realized that the building would have to succumb to the laws of decay and destruction. Wood, therefore, became the ideal material. No longer used for building, stone went out of fashion; apart from a few large carved figures following naturalistic lines of development, it was used less and less even in small pieces and ended by disappearing almost completely, to the advantage of wood and bronze; it was used in the end only for carving certain traditional pieces.

Pl. 66 Apsaras. Phimeanakas, Angkor. Dépôt archéologique de la Conservation d'Angkor. Height: 54 cm. Early 13th century.
Pl. 67 Decorated figure of Buddha. Angkor Vat. Dépôt archéologique de la Conservation d'Angkor. Height: 62 cm. 17th century (?).

Pl. 68 Asura Bāna. Bas-relief from the east side of the north gallery, Angkor Vat. 16th century.

FREE-STANDING SCULPTURE

The conversion of Cambodia which took place after the introduction of Theravādic Buddhism resulted in a radical change in the iconography of three-dimensional carving. Brahman images disappear almost entirely while the greater part of the artistic production is dedicated to the glory of the Buddha, Śākyamuni. Sometimes carved figures of a praying disciple or *arhat* would be added to the innumerable statues of Buddha, their hands joined in the position of *añjali*. The iconography of the Buddhas of the thirteenth and fourteenth centuries is directly descended from the Bayon style. The most popular theme is that of Buddha seated in meditation on the *nāga* coils and of Buddha standing with outstretched arms in the gesture of reassurance. The latter clearly shows the influence of Dvāravatī. During the same period Buddhist scenes were often carved on steles: Buddha conquering Māra, receiving the offering of the Lokapāla, the guardians of the four quarters of the earth, or simply accepting the homage of the *arhats*.

Pl. 69 Sīmā decorated with an arhat. Phum Dun, Battambang. Museum of Vat Po Veal at Battambang. Height: 63 cm. 18th century (?).

Physically the thirteenth-century Buddhas scarcely differ from those of the Bayon. They are supple with a well-carved muscular frame. The faces still have a gentle expression, almost smiling; but the eyes, closed in the Bayon, are now open and seem to shine between lowered lids. The treatment of the eyes and the slight hook to the nose speak of Thai influence. Now the flame, symbol of the Blessed One, appears on the *uṣṇīṣa* which is very elaborate with many spiralled curls. Post-Bayon art still produced some very fine works. Especially remarkable is a thirteenth-century statue in the Phnom-Penh National Museum, the so-called *Buddha de Commaille*[2], which is not only brilliantly carved but has a serene and beautiful face. That the skill of the stone-carvers did not diminish during the centuries that followed is shown by the very fine large Buddhas of Tep Pranam. They are made in dressed stone and the meditating Buddha is eighteen feet high. The standing Buddha's face has gone, but although the proportions of the body are short the reassuring gesture of the hands is very beautiful. The seated Buddha has a rather flattened face, but this is compensated for by the half-veiled, thoughtful eyes. Another Buddha of the same size stood in the eastern part of Angkor Thom; the body is broken and only the head, with an intense expression, was found intact leaning against a tree trunk in the middle of the jungle.

During the fifteenth and sixteenth centuries the technique degenerates; muscles no longer ripple beneath the skin, the legs grow spindly and the oval face is lengthened. Thai influence becomes more and more insistent and the bodies are stiff beneath rigid clothing. Sometimes the costume has a decoration on the front panel of the *antaravāsaka* as well as on the hips and a large pectoral hangs from the neck. It is unfortunate that all the jewelled Buddhas have been decapitated. On the oldest idols the most important decorative element is a flower inscribed within a lozenge. Subsequently this *motif* changes and is embellished with mitres while the border of the front panel, folded through the belt, takes the form of an anchor. These carved ornaments were nearly always encrusted with pearls or glass. It is clear that the jewelled Buddhas are an imitation in stone of wooden images, because after the sixteenth century, and even before, wood was the medium preferred by sculptors. The study of post-Angkor jewelled Buddhas must therefore begin with the wooden prototypes.

At Angkor Vat, in the Preah Pean, where fortunately so many of the later works have been preserved, there are stone statues of people praying with their faces towards the Buddha. One of these is astonishingly realistic. The figure is
*Pl. 68 dressed in a monk's robe with very clean lines and is treated with extreme simplicity; the head, placed on a neck which has been restored, and is too long, is emaciated and bald, with high cheek bones and the cast of an ascetic. This face burns with the ardent expression of the mystic. The piece clearly prolongs the realist tradition of the Bayon and is probably not later than the sixteenth century. Some *arhats* around a pagoda at Oudong are almost certainly slightly later. They are seated with their legs tucked to one side and although the hands are broken they must have been in the *añjali* position. Their ornament, which is not unlike that of Buddha, is directly inspired by wood-carving. Fate has decreed that every one of the figures should be headless. It is therefore even more essential to refer to the wood-carvings and reliefs if one wants to know more of the faces and coiffures of the ornate pieces made after Angkor.

The Khmer abandoned their stone buildings but they continued to worship at some of the ancient sanctuaries and when these became monasteries began to restore them. They carved surfaces which had been left plain or which were intended to be simple portals. Thus the great bas-reliefs of the north-east quadrangle of Angkor Vat were completed, besides the pediments of the central sanctuary of Vat Nokor near Kompong Cham, and the last *devatās* of the royal terrace of Angkor Thom.

There is no comparison between the bas-reliefs of the north-eastern quadrangle and those on the galleries carved at the finest Angkor Vat period, but the sculpture of the eastern gallery of Angkor Vat's north side is really mediocre; on the other hand the main figures on the wall of the adjacent gallery, where the artists illustrated the struggle of Krishna against the *asura* Bana, are still very fine even if the soldiers are clumsily done. Garuḍa carries Krishna proudly on his shoulders; standing in his chariot Bana leans forward in the halo of his many arms. The movements are well-composed and the drawing of the outlines is clear and sharp. In its best sections this bas-relief of Angkor Vat is important aesthetically and it is an interesting study because of the new developments it shows. We can see how the physical types and clothing, even the instruments have evolved since the days of Angkor Vat. The oval faces are longer, the nostrils flaring and the nose slightly aquiline. Several different kinds of costume are used at the same time. Drapery becomes complicated; sometimes the sampot is knotted in front with two soft panels back and front; another style has a turned edge which forms a kind of basque on the hips, and finally a type of trouser is evolved which passes beneath the sampot and this fashion marks the domination of Thai influence. The modifications are most clearly seen in the jewelled ornament; the diadem, an integral part of the mitre and prolonged down to the nape of the neck, forms a real tiara; sometimes it has a vertical rib placed above the ear, a *motif* which is typical of Ayudhyā.

In a period when work in stone is dormant, in which there are no buildings nor dated pieces, the reliefs of the north-east quadrangle of Angkor Vat seem to hold one of the keys to post-Angkor art. The façades of Vat Nokor were carved at the same period and can be dated by inscription.

They recount four of the principal episodes in the life of Buddha from the moment when he decided to leave his father's palace up to his victory over Māra. The composition on the southern façade is arranged in registers, whereas the eastern pediment contains a single scene in which Buddha sits impassive before the attacks of the army of Māra. The clothes consist of floating panels, the sampot and trouser.

The reliefs of Angkor Vat and Vat Nokor show only a single moment in the development of finery and costume in the post-Angkor period. If we want to follow the developments it is necessary to study the *arhats* who often decorate the *sīmās*, the enclosures limited by steles marking the sacred courts of the pagoda. The oldest narrative-*sīmā* may be as early as the fourteenth century and the tradition is still carried on. The *sīmās* never have a date, but their chronology can be established by studying the decoration. On one façade the praying disciple is heavily bejewelled, the hands in *añjali*, and the legs crossed in the Indian position. The earliest *arhats* wear costumes with floating panels and a diadem which is rather like the headdress worn by the *deva*-giants guarding the gates of Angkor Thom. Later the tiaras begin to degenerate as the lower part of the figure becomes more stylized in an evolution not unlike that of Kut Cham. The diadem is decorated with a rib just above the ear. Then it gives place to a richly designed ring of jewellery during the years contemporary with the last period of the Ayudhyā style. However, the lower limbs are hidden in a lotus flower which degenerates in the nineteenth century into foliage scrolls from which only the torso of the praying figure emerges.

Statues of bronze, free-standing wooden images and panels in relief have taken the place of stone-carving, which had known such splendour in the period of Angkor. Nowadays stone-carving is only done by the humblest artisans who carve pious images, oblivious of the glorious traditions of the past.

II. BRONZE

Pl. 70 Lokeśvara. Unknown provenance. National Museum of Phnom-Penh. Height: 16 cm. 7th century.

Khmer bronzes have been found scattered all over the former empire and they only appear occasionally in their original home. They were the booty of robbers and conquerors, and even the faithful who concealed them for safety are partly responsible for their loss. Some have been discovered when temples were cleared; some have been preserved in the monasteries and others have been found by chance during irrigation work. These pieces are very diverse in date and iconography. Their owners, after they had buried them or hidden them in a bronze or pottery vase, lost track of their cache.

Such pieces are extremely elaborate. The Khmer bronze founders cast both very large idols and delicate statuettes, cult-objects as well as useful wares, and the production of their workshops is undoubtedly the most varied and interesting of all Indochina.

Most of the figures, whatever their size, are images of gods. Very few sanctuary-idols have survived, but whether this is because they were destroyed or just that few were made is not known; those which have been preserved are remarkable for their size and fine workmanship. More numerous are temple-images presented to the temple by rich donors to be carried in procession, and they are nearly all very elaborately carved. The small figures made for family altars are of very uneven quality: sometimes they are sensitively modelled but often they are horribly clumsy. Representations of humans and animals are rarer and usually formed some kind of support such as atlantes at the base of a pediment; sometimes they would be used as finials on a military staff. They were worked just as finely as the decorative pieces and must have fulfilled a purely aesthetic role. The Khmer people had cultivated their love of fine bronze

Pl. 71 Maitreya. Acquired in Thailand. National Museum of Phnom-Penh. Height: 32 cm. 7th century.

and it was immaterial whether a piece was a cult-object or simply something useful. Therefore they ordered pieces to decorate their furniture, finials for chariots and chiselled plaques to embellish the buildings.

It is probable that the only technique known to the Khmer of Angkor, and even later for many years, was the "*cire-perdue*" process. Small statues made by this method could be solid, but anything of any size was cast hollow. Very large statues were cast in several pieces which were assembled later. The bronze surface would be nearly always gilded and traces of this can still be seen despite corrosion. Incrustation became frequent in the thirteenth century though formerly it had been rare. We cannot say exactly what material would have been used because the settings are now always empty; perhaps precious stones, but it seems more likely that they were some kind of glass-paste such as is found on wooden statues later than the Bayon. Sometimes filigree ornament was added later with fine decorative effect.

The bronzes have a patina which varies in colour from a more or less dark greenish-grey to a luminous green and here and there one finds bluish reflections in the polished surfaces. Some have a black or very dark brown patina of great brilliance, with spots of green corrosion in the fractures and deep incisions. The variation in patina is the result of differences in the alloy. Georges Coedès describes the many differences in composition. Traditionally bronze pieces were cast in a conglomerate of new metal and of a variety of old pieces of unknown composition. Apart from brass with a more or less strong copper content, the Cambodians preferred an alloy which they called *samrit*; this they believed produced the finest bronze. They boasted of its brilliance and traditionally it was a mixture of gold, silver and copper.

Pl. 72 Face of a statue. Basak (Svay Rieng). National Museum of Phnom-Penh. Height: 17 cm. 11th century.

Coedès cites the different formulae of *samrit* which appear in Siamese texts. In addition to the three metals already mentioned, zinc, mercury, tin, bismuth and lead were used. One thing, however, is certain, that Cambodia as well as Siam insisted on a very high gold content.

The bronze images, like the stone-carvings, represent Brahman or Buddhist divinities, but their iconography differs in several respects. Some gods have been cast in bronze, who are almost unknown in stone-carving. For instance, there are several statuettes of Maitreya, dating from different periods and all finely made, while there is scarcely one in stone from the pre-Angkor period. Of course the problems of balance in a metal figure were not the same as those posed by a stone-carving. Some shapes which were impossible in sandstone were easily cast in bronze. Stone idols of Śiva in the sanctuaries always had two arms, the only exception to my knowledge being the dancing Śiva of Koh Ker; but images of this god with his many heads and arms are not rare at all in bronze. Iconographically it is interesting that almost no Brahman representations have yet been found among pre-Angkor pieces. The images of this period almost without exception represent Buddha and the Bodhisattvas.

Khmer bronzes, their iconography apart, exhibit many peculiarities and the differences inherent in the metal sometimes make dating a hazardous affair. It is true that one often finds costumes and ornament on the bronzes analogous to those on the stone-carvings, and one is tempted therefore to treat them as contemporary. However, the artists often exploited the possibilities of the metal to enhance the drapery, to cut a panel free from the figure, to make a looser tie, or more elaborate ornament, so we must have recourse to the

Pl. 73 Hand of a statue. Western Mebon at Angkor. National Museum of Phnom-Penh. Height: 26 cm. 11th century.
Pl. XI Standing Buddha. Eastern Barai, Angkor. National Museum of Phnom-Penh. Height: 27 cm. 7th century.

bas-reliefs for comparison before tentatively suggesting a date. Often we get the impression that a certain type of costume or jewellery must have appeared earlier in bronze than in stone, or that the style lasted longer. Finely-made pieces, even if they are complicated by unusual additions, remain very close to traditional shapes; more mediocre pieces on the other hand tend to vary a great deal. Another difficulty is that Angkor idols were copied for a long time after the Bayon period. Sometimes a copy is given away by anachronisms, but it is often hard to distinguish a piece which is genuinely early and authentically clumsy from a late and decadent piece. Nevertheless a copy of a well-made piece is always easier to detect because the artist, although he tries to reproduce it faithfully, is betrayed by his own taste and gives himself away in some anachronistic detail.

In the face of the fantasies which the bronze-founders permitted themselves technique is undoubtedly the safest way of dating. The technique is flexible in the Angkor period; elegant and careful in the art of the Baphuon; impeccable and a little dry at Angkor Vat. The expression of the faces and physiognomy is also important. The figure stands in the oblique position and is naturalistically handled during the pre-Angkor period; firmly fixed on rather stiff legs during the tenth century; slim with a large head in the Baphuon style and upright with square shoulders at Angkor Vat. The pre-Angkor Bodhisattvas have a rather fixed smile; in the eleventh century the expression is pleasant; at Angkor Vat the disdainful lower lip is pronounced, as it was in the stone-carvings, while in the Bayon the eyes are closed in meditation.

However, if only the fine works are capable of precise dating a careful study will often enable one to decide on the style and approximate date.

Fig. 74 Viṣṇu. Unknown Provenance. Musée Guimet, Paris. Height: 87 cm. 11th century.

STATUARY

THE PRE-ANGKOR PERIOD

Unfortunately very few bronzes of the pre-Angkor period have survived, but those that have are nearly all small figures of real artistic merit. It does not follow that the Khmer of the period did not know how to cast large bronzes. At Phnom Bayong the broken feet of a statue of fine workmanship were found which must have been over life-size. I have already mentioned that apart from a small group representing Śiva and Umā riding on the bull Nandin almost all the images belong to Buddhist iconography, but Chinese historians record that the people of Fu-nan made bronze images of the "Heavenly Gods". The whereabouts of these pieces is unknown. The answer must be that the earth still guards most of the pre-Angkor bronzes. The most important of those which can be identified have been found to the west of Angkor in the sanctuary of Ak Yom, and in the region of Battambang. But perhaps one day the words of the Chinese historians will be corroborated.

The group showing Śiva riding on the bull is probably an Indian image because Umāmaheśvara is never represented thus in Khmer art. Śiva is seated cross-legged on Nandin's back, resting. On his left knee sits his companion, Umā, depicted here as quite small. The snake worn across the breast by Śiva and the ogival crown of both gods are imported directly from India. This small bronze is undoubtedly a faithful copy of an Indian model.

There are many images of the seated Buddha with gentle smiling face and head dressed in large curls. Two standing

Pl. 75 Monkey. Unknown provenance. Museum of Vat Po Veal at Battambang. Height: 20,5 cm. End of the 11th / early 12th century.
Pl. 76 Kneeling girl. Banteai Chakrey (Prei Veng). National Museum of Phnom-Penh. Height: 95 cm. Second half of the 11th century.

figures of Buddha are of finer quality. One of them was found on the shores of the Western Barai at Angkor. This Buddha must have had a support for there is a ring between his shoulders at the back. With his right hand he makes the gesture of preaching and his head, with the big *uṣṇīṣa*, has large curls. A monk's robe covers his shoulders, clinging closely to the torso and allowing the *antaravāṣaka* to show through. The long face is thin and the whole figure finely executed. Covered with a luminous green patina this Buddha emanates an aura of sweetness and peace. A black bronze Buddha, with spots of green corrosion on the shining surface and unfortunately very badly damaged, was discovered at Vat Banon in the province of Battambang. The Buddha stands in *tribhanga*. The monk's robe, leaving the shoulder bare, passes under his left arm and is wound round the wrist; the end of the material is held in his hand in the Indian manner. A wooden Buddha found in the Plain of Reeds, also holds a robe like this. The long thin body is comparable with seventh-century Buddhist art; the oblique lines of the hips and slight ripple of flesh at the belt above the lower drapery are characteristic details. The Buddhas are dignified but have a benevolent aspect.

Pl. XI
Pl. XII

A study of the Bodhisattvas reveals a foreign influence that is far more pronounced in the bronzes than in the carved statues; it is particularly well seen in three small figures of Avalokiteśvara which must be among the earliest pieces. One was found at Kompong Luong not far from Angkor Borei. The figure stands slightly flexed towards the left, one hand raised, probably to hold a detachable attribute, the other holding a lotus-bud. Avalokiteśvara wears a foreign headdress – a mitre spreading at the top and decorated with three flowers at the base and in front with the image of

Pl. XII Torso of a standing Buddha. Banon (Battambang). National Museum of Phnom-Penh. Height: 21 cm. 7th century.

Thommanon, lintel

Amitābha. This mitre and short costume, draped with a rather complicated panel is reminiscent of the headdress and sampot of the reclining Viṣṇu of Tuol Baset, which I have already mentioned in connection with Cham art. This bronze Avalokiteśvara wears a robe supported by a cloth belt folded twice round the hips; a type of belt, which is Indian in origin. It had been adopted by Indo-Javanese and even Cham art; in pre-Angkor art, however, it is quite exceptional. Two other images of Avalokiteśvara also show strong Indo-Javanese influence. They were discovered recently in the west of Cambodia and are to be seen in the museum of Vat Po Veal at Battambang (numbers 279 and 280). The figures are almost identical. They stand on a base decorated with lotus petals. An oval halo is fixed to the back of the head by a vertical pin and the hair is piled on top of the head in a chignon, held in a ring at its base and broadening towards the top. Amitābha is carved into the front of the chignon and a tiara with three rosettes crowns the forehead. The skirt, draped with a floating panel in front is held by a belt with a scrolled and jewelled clasp; it is very like the costume of Avalokiteśvara at Rach-Gia. Number 279 is in the flexed position; he holds a bottle in the left hand and makes the gesture of reassurance with the right. The other image, number 280, stands in the same position holding a bottle and a rosary. Although the iconography, position and ornament of these two pieces is similar, their modelling is very different. Number 279 for instance is rather dryly handled, the other shows greater sensitivity. The body is supple and free, the hands graceful and delicate; the smiling face has a light patina. There are several features which lead one to attribute this Avalokiteśvara with some diffidence to Khmer art; nevertheless its elegance of line and gentle facial expression relate it very closely to pre-Angkor art of the seventh century. *Pl. XIII

Another Avalokiteśvara of unknown provenance stands in the flexed, oblique position, the body visible through folds of a long clinging *dhoti*. His left hand is outstretched holding the bottle; the rosary hangs like a bracelet on the Pl. 70

Pl. 77 Female statuette. Beng Mealea (Siem Reap). National Museum of Phnom-Penh. Height: 14 cm. First half of the 12th century.

Pl. 78 Viṣṇu dancing. Phnom Bayong (Ta Keo). National Museum of Phnom-Penh. Height: 14 cm. 12th century.

right wrist, which is raised, the elegant fingers closed in the *kaṭakahasta* position. This delicate figure, with its flowing lines, appears to date from the seventh century.

*Pl. 71 Several statuettes discovered at Ak Yom belong to the style of Prei Kmeng. With a tall chignon and hair braided in loops, their short robe covers the hips and is tied by a knotted cord at the side. The Maitreya of Ak Yom has been severely damaged, but an Avalokiteśvara from the same Pl. XIV site is a remarkable piece. This standing Bodhisattva holds a bottle in his left hand and carries a lotus in the right. Beneath the sombre green-toned patina the body, stripped of all elaboration, displays great elegance. The hands are delicate and the face, with elongated eyes, is lit by an almost malicious smile. A Maitreya in the National Museum of Phnom-Penh of unknown provenance may date from the same period. The body is thin and upright and dressed in a very short sampot. The four hands with long, tapering fingers must have carried detachable ornaments. The chignon decorated with loops surrounding a small *stūpa* has been closely chiselled. The delicate features of the face have

Pl. 79 Apsaras. Plantation of Christianville (Kompong Thom). National Museum of Phnom-Penh. Height: 25,5 cm. 12th century.

been carved with unusual care. A polished black patina shows up the fine treatment of this idol but there is something rather precious in its delicate sophistication.

There are no bronzes which can be attributed to the end of the eighth century; but as far as one can say in the light of present knowledge the art of bronze was not apparently affected by the impoverishment which characterized the last idols of pre-Angkor art.

THE TENTH CENTURY

Very few bronzes from the tenth century have been found; those that we possess are of a quality to make us regret their scarcity. Every piece repays individual study. The first is a statuette of Śiva in a private collection in Bangkok, discovered in the region of K'orat and illustrated by Coedès in his book *Khmer Bronzes* (plate 10, number 2). The richly carved diadem and pleated robe decorated with a folded border, draped pocket and double-anchor panel encourage us to date it to the mid-tenth century. Beneath the forehead, engraved with a third eye, the joined eyebrows are square and straight but the sweetness of the art of Pre Rup can be seen in the expression of the eyes and mouth. The treatment is painstaking, the modelling tense. Another standing male statue of the early tenth century was found at Basak, but unfortunately in a very damaged condition.

The other tenth-century pieces pose more difficult problems. About thirty years ago near the village of Anlong Top the fragments of a small four-armed figure were found in the river Stung Mung which flows between Battambang and Pursat; the head and two right arms are lost. The body is well-proportioned with broad chest, thin waist and

Pl. XIII Lokeśvara. Phnom Ta Kream (Battambang). Museum of Vat Po Veal, Battambang. Height: 24 cm. 7th century.

powerful hips. The line of the arms is finely composed and although the left upper arm is damaged the lower hand, even without its fingers, moves in a graceful gesture of giving. Its rather long sampot, held by a flat belt and draped into a double-anchor panel, recalls the well-known costume which characterizes the Koh Ker style. But the sampot of the figure found at Anlong Top lacks a draped pocket and folded border, whereas one or other of these styles is always found on the male images of Koh Ker. Such fine pleating is remarkable for a mid-tenth-century costume. However, a Sanskrit inscription on the base fixes the date of casting exactly to 892 in the *śaka* period, that is A.D. 970. So the Anlong Top figure was cast five years after Koh Ker had been abandoned, just after the foundation of Banteai Srei. This means that the Koh Ker tradition survived for some years, exemplifying the prolongation of styles often encountered in bronze. The inscription corroborates our tentative attribution.

An eight-armed Maitreya from the monastery of Ampil Tuk (Province of Kompong Chnang) must have been cast a little earlier. At first sight the high cylindrical chignon decorated with looped plaits and the smooth costume strongly recall the style of Preah Ko; but the glossy sampot is draped, not only with a naturalistic pocket on the left hip, but with a double-anchor pleat of the Phnom Bakheng style, the long panel passing in front of the short one. This type of costume could belong to the early years of the tenth century, but examination of the headdress leads us to very different conclusions; in fact the plaits of hair on the top of the head are braided; little plaits of this kind and the tassel-like loops and curls which cover the chignon foreshadow the coiffures of the eleventh century. A garland covers the hair

Pl. XIV Lokeśvara. Ak Yom (Siem Reap). National Museum of Phnom-Penh. Height: 35 cm. 7th century. (cf. Cat. 131).

at the back, but the roots are clearly indicated on the forehead. The face is square in the manner of the late ninth century, the eyes carefully handled beneath straight rectangular eyebrows; the gaze is enlivened by relief carving of the iris between the lids. The frank smile and young face recall the statues of Koh Ker. Six upper hands with slightly bent fingers lack their attributes, while the two lower hands make the gesture of sacrifice. A *cakra* is carved on the palms, while the wrists and tapered fingers are very graceful. This supple and easy stance is almost entirely restricted to the tenth century. Hence the costume of this particular Maitreya recalls the late ninth century whereas the headdress looks forward to the eleventh; moreover, it must not be forgotten that the style of Banteai Srei was to copy that of Preah Ko and to adopt the smooth clothing on some pieces. Far from wanting to reduce the age of the piece by attributing it to the time of Banteai Srei I would prefer to date it to the middle of the tenth century noting a certain nostalgia for the preceding style, and the features which foreshadow the end of the tenth century, and, here and there, even the early years of the following century.

THE ELEVENTH CENTURY

Although it is true that Cambodian bronze probably reached its peak sometime in the second half of the ninth century we cannot recognize a single piece as genuinely of the

Thommanon, lintel showing Rāma and Lakṣmaṇa caught by the snake-arrows of Indrajit

Pl. 80 Seated male figure. Plantation of Christianville (Kompong Thom). National Museum of Phnom-Penh. Height: 17 cm. 12th century.

Khleang style. It would be surprising if nothing from the beginning of the century had survived, when the bronze founders of the Baphuon left so much which is remarkable. However, since characteristics of a given style appear earlier in bronze than in stone we may be permitted to think that the bronzes which approach the Baphuon style may well cover almost the whole century.

Bronzes cast at this period were either small images or very large idols. An enormous figure of Viṣṇu reclining has
Pl. xv been found in the Eastern Mebon, but no other large piece is intact. The exceptional quality of the fragments makes the damage even more to be deplored. Khmer bronze images of the Baphuon period were characterized by the features of stone-carving of the time and it is therefore possible to date them fairly accurately. And at this period artists, bronze or stone-workers, aimed at an ideal of elegance exemplified by the suppleness of the body balanced on slim legs, the smooth, even precious movements of the hands and the finely-pleated costume tied with a loosely-knotted bow and held by a belt delicately chiselled in loops. When working on the costumes and jewellery of their images the bronze workers permitted themselves innovations which only really became common after the appearance of the Angkor Vat style; for instance the short sampot such as we have seen in the Baphuon style has a border of piping. Bronze allowed a freedom which the stone-carvers did not enjoy. The bow holding the tail of the sampot behind is a metalworker's conception, borrowing its broad, delicate wings from the butterfly. This knot was often cast separately and fixed by a rivet. It is obvious that the artist who made the bow of the Phnom Bayong male idol was preoccupied with the idea of conferring on the god the lightness of the butterfly's frail, spreading wings. Thus in the eleventh century the stone-carvers sought simplicity while the bronze-workers had a pronounced taste for sumptuous jewellery and ornament. Simply plaited hair in a chignon is rare. Sometimes a dancing girl or small figure wears her hair knotted high over her head. The two divinities in a group representing Śiva and Umā wear their hair in a chignon with four lobes, fastened with a jewelled clasp. Other images wear a tiara and a chignon-cover, though they are sometimes missing.

Pl. 81 Harihara. Pursat. National Museum of Phnom-Penh. Height: 29 cm. 12th century (cf. Cat. 20).
Pl. 82 Female statuette. Unknown provenance. Jean Fribourg Collection, Paris. Height: 22 cm. 12th century.

Although the costume and jewellery are extremely valuable guides in dating a piece, the style of the Baphuon is best seen in the handling of the design, the eloquent pose and above all the modelling of the face. The Viṣṇu of Mebon, the fragmentary mask of Basak and the masculine god of Phnom Bayong all display the round face with cleft chin, fleshy mouth and straight eyes whose lids are drawn in a line continuing up towards the temple. The Mebon Viṣṇu and Śiva of Por Loboeuk must have had precious stones embedded in the eyes, lids, moustache and beard. The eye in the forehead of the Śiva of Por Loboeuk still retains the metal plaque which supported the encrusted stones. Pl. 72

The fragments of Śiva found when the swamp was drained near the monastery of Por Loboeuk suggest that the perfect figure would have radiated a serene authority. Conforming with the Baphuon style, the head is rather large, exemplifying one of the features, which we associate with stone-carving. Only two hands have been found; one is finely-modelled, the other, which was separately cast and fixed with a rivet, is less vigorous and seems to have been cast by a different method. It may have been added later because the eleventh-century bronze-founders generally paid special attention to hands. It is unfortunate that the hands of the Viṣṇu from the Western Mebon have also been damaged, for they seem to have been very beautiful. Perhaps the most graceful expression of the beauty of tapering fingers is a hand, making the gesture of *kaṭakahasta*, now in the National Museum of Phnom-Penh. Pl. 73

The peculiar features of the faces, jewels and lines of the body give the Baphuon bronzes almost a family air. Nevertheless no other style is so varied, nowhere else is such virtuosity displayed in the attitudes, expressions and size of

Pl. xv the idols. The bust of Viṣṇu reclining, found in the Western Mebon, is certainly the most remarkable of all the bronzes of South East Asia. Could this be the very one which Ch'ou Ta-k'uan described as "a Buddha of bronze reclining", from whose navel water always flowed? If this is so there would have been lotus petals – the symbol of water – and a fountain. But this is relatively unimportant, for the bust is strikingly beautiful. Diadem and chignon-cap have disappeared, no sign of incrustation remains, but stripped thus of its ornament the figure is no less admirable under its luminous green patina. Leaning on one elbow, the god reclines in dignified ease. There is perfect balance between the lines of the shoulders, arms and hands. The hollow iris confers intense life on the slightly smiling face. The artist seems to have tried to depict the god in that state of conscious repose which would be the prelude to universal renaissance.

Although they are scarcely comparable with such a huge
Pl. 74 figure, a Viṣṇu in the Musée Guimet and a torso from Basak are still among the largest bronzes of Cambodia. The statue of Viṣṇu, acquired some ten years ago, is alien to the general flexibility of this style. Standing on rather stiff legs it is unusual in having a belt across the torso. The head has almond-shaped eyes but no diadem or chignon-cover. All the same
Pl. xvi the disappearance of the headdress gives the god a bald, strange appearance. The Basak statue, now nothing more than a torso, must have been about four and a half feet high. Badly damaged and corroded, deprived of all the front part of the clothing, the bust impresses by its intense power. Its patina is moss-green. The small pieces are even more varied. When the artist modelled the group of Śiva and Umā, which was exhibited at the Royal Palace of Phnom-Penh during the festival of Tangtok in 1925, he followed his

Pl. XV Torso of Viṣṇu reclining. Eastern Mebon, Angkor. National Museum of Phnom-Penh. Length: 217 cm. Second half of the 11th century.

Preah Khan, Kompong Svay, boundary pillar with Lokeśvara

own spontaneous inspiration and placed the divine couple in the intimate atmosphere of a family; the severely-pleated costume and the hairstyle, arranged high on the head with no jewellery, is devoid of all ornament. The god holds his wife in a tender, almost human embrace. Unfortunately it is impossible to find the actual carving which is known only from a photograph.

Animal-subjects add much to the originality of the Baphuon style. The bronze-founders of the late eleventh century must have had a sense of humour and mystery. A good example is the little monkey in the museum of Vat Po Pl. 75
Veal. He stands upright with his hands before him, his head crowned with a jewelled tiara, and seems to be crying out.

A female figure found in a hiding-place near Prei Veng Pl. 76
unites all the features of Baphuon art. Resting back on her heels this slim young woman holds out her hands in a gesture of giving. A lightly-pleated dress decorated simply with a narrow tasselled belt moulds her body. Beneath the jewelled headdress her face with its wide-set eyes, fleshy lips and cleft chin has a serious expression. She wears a rich necklace, but it is not possible to say what this exquisite figure could have been holding in her hands. The gesture does, however, recall those women of the bas-reliefs who held a lotus to receive the foot of Viṣṇu. The treatment is restrained, the figure aristocratic.

Two female statues mark the transition towards the style of Angkor Vat. Overflowing with life, a young woman is dancing on one foot, her legs flexed. She must be an *apsaras*, but she has been chiselled with a realism which is rare among the bronze-workers. Although she has rather a square jaw, the face is delicate; a mass of hair is arranged on the top of her head in a tall coiffure, the ends knotted with a large plait

which falls loosely down. Graceful and naturalistic, she does not belie the restrained and sensitive workmanship. A similar headdress can be seen on a female figure in the National Museum of Bangkok. The lower part of the body and the left arm are broken, the right arm, with sadly damaged fingers, appears to make the gesture of reassurance. The thin body is that of a very young girl whose smile is graceful but malign.

THE ART OF ANGKOR VAT

The transition between the styles of the Baphuon and Angkor is scarcely noticeable. Some of the details which are typical of Angkor Vat are already discernible on some eleventh-century pieces; even at the end of the following century some figures were still dressed in costumes popular with the bronze-workers of the Baphuon period.

Pl. 83 Decorated Buddha making the gesture "which reassures". Angkor Vat. National Museum of Phnom-Penh. Height: 75 cm. 12th century.

A study of the changing features on the bronzes attributed to this school shows that certain attitudes and expressions proper to the Angkor Vat style gradually took precedence. The style of the Baphuon produced some examples with a rather hieratic flavour, for instance the statuette found at Prei Veng. The kneeling woman is doubtless meant to imply a respectful religious attitude, but at that time the hieratic style had abandoned its former rigidity and was expressed more freely in a religious context. At Angkor Vat the hieratic approach is often indistinguished from the rather dry stiffness which we have already seen in the stone-carving. The gently falling line of the shoulders of the eleventh century becomes a straight line; the lower jaw grows heavy and the dimple vanishes from the chin, while the scornful lower lip too often effaces the smile. However, in bronze, just as in stone-carving, these characteristics are not always present on the best pieces.

It is not surprising that the hieratic treatment affected primarily the idols, small altar-images and processional statues. More than any others these bronzes resemble the stone idols of the sanctuaries. The Harihara of Kapilapura, standing upright and gently smiling, seems too large – twelve inches – to have been an unimportant altar idol, especially as it was found in a ruined temple. A light olive-green patina shows up the beauty of the workmanship. The iconography of this restrained and perhaps rather cold figure is extraordinary, for the Harihara lacks the usual combination – the left side representing Viṣṇu and the right Śiva. The composite god bears all the attributes of Viṣṇu in his four arms, but a third eye in the forehead and the sign *om* on a medallion in his high cylindrical chignon impart to the crowned head the aspect of Śiva.

Pl. 84 Lokeśvara. Unknown provenance. Museum of Vat Po Veal at Battambang. Height: 23 cm. End of the 12th / early 13th century.
Pl. 85 Hevajra. Banteai Kdei, Angkor group. National Museum of Phnom-Penh. Height: 30 cm. End of the 12th / early 13th century.

A very small and finely-worked, but more rigidly hieratic, female statue found in central Vietnam must certainly have been a family altar-piece. We shall never know the course of events which led to this incontestably Khmer piece being found in the heart of the Cham country. Could she have been looted in the course of the Cham invasion of 1197 or carried there by the Khmer when Sūryavarman II or Jayavarman VII occupied Champa? Perhaps she was brought by an innocent Cham traveller to Khmer country. With her serious face beneath a broad crown, her straight, well-set figure in finely-pleated square skirt, she is an exact replica in bronze of the stone Lakṣmī of the sanctuaries.

Pl. 77 A female figure found in the library of Beng Mealea escapes the stiffness of the idols. She was modelled with care and an eye for beauty. The pleated costume leaves her belly uncovered, clinging to the hips and thighs to flare out at the bottom in traditional Baphuon style. The body is slim, finely carved with broad hips and a double line beneath the breasts. Perhaps it could be Lakṣmī, since she is holding a lotus? Her right hand is held forward while the left arm falls beside her body, the hand and wrist just raised in a graceful pose. The face, however, is hard, with a haughty expression and an absence of charm which is out of keeping with this otherwise beautiful bronze.

Representations of Viṣṇu riding on the shoulders of the *garuḍa* bird are free of the rigid, hieratic character of the other idols. Usually the god balances on his mount, one foot on the tail and the other on the shoulder of the mythical bird, which advances triumphantly. In another group of
Pl. 78 three figures, each with an arching background, Viṣṇu is dancing. The influence of the Baphuon style persists in the handling of this piece, and the face still smiles with the sweet

gentleness of the eleventh century. Although the short sampot is draped with a broad, folded border proper to the late Baphuon style, its decoration of striped ribbons divided by piping is clearly later. A three-lobed nimbus in an aureole of foliage forms a background to Viṣṇu who balances on his toes with legs bent. The torso is upright and the gesture of the hands symmetrical. It is a formal movement, slow and ritualistic.

The dance of Viṣṇu can scarcely be compared with the graceful, lively spirit of an *apsaras* in a private collection in Bangkok, and illustrated by Coedès in *Khmer Bronzes*. The young goddess is dancing on a lotus flower, wearing the costume with the folded border and flying panels to be seen on many *devatās* at Angkor Vat. The diadem with florettes could not be earlier than the twelfth century. Her foot is planted firmly on the lotus while her hands are in a position commonly affected by Cambodian ballet dancers. The breasts are well-defined on the slim body and the long legs and supple arms are finely modelled. One is tempted to think that this figure must have been part of a group such as the two large bronze *motifs* found in the plantation of Christianville near Kompong Thom and now partly destroyed. The *apsaras* are among those parts which survived. One of them is complete. The *apsaras* in the Bangkok collection is dancing on a lotus flower with her feet poised on the flower's corolla. Knees bent, she holds her hands to the sides of her head. A short sampot, striped and folded over is draped with long soft panels. The diadem is on the front of the head while the chignon-cover has a large florette flanked by two ears of corn. The strong, square-jawed face has slanting eyes and a thin smile. These *apsaras* are considered to be among the finest bronze-work done in Cambodia. They are the most important fragments that were saved from the fire in the Christianville plantation. Of the other figures which were with the *apsaras* there remain only a nimbus, chiselled like lace, some small *garuḍas* with outstretched wings and a male divinity seated in the Indian position. Pl. 80

One female statue can certainly be attributed to the late Angkor Vat period. Pl. XVII Her hands are raised, supporting an object long since lost, a mirror perhaps or a screen. Balanced on the right heel with raised knee, she appears to be making *Pl. 79 an offering. Her hair is not bound into a cone-shaped, jewelled chignon, but arranged unusually in the shape of a fan. A rosette decorates the crown above the forehead and similar floral *motifs*, such as decorated the tenth-century coiffures, reappear on some diadems of bronze made by artists working in the style of the Bayon. The narrow pleated costume with a folded border encircling the figure is the clothing worn by a Prajñāpāramitā of the late twelfth century. However, we can hardly attribute such a late date to the screen-bearer, because the crown engraved with oval flowers and the fish-tail panel at the front of the skirt could not have survived the Angkor Vat style. The most likely date seems to be the end of Angkor Vat. An examination of the face confirms this hypothesis; the characteristics of Angkor Vat are still faintly seen but the sweetness of the expression foreshadows the lively spirit of the Bayon style. Hieratic but supple, the growing girl is finely modelled and ranks among the finest pieces of Khmer bronze. Another female statue Pl. 82 from the Fribourg Collection has a very gentle expression and the workmanship is magnificent. A statuette of Harihara found at Pursat well illustrates the tendencies of the late Pl. 81 Angkor Vat style. The iconography is the same as that of the Kapilapura Harihara. The oval face with almond-shaped

Pl. XVI Male torso. Basak (Svay Rieng). National Museum of Phnom-Penh. Height: 68 cm. Second half of the 11th century.

eyes beneath arched and joined eyebrows seems to smile. Only the three rosettes on the diadem hint at the style to come. The sampot is very different from the male costume of the late thirteenth century; it has an unusual fan-shaped panel, an upper border folded like a petal, a row of disc-like coils on the hips and a broad border on the thighs.

The transition to the Bayon style is more clearly seen on some other pieces, for instance the figures of Buddha on the *nāga*. The Blessed One is crowned with a diadem engraved with flowers and wears a chignon-cap carved with lotus petals. One of these figures comes from Anlong Sla (a province of Battambang); the other was found near the Silver Towers in central Champa. The Buddha is adorned in the manner of a royal prince and is seated meditating on the *nāga* as if on a throne. The position of the body and the robe, which lies in a folded panel across the left shoulder, are the only clues to tell us that this regal figure is a monk.

Similar rich jewels adorn a figure, which may be Prajñāpāramitā, owned by the Brahman temple of the Royal Palace at Bangkok. The robe of this female figure is straight and pleated in the style of Angkor Vat; but the end of the skirt, folded back in front, foreshadows the triangular panel characteristic of the Bayon female costumes.

THE BAYON STYLE

Artistic taste developed and iconography changed as the Bayon style gradually matured. The bronze-workers, like the stone-carvers, tried to express the gentle, meditative appearance even on figures which are sometimes still Brahman, though more often Buddhist; figures of Buddha, Lokeśvara, of Prajñāpāramitā, alone or occasionally in

Pl. 86 Military ensign in the form of a monkey. Phnom Bayong (Ta Keo). National Museum of Phnom-Penh. Height: 16 cm. End of the 12th century.

Pl. 87 Conch. Angkor region. National Museum of Phnom-Penh. Height: 28 cm. End of the 12th / early 13th century.

Bayon, pillar

groups of three, and later images of Vajrapāṇi and Hevajra. Like the stone-carvers the bronze-workers received more and more commissions as personal cults increased, for never before had so many people sought to fill their chapels with private images. The feeble workmanship inherent in mass-production has been mentioned in connection with stone-carving, but it affected the work of the bronze-casters in an even more disquieting way. There are, it is true, one or two works of real beauty in the Bayon period, but most of the statuettes are simply pious images, no doubt touching in their fervour, but with a painful absence of taste. And for many years after the eclipse of the Bayon style these unaesthetic bronzes were still made, outbidding one another in mediocrity. To ignore this side of bronze production completely would give a false impression of the post-twelfth-century works, and one must realize that there is as great a difference between this decadent work as between tourist plaster-saints and the finest modern art.

The art of the Bayon produced fine-quality works but it must be recognized that the art of bronze fell away little by little after the great heights attained in the eleventh century. Very few large pieces were cast, statues scarcely ever measuring more than nine inches. It was almost impossible to give the faces of these small figures the depth of feeling achieved by the stone-masons at this period. Nevertheless the heads of one or two exceptional pieces are meditative and expressive. In general, however, it was the pose, the movement and the modelling that interested the artist. The costumes of many of the bronze images scarcely differ from those of the stone statues; but the best statuettes have more elaborate ornament and at the end of the period excessive decoration overwhelms even well-cast pieces.

Pl. XVII Screen-bearer. Angkor region. National Museum of Phnom-Penh. Height: 30 cm. 12th century.

A Lokeśvara and a Lakṣmī from the museum of Vat Po Veal wear costumes in the Bayon style, which have been described in the section on stone. Considerable care was taken to carve out in high-relief, but in rather a dry way, the triangular panel of the skirt and the meticulous engraving of the decoration. On some other images it is possible, here and there, to discern traces of the preceding styles. Thus the hips of the Hevajra of Banteai Kdei are draped in the notched sampot so characteristic of the Baphuon style, but embellished in front with a long pleated panel ending in a double anchor. A statuette of Prajñāpāramitā with multiple heads and arms, now in the National Museum of Phnom-Penh, is dressed in a long skirt with folded upper edge, similar to that of the screen-bearer in the same collection. On the other hand on the later bronzes which prolong the Bayon style, costume is treated with more fantasy but an increasing lack of comprehension.

Although the figures were so small the artists occasionally tried to express the idea of gods in meditation. Of course they could not achieve the intensity of expression of the large stone figures, but some of the faces are vital and alive. The asymmetrical face with wide-open eyes of the Lokeśvara of Vat Po Veal smiles benevolently upon all those who invoke the aid of the Bodhisattva. Some Buddhas are depicted in the gesture of preaching, or of reassurance, but the god is more often seated in meditation on a *nāga*. If their skill and artistic sense allowed, the bronze-workers tried to invest the faces with meditative gentleness. A young woman kneels in prayer, her hands in *añjali* and the calyx of an open lotus flower poised like a vase on her head. This image, which was found in the region of Mongkol Borei, emanates a charm which was rare in this period.

The National Museum of Phnom-Penh owns a Prajñā- *Pl. 84
pāramitā, with its eleven-faced head, seated in the Indian fashion. It has an aureole of twenty-two arms which are deployed like wings around the goddess. The faces are arranged in two registers, the principal and lower one being in a frontal position. The rest are in profile. Three more faces crown the group. The workmanship is vigorous and betrays the hand of an artist. Representations of the many-headed *Pl. 85
and many-armed Prajñāpāramitā are very rare, although there are several examples of Hevajra, both in Cambodia and Thailand, which has eight faces and sixteen arms. The pose of the Mahāyāna god dancing on a demon is more or less limited to that of Śiva, the King of the Dance, who in his cosmic choreography stamps on the demons of ignorance and epilepsy.

The statuettes of the Hevajra are listed in the catalogue of the National Museum of Phnom-Penh. One comes from Banteai Kdei, the other was found during excavations in the royal palace at Angkor near the Phimeanakas. The latter has retained heavy traces of gilding; it gives an impression of over-elaboration with its rich ornament and highly chiselled costume. This excessively sumptuous decoration was only adopted towards the very end of the Bayon style, or even early in the thirteenth century. The image found at Banteai Kdei, simpler and with a freer line, is probably earlier. But when it comes to dating one should not lay too much stress on the costume derived from Baphuon art and described elsewhere. This kind of nimbus which frames the heads of gods is a symbol of power, and the fan-like arms, suggest the rapid movements of the dance. The curve of the body, gentle inclination of the head and the sweep of the arms make this a very elegant figure. The re-

Pl. 88 Incense-burner. Danrun (Battambang). National Museum of Phnom-Penh. Height: 24 cm. 12th century (cf. Cat. 102).

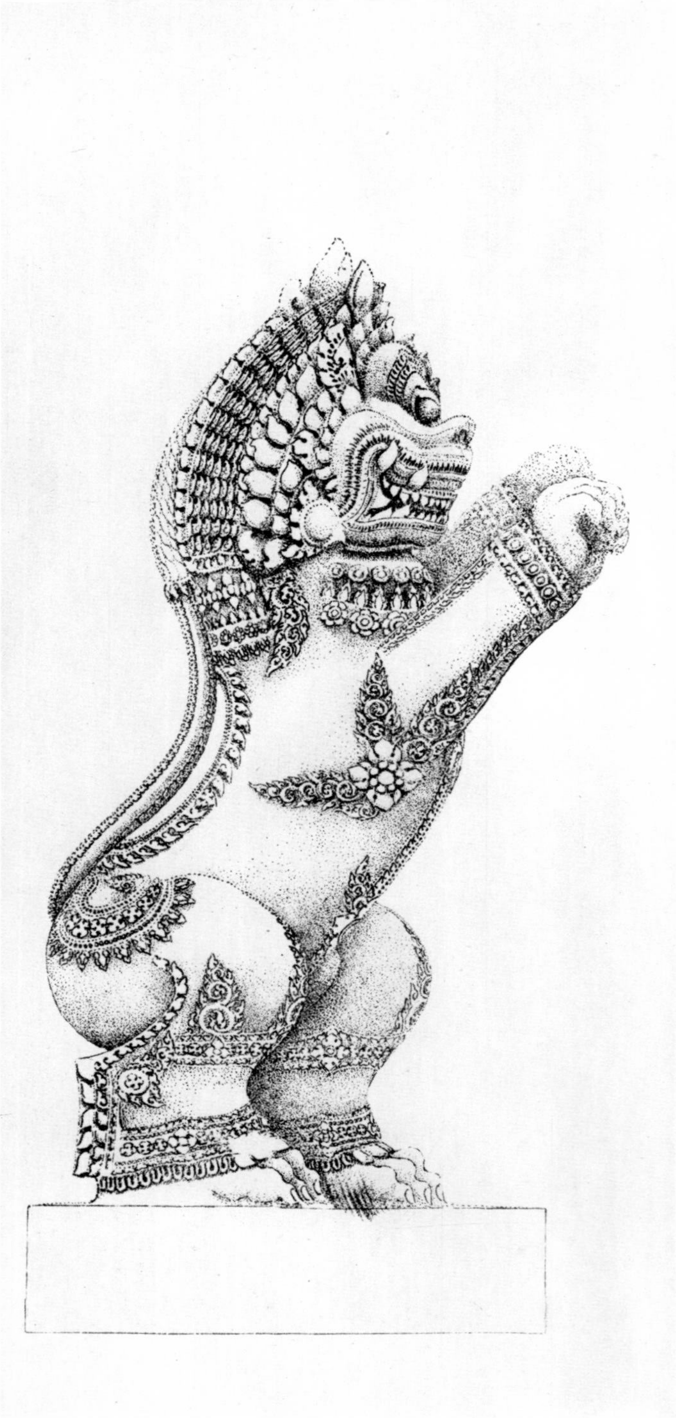

Preah Khan, Kompong Svay, lion rampant

gal simplicity of its lines renders it worthy of the best traditions of Khmer bronze.

BRONZE IN THE POST-BAYON PERIOD

During the thirteenth century, at a time when stone-carving was almost entirely dedicated to Buddhist iconography, the bronze-workers went on casting Brahman images. Unfortunately they lacked originality. They are merely altar images cast by workmen who, for good or ill, repeated the tradition of the Bayon. Sometimes they tried, apparently, to copy an image of the Baphuon or Angkor Vat style, but the clumsy workmanship and the failure to comprehend the draped costumes demonstrate the late date of the pieces. One piece, however, is worthy of note: the Prasat Khleang statue of Viṣṇu. It is a beautiful figure, inspired by the traditions of Sukhodaya, but handled with great originality.

The Brahman figures now became degenerate, whereas Buddhist art enjoyed a renaissance. After the Theravāda was generally adopted, images of Lokeśvara, Prajñāpāramitā and other Mahāyāna divinities were gradually proscribed and we know of none later than the thirteenth century. The bronze-workers tried to represent Śakyāmuni almost exclusively. Standing upright, the Buddha holds out his protective hand, sweeping fear aside. In the seated figures the gesture of meditation, in which one hand is placed above the other and resting on the knees, tends to disappear; the artisans substituted the "earth-touching" gesture, in which the left hand reaches the ground. It is natural that this should have been one of the poses to be retained, because it symbolizes the triumph of Buddha over Māra; and this victory, the prelude to the Awakening of Knowledge, is depict-

Pl. 89 Chariot finial. Phum Khal Khmauc (Battambang). Museum of Vat Po Veal at Battambang. Height: 21 cm. End of the 11th century.

ed increasingly as the most important moment of Buddha's life. Moreover, it is in the course of the thirteenth century under Singhalese influence that a flame, the symbol of the Awakening, appears above the Buddha's *uṣṇīṣa*. In this context a statuette from Kong Pisei may be taken as the most representative of thirteenth-century bronzes. It is fairly tall – three feet – and the hands are broken. The figure is rather dumpy, having legs which are clearly too short. The face, however, is peaceful and serene.

The stone- and wood-carvers managed to maintain an independent Khmer art during the sixteenth century despite strong pressure from the Thai, but bronze is quite another story. After the fifteenth and at the latest the sixteenth century it becomes very difficult to distinguish between a Khmer and a Thai Buddha, because the iconography of the two countries was the same. Portable bronze images introduced from Siam influenced the bronze-workers just as strongly as some of the Buddhas, which were venerable pieces of Singhalese origin and which had to be copied absolutely faithfully to retain their magic power.

Apart from the productions which sprang from the schools of Uthong and Ayudhyā, there is a statuette in the National Museum of Phnom-Penh which is quite exceptional. It is an idol representing Nang Thorani, the Khmer name for the Earth-god, Preah Dharani. Here once again we are confronted with a symbol of Buddha triumphing over Māra. Cambodian texts reiterate the legend in which Buddha, having overcome the daughters of Māra and the fear which the armies of demons were meant to inspire in him, calls the Earth to witness his unshaken constancy in the face of temptation. The Earth, hearing the voice of the Sage, appears in the aspect of a woman who wrings her abundant hair and brings forth torrents of water, to testify to the courage of Buddha in his former lives, and which, in Cambodian iconography, lead the demons to destruction. The goddess leans forward in a kneeling position. She gathers her hair on the top of her head with one hand while the *Pl. XVIII other holds a long snake-like plait. The figure is nude, which is unusual in Khmer art. The modelling is simple, almost crude, but the bent head harmonizes well with the long curves of her arms and tresses. This simple little figure emanates a youthful, almost childlike, charm. Another small figure, of a kneeling wrestler, deserves attention because of its vigorous modelling and realism. The quiet elegance and vitality of these two figures prove that naturalistic art of the fourteenth and fifteenth centuries – which must be the period of these two statuettes – had not entirely lost the spirit of the golden age of Khmer bronze.

*Pl. XIX

Pl. XVIII Standing Buddha. Kong Pisei (Kompong Speu). National Museum of Phnom-Penh. Height: 85 cm. 13th century.

DECORATIVE ART IN BRONZE

A study devoted to the statues alone could only give an incomplete idea of the art of bronze of the Khmer people. Excavations and chance finds have produced a large number of decorative pieces such as ritual objects and ornaments for buildings and chariots, apart from quantities of domestic ware. Bronze was a noble material and was often used to add the luxurious gilded element to a piece; so the unusual richness of the collections of decorative bronzes, which date from the period when the Khmer state was at the height of its power is not surprising. Nevertheless it is odd that there are almost no bronze pieces before the late eleventh century. The complete absence of decorative pieces from earlier periods does not mean that they did not exist. In fact Chinese historians and the Khmer stone inscriptions mention numerous bronze idols, some of which have survived. Clearly there was less hesitation about melting-down everyday objects than the idols and this must be the reason for their scarcity.

We can recognize very few decorative bronzes of the late eleventh or early twelfth century, but those which have survived are of exceptional quality. The restrained beauty which makes the Baphuon school bronzes so admirable is still seen in the fashioning of the Angkor Vat pieces. By the end of the twelfth century virtuosity had triumphed over taste; at the beginning of the thirteenth the bronze-workers were intent on overloading the decoration, more often achieving a *tour de force* than a work of art. The decline of the Khmer kingdom and degeneration of its fortunes resulted in impoverishment of the bronzes. The only pieces we know from the post-Angkor period are a few cult-objects,

Pl. 90 Chariot finial. Unknown provenance. National Museum of Phnom-Penh. Height: 27 cm. 12th century.

Pl. 91 Finial in the form of a haṃsa. Unknown provenance. Museum of Vat Po Veal at Battambang. Height: 16,5 cm. 12th century.

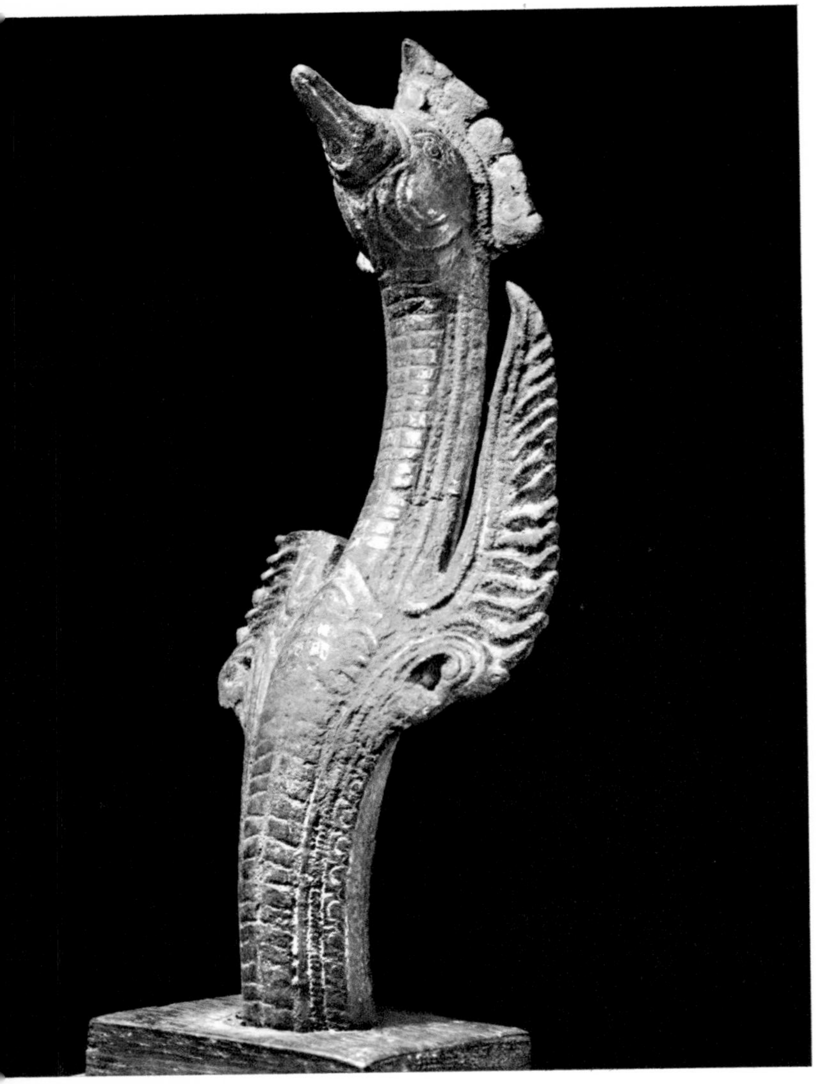

some domestic wares and harness-ornament. Restriction in the use of bronze was accompanied by a change in technique. Relief decoration was abandoned and replaced by engraved or filigree *motifs*, which were later encrusted.

CULT-OBJECTS

Idols were sometimes embellished with bronze. Often altar-images would have a bronze pedestal, a miniature copy of the stone ones in the sanctuaries. Sometimes an image or a group in bronze would be mounted against a background. The delicately chiselled fragments of such a nimbus on the bronze groups in the former Christianville Collection have already been discussed. The decoration on an altar-pedestal discovered in the Battambang region consists of two concentric arches festooned with foliage; two beautiful curves, one joined, the other free. A piece of such pure design could not be later than the beginning of the Angkor Vat period. Sometimes a divine statue had a richly chiselled nimbus, the lines of which are reminiscent of the curves of rampant arches on contemporary façades. The architectural features of small bronze idols sometimes took on the aspect of a miniature sanctuary enclosing the object of veneration like a tabernacle.

Apart from these elements which were supposed to exalt or protect a small idol, some objects were designed expressly for ritual purposes. Bells were rung during the ceremonies. Conches had a dual purpose: used as a musical instrument their deep tones filled the vaults of the sanctuaries, echoing from gallery to gallery: as receptacles they held the holy water which was employed in the rituals. Candles fixed on the walls or carried by *torchères* cast their flickering light on

Pl. 92 Palanquin hook. Mongkol Borei (Battambang). National Museum of Phnom-Penh. Height: 20 cm. End of the 12th / early 13th century.

Pl. 93 Palanquin ring. Tonleap (Ta Keo). National Museum of Phnom-Penh. Height: 25 cm. 12th century.

the idols hidden in the half-dark of the sanctuaries. The holder alone is decorated, either with the five-pronged *vajra*,
*Pl. 87 symbol of lightning, or the *triśūla*, Śiva's trident. Sometimes a small praying figure decorated the central branch.

The long curve of the conches is always graceful. Decoration consists of a denticulated border or dancing *Hevajra* at the base of the mouth. Bronze conches were supported on a tripod with feet in the shape of *nāga*-heads. The National Museum of Phnom-Penh has a most remarkable conch with a clear-cut décor of denticulations and festoons and a magnificent composition showing *Hevajra* dancing surrounded by *apsaras*. The iconography and especially the

Pl. XIX Nang Thorani. Khum Prasat, Kong Pisei (Kompong Speu). National Museum of Phnom-Penh. Height: 16 cm. Circa 15th century.

treatment of the figures on this conch enable us to date it to the Bayon period.

No lamp-holder exists which can be attributed to the Angkor period; but a very fine incense-burner of a type known in India was found at Danrun in the province of Battambang. The cup represents the chalice of a blue lotus; a *nāga* in profile springs from the beautiful curve of the branch like a slim leaf. Its lacy nimbus recalls the broken-arched aureole of the Beng Meala *nāga*. So we can attribute this burner to the twelfth century. Its simple line and fine workmanship bear this out.

Of the post-Angkor lamp-holders some are simple candle-holders with one or two branches. Others are more elaborate. One of the faithful kneels holding a branch or sometimes almost a leafy bush to which the candles were attached. The *popil* are probably later and we know of none which can be dated earlier than the nineteenth century. These are small plaques of bronze or copper in the form of a banyan leaf to which two candles were fastened. In certain ceremonial rites the believers seated in the pagoda or surrounding a young married couple, would pass the lighted *popil* from hand to hand, lighting up the faces of the people and the objects within the circle. Their decoration varies, but they often have a praying figure, or Hanuman, the monkey, or an image of Nang Thorani. *Pl. 88

Bowls and cups must also have been used in the ceremonies but they would differ little from ordinary domestic pieces.

ARCHITECTURAL ORNAMENT

It is impossible to imagine the decoration of the brick and stone buildings which, apart from one or two wood-carvings, have been stripped of their doors, ceilings and all the frames and carvings of wood and metal. Palaces and

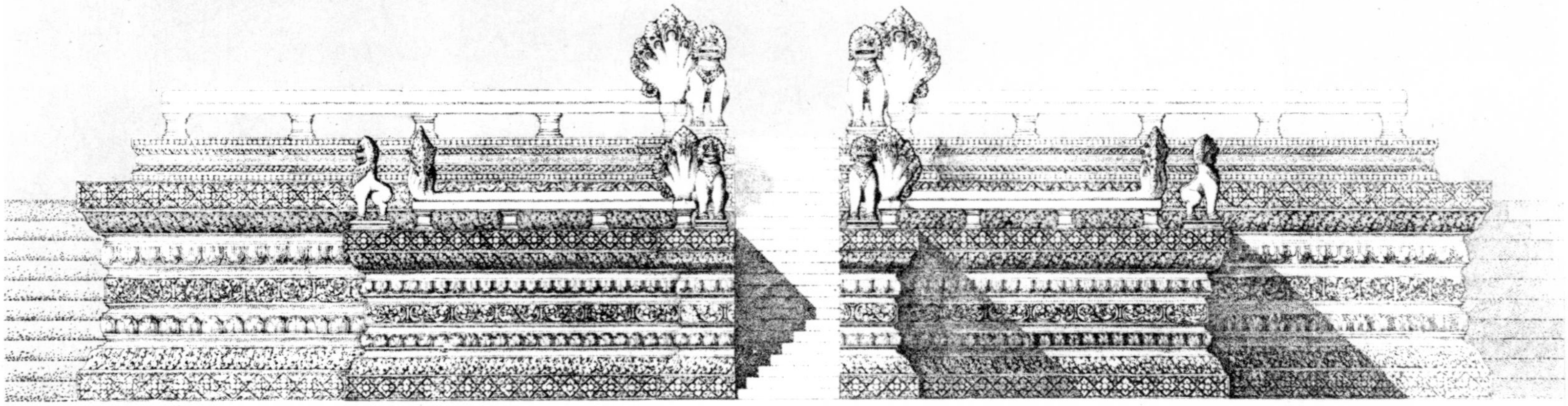

Sras Srang, elevation of the departure steps and quayside

Pl. 94 Plaque in the form of an elephant. Beng Mealea (Siem Reap). National Museum of Phnom-Penh. Height: 94 cm. 12th century.

houses were all made of wood but some metal-decoration was probably used. Iron has completely rusted away and the very few traces which have been found are so corroded that their use is indistinguishable. Although the bronzes have often been severely damaged, they have not corroded entirely; but apart from door-hinges, sockets and other objects of no artistic interest very few architectural pieces are known. A kind of staff might be a roof decoration and is probably a side-piece to one of the *triśūla*, tridents adorning the roof of the sanctuaries. The temples represented on the bas-reliefs bear witness to the Cambodian adoption of this Indian custom. The *triśūlas* which were fixed to the ridges of the sanctuaries fell when the roof collapsed and generally they were picked up by looters and melted down. The arm of the *triśūla* found at the Gate of Victory in Angkor Thom has three fine curves and a restrained engraved decoration of parallel lines and rosettes.

The door panels had applied *motifs* of lotus flowers similar to the sculptured prototypes carved in the false doors of the temples. Several of these applied pieces have been found; they are square and have a lotus flower in high-relief. Comparison with the ones on the buildings suggests that they can be attributed to the twelfth century. The gilding on these ornaments must have made them shine in the semi-darkness of the sanctuaries.

FURNITURE-ORNAMENT

The bas-reliefs and inscriptions are our only guide to the sparse furniture which decorated the palaces and the houses of the people. The only furniture to reappear constantly on the bas-reliefs in scenes of palace-life are thrones and beds. They must have been made of wood and decorated with bronze. The feet and terminals usually ended in *nāga*-heads and these are fairly common. They date more or less to the twelfth or early thirteenth century. However, a small three-headed *nāga* was found at Phnom Bayong wearing a diadem of mid-tenth-century style on each of its heads; this piece could therefore be hardly later than the Khleang style.

A bronze *nāga*, probably late-twelfth-century, was found at K'orat and is now in a private collection in Bangkok. It seems to have been part of a strangely-designed balustrade. The *nāga* rears its head and two *garuḍas* stand on its body.

The serpent is finely modelled and the triumphant air of the *garuḍas* is not without humour.

However, the first known pieces of medieval furniture are undoubtedly the bronze feet recovered at Beng Mealea. These are two rather short feet from a chair and two others larger and very slim, which perhaps supported a console or pedestal table; their tapering legs imitate a *nāga* slipping to the ground, its erect body stiffening and the hoods swelling on the heads which are crowned with a diadem. A marvellous light green patina shows up the purity of line, the slight swelling of the body and tense modelling of the heads.

HARNESS AND CHARIOT-ORNAMENT

Harness- and chariot-ornaments have contributed more towards collections of Khmer bronze than any other decorative pieces; especially chariot-finials, and hooks and rings and bells for palanquins. It is easy to imagine the use to which these pieces were put. On the bas-reliefs of Angkor Vat, of the Bayon and Banteai Chmar, long processions of vehicles are depicted. Officers ride to battle in their chariots, princes ride in litters on their way to some place of pilgrimage and women are carried in palanquins as part of the royal train. Elsewhere the king progresses surrounded by his warrior chiefs. He stands on the saddle of his elephant which moves solemnly forward to the sound of the bells hanging round its neck. In the long procession following after, the army-bullocks pulling carts also wear a cowbell.

The ornaments adorning the racks of carts and elephant saddles are not very different from the applied furniture ornament and many a bronze *nāga* with its tubular body could as easily have served to decorate the arm of a chair as the shaft of a wagon.

The earliest chariot-fittings to have been found date from the late eleventh century, as instanced by the two finials in Pl. 89 the museum of Vat Po Veal at Battambang. Like most other finials they spread out into a *nāga*-hood with five heads, but beneath the throat the serpent's body is crossed by a horizontal branch terminating in a poised *nāga*. A charioteer stands on this arm and is apparently driving the small *nāga*; the principal character rides behind – a female figure in one of the two pieces, and Viṣṇu on the *garuḍa* in the other. Although the Viṣṇu is remarkable for its feeble modelling, the female figure is correspondingly graceful and her pleated costume recalls the style of the Baphuon. Her right hand is held forward as though to grasp something, perhaps the reins, while her left arm falls with the hand slightly raised in a charming gesture; she appears to be mesmerized by the undulating movement of the snake. One is inclined to date this figure to the Baphuon period because of the costume, but in my opinion this is too early. Twelfth-century *nāga*-heads of a very similar design on staff-finials may have been used as supports for a divinity (Viṣṇu mounted on *garuḍa* is very frequent) or, later, a seated Buddha in meditation. The bronze-workers regarded the modelling of the *nāga* as the most important part, taking infinite pains with the flexed body, spreading hood and the denticulated nimbus. Sometimes, while preserving the shape of the *nāga* the artist would substitute a broad aureole for the mythical serpent and place Vajrapāṇi – the lightning carrier – of the Buddhists in front. The National Museum of Phnom-Penh has an example of these strange finials; Vajrapāṇi is seated on a base Pl. 90 supported by lions with a pierced structure behind.

Pl. XX Nāga. Angkor. National Museum of Phnom-Penh. Height: 46 cm.

The finial is sometimes differently handled. The museum of Vat Po Veal contains an especially interesting specimen,
Pl. 91 in the shape of a stylized bird, the *haṃsa*, or sacred swan, Brahma's mount. The body of the bird is etiolated, the short wings being spread parallel to the body. The long, outstretched neck is crowned with a diadem of leaves. Large traces of gilding harmonize with the patches of green patina.

The finials of the late Bayon period develop into plumed *nāga*-heads with a hooked beak, while a many-headed *garuḍa* tends to replace the *nāga*. At the same time the image of Buddha on the *nāga* becomes more and more prominent. But the workmanship is not so careful and the decoration is less restrained.

The various pieces made for palanquins were hung on a transverse pole slung on the shoulders of the bearers. Hooks, supplied with a ring, were fixed to the end of this pole, and a ring marked the centre; the litter was fastened to the rings. These pieces were all done in gilded bronze and very finely worked in vigorous relief. The earliest pieces have clean, simple lines which grow more complicated as the twelfth century advanced and as art gradually gave way to virtuosity during the next hundred years. The ring in the centre, which was the richest ornament, often has a freely-worked lotus-bud poised on tapering petals. A rosette decoration of much later date is dry and uninteresting. A curious ring at Vat Po Veal is formed from a figure of a monkey whose arms form the circle.

The earliest hooks usually have lotus-buds and some fine specimens are to be seen in the Dépôt de la Conservation at Angkor. They grew richer as time went on, terminating in *nāgas* ridden by *garuḍas* until the *garuḍas* displace the *nāgas* altogether. Feathers treated like foliage surround *garuḍas* and

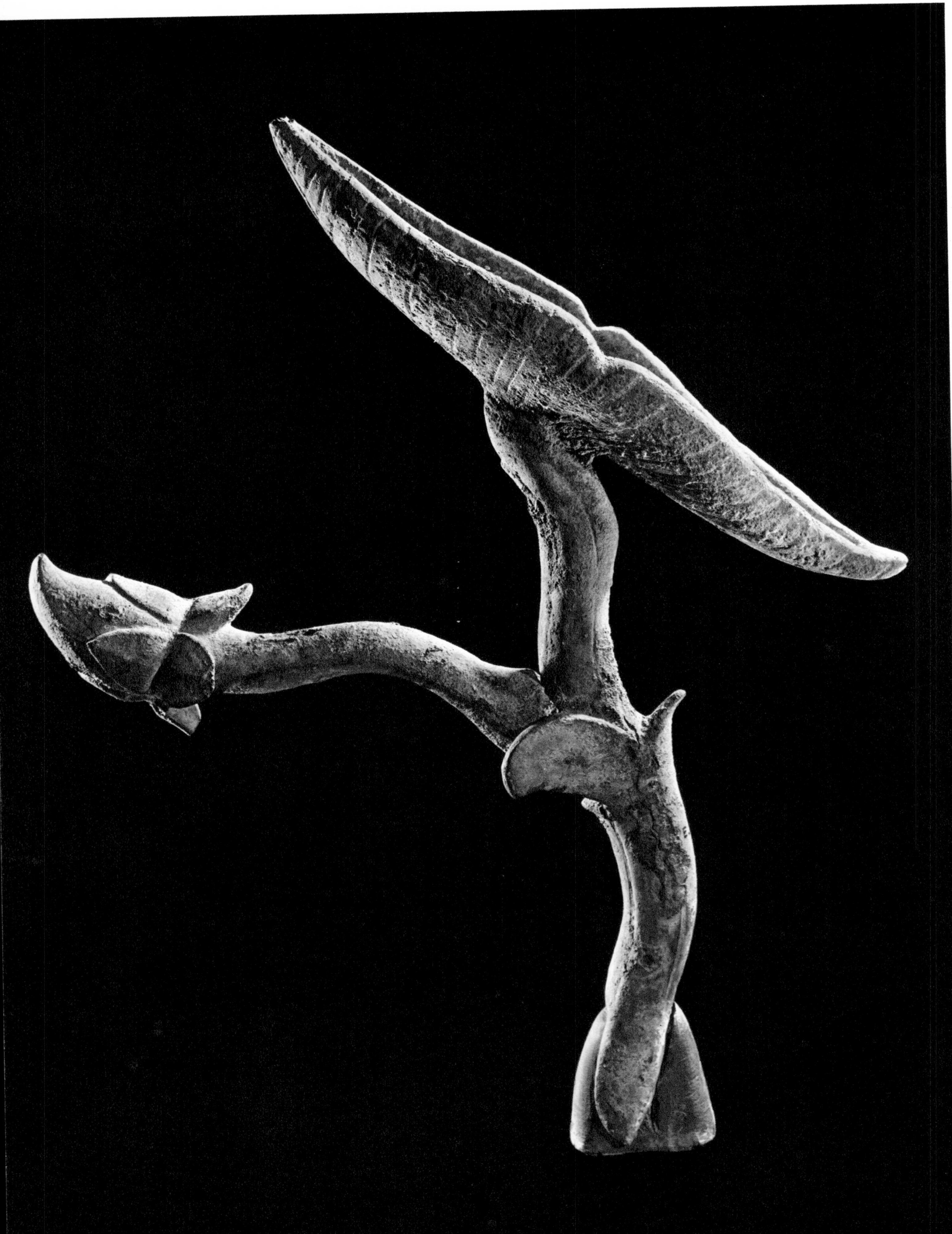

Pl. 95 Lotus. Angkor region. National Museum of Phnom-Penh. Height: 45 cm. 12th century.

young women praying – leaves, fruit-spurs, human-figures and animals swarm all over the surface of the hooks. The technique is good but the balance of the piece is completely spoiled by such uncontrolled proliferation of detail.

The rings which were slung on the hooks were of stirrup-shape. The top of the ring was sometimes carved into a lotus-bud, but it could describe a polylobed and leafy curve. In the early thirteenth century the decoration grows more involved but fortunately without the surfeit of ornament

Pl. 93 which spoiled the hooks. A very fine ring, found at Tonleap (Ta Keo province) is now in the National Museum of Phnom-Penh. Its curves imitate the serpentine body of the *nāga*, whose reared heads are crowned with a beautiful diadem of notched form similar to the nimbus on the *nāga* of

*Pl. xx Beng Mealea.

Of the bronze accessories which must have embellished the harness and saddles of the animals some bells alone remain. Cow-bells, usually post-Angkor and done in filigree, and huge elephant-bells, often ribbed and decorated

*Pl. 95 with a chiselled triangle near the mouth and a kind of small collar below the ring, are the only relics.

Although their line is admirable and the patina of great splendour, the bowls, cups, plates and mirrors must be omitted since they have no relief decoration. Some decorative pieces, on the other hand, leave us in the dark as to their use – plaques, probably applied to wooden or metal objects, fragments of big groups long since destroyed and fine pieces made perhaps as offerings.

In the course of excavation in the interior library at Beng Mealea, some symmetrical small plaques came to light.

Pl. 94 They were cut in the shape of elephants with erect tail and with lotus-buds held in the trunk. They emanate a familiar, almost malign air. Although the head and body are in relief, the trunk and lotus are carved in the round; there is therefore no ground for thinking that they are the two halves of the same elephant. They were probably applied ornaments. They could scarcely be later than the temple itself.

A rearing lion with its claws out, found in the Royal Palace of Angkor, and a *garuḍa* raising the long spike which crowns its head might be slightly later, probably early thirteenth-century. The lion, which is supported on a socket, must have been a finial. The *garuḍa* with flattened feet, pierced in the shape of a ring, was perhaps supported by a *nāga*. Both these pieces are of fine and vigorous workmanship but they are rather over-decorated, a sure sign of late Bayon art.

There is an altogether remarkable *nāga* in the National Museum of Phnom-Penh. It is pierced with cavities for incrustation of stones, and has a powerful presence and admirable patina.

The National Museum of Phnom-Penh also possesses several fragments of a bronze lotus branch. This is composed of separate articulated elements: a bud and a leaf which can be inserted into the branch. The piece illustrated, though incomplete, is very graceful. The branch bends to hold the opening bud while the folded leaf follows a long curving line. This lotus unites all the characteristics of Khmer bronze art at its finest: elegance and purity of line, simplicity, vigorous modelling and brilliance of technique.

III. WOOD

Pl. 96 Standing Buddha. Banon (Battambang).

Wood-carving, although it is richly gilded and brilliantly decorated is the least familiar aspect of Khmer art, and one may look in vain among the few statues and reliefs that we possess for the remarkable homogeneity evinced by the stone-carvings. The wide variety of wooden images is really striking. One or two pre-Angkor statues have been found, but apart from some rare exceptions, we are faced with an immense gap lasting throughout the finest Angkor period; many pieces survive from the post-Bayon and later periods, however. Curiously enough these statues, whatever their period, style, or school, are all Buddhist in iconography. To my knowledge no single Brahman idol made of wood has ever been recovered in Cambodia.

Although most wood-carving stems from the post-Angkor period it is difficult to date the pieces exactly. Much has been lost and any study of the development of the art is continually hampered by missing pieces. Termites and damp have accounted for the wooden images of the temples which lay in ruins beneath the undergrowth of the jungle. Since our information on the subject is so sparse and dating perforce very imprecise I propose to limit my discussion to the different schools, outlining the characteristics of each and the influences to which they were subjected, arriving thus at a rough chonological order.

Not a single wooden statue is dated. The only solid ground on which to build a chronological sequence is a comparison with some late stone bas-reliefs cited above, and with contemporary foreign art, especially Thai. Provenance is no guide. Cambodia possesses no monasteries built before the nineteenth century. Some Angkor temples show traces of carved ceilings of the period and there are several folding doors from the seventeenth and the eighteenth centuries.

Some of the post-Angkor period statues were worshipped in old temples and occasionally one comes across them by chance in modern monasteries. Many statues, jumbled together with stone Buddhas, used to be at Angkor Vat until the finest of them were placed in the safe keeping of the Dépôt de la Conservation at Angkor. They stood in rows in the long galleries of the temple disappearing into the shadows or brilliantly outlined by a shaft of sunlight filtering through the window carvings. In the Preah Pean of Angkor Vat they were crowded one upon another, half-hidden by incense-clouds wreathing in the sunlight.

Carved wooden pediments and façades are often found decorating the sanctuaries and even the hostels of the religious communities. None is earlier than the nineteenth century. The only collection of old reliefs which we possess comes from the monastery of Babaur, near Kompong Chnang; save for one pediment they are all large wood panels. Their very fine workmanship makes it feasible to attribute them to the late sixteenth or early seventeenth century.

In the minor arts we find some fine pieces of furniture: pulpits, desks and *torchères* still add a rich note to the old monasteries. Carved *motifs* sometimes decorate a chariot finial or the rails of a howdah. Even domestic pieces are made artistically. The struts, pulleys and combs of looms were carved and delicate engraving covers the smooth shuttles of bamboo.

TECHNIQUE

Only pieces carved in hard wood were able to resist attack by insects and damp. Koki wood[3], popular still in temples, was probably favoured by artists of the past too and the huge size of the trunks gave immense surfaces. The early pieces, both large and small, are carved from a single block but I have noticed that post-Angkor images, unless they are very small, are made out of several pieces of wood carefully fitted together. Methods of carving are diverse. The body is usually cut out of one piece, but occasionally one sees statues made of two vertical fitted planks. Hands, held forward in *abhaya mudrā*, are usually assembled separately and the adoption of this technique from the art of Dvāravatī is logical. To cut the statue and the hands in this position out of a single piece of wood would have required huge tree trunks. Sometimes, in an attempt to strengthen the figure, not only the hands but the wrists, forearms and occasionally even the front of the robe were carved and attached separately. Shoulders and parts of the feet are most often found. The feet are made in a curious way. When the Buddha is not carved in one with the pedestal, the front part of the feet will be cut out of the base; the heels, however, which are carved normally at the end of the legs, have a pin to hold the figure firmly in place.

Assembly of the different parts was sometimes done by means of wooden pegs or clamps set athwart the joints, or the pieces would be stuck together by means of a lacquer glue of varying density. I have observed traces of cloth still clinging to this glue on the inside of figures. The seams were not visible to the eye because the whole figure was covered with lacquer. The thickness of the covering varies enor-

Banteai Kdei, garuḍa on a nāga

mously. Often no more than a millimetre or two, it can be nearly a centimetre thick. The covering usually comprised a black priming coat, followed by another of red lacquer which was then decorated with gold leaf. When the covering is very thick the black coating is preceded by a base of yellowish-brown lacquer glue. Since nearly all the statues have only traces of gilding, the black and red lacquer can be easily seen.

The pre-Angkor pieces show only the natural wood; the lacquer on twelfth-century statues may have been applied later, but post-Angkor sculpture always has one or two coats of lacquer, which has preserved both the wood and the decoration. Generally the decorated Buddhas and *arhats* were given only a very thin coating lest the sharpness of the relief carving be impaired.

Ornament on the decorated Buddhas was often carved into the wood. This relatively fine chiselling had a vigorous and free relief on the earliest statues, those pre-dating the seventeenth century, but it degenerated as time went on. Post-Angkor wood-carving adopted new techniques. At one time only carving on wood was allowed but later schools also used incrustations of stones and lacquer fillets. The jewelled inlay coloured the petals and corollas of flower-heads and rosettes. Probably the incrustations were of ivory, mother-of-pearl or glass-paste in blue turquoise, green or gold. The ivory and mother-of-pearl have long ago lost their lustre, but the glass still glitters on the diadems and panels of the robes. Wooden façades on the earliest sanctuaries have gilded reliefs which stand out against an iridescent background. Although the gleam of the gold has faded, the splinters of coloured glass still glitter in the sunlight.

Preah Khan, Angkor, drawing of the reconstructed boundary walls

Pl. XXI Standing Buddha. Angkor Vat. Dépôt archéologique de la Conservation d'Angkor. Height: 208 cm.

WOOD-CARVING IN THE PRE-ANGKOR AND ANGKOR PERIODS

A few pre-Angkor statues have survived the centuries, though not one was actually found in modern Cambodia. They all come from the Plain of Reeds. Excavated figures from the old Fu-nan territory are part of the Buddhist art which spread from eastern India towards South East Asia and Champa. The oldest Buddha, long, skinny and half rotted away, is still an impressive figure. It was found on the site of Thap muoi. It stands obliquely, the monk's robe revealing a roll of flesh above the *antaravāsaka*. On the right the drapery falls in a supple line running from shoulder to heel, pinched in at the waist, filling out on the hip and thigh and outlining the nervous modelling of the muscular legs. This extraordinary figure, poised on two thin feet, is nearly nine feet high and dates from the pre-Angkor period.

Two much smaller statues of Buddha were also found in the Plain of Reeds, at Binh-hoa. The monk's robe leaves one shoulder bare. One figure holds his right hand in the gesture of preaching (*Dharmasakra mudrā*) while his left hand holds the end of the robe which encircles his waist, covering his body like a toga. This is the gesture of the admirable bronze Buddha of Amarāvatī which was found at Duong-dzuong in Champa. The second figure makes the gesture *abhaya* – reassurance – but the close relationship between the two figures is established by their similarity in size, workmanship and pose. The long sojourn in the swamps of the Plain of Reeds doubtless saved these pieces from destruction. Unfortunately wood-carvings of later periods lacked this

Pl. 97 Decorated standing Buddha. Angkor Vat. Dépôt archéologique de la Conservation d'Angkor. Height: 177 cm. Circa 17th century.

advantage, but it seems unbelievable that no images at all should have been carved in wood between the seventh and the twelfth centuries. But the gap is there and is only stopped at Angkor Vat. It must, however, be realized that apart from a few fragments of ceiling decorated with lotus-flowers only two large Buddhas are known to have come from Angkor Vat. The two pieces are very alike in style, size and iconography. The Buddha is standing, richly adorned, his broken hands undoubtedly in the gesture of reassurance. One figure of rather dry workmanship is spoiled by a somewhat morose expression, but the other is eloquent and beautiful, the naturalistic torso modelled with power and restraint. A gentle smile softens the harsh Angkor Vat style and the face is benevolent despite its strong jaw and too-pronounced lower lip. Beneath the high conical chignon-cap and richly chiselled diadem the Buddha stands, majestic and radiant.

This piece was probably greatly venerated and the fervour and admiration of the faithful were doubtless responsible for the formation in years to come of an imitative school which will be discussed in relation to the development of post-Angkor art.

SCHOOLS OF BUDDHIST SCULPTURE IN THE POST-ANGKOR PERIOD

THE HERITAGE OF THE BAYON

The Bayon period, so rich in stone sculpture, has left no wood-carving at all. However, the Dépôt de la Conservation at Angkor has a statue which still bears the imprint of Bayon art, although it is slightly later. It is a tall standing Buddha. Parts of the face and chest have been eaten away by insects but it is still impressively beautiful. The body is sturdy and the monk's robe covers both shoulders, moulding the naturalistically modelled torso. The *antaravāsaka* clings to the hips and hangs a little below the edge of the cloak. Very small curls cover the head, topped by a well-developed *uṣnīṣa* which served as a ground for the flame. Only the right side of the face has survived, but the fine modelling of cheek and chin can be discerned even in this fragment. The eyes are half-closed beneath the arch of the brows, and cast down; but the shape of the eye can be sensed beneath the lid. A peaceful serenity emanates from this figure of the Sage on which the scarcely tarnished gilding still gleams over the red lacquer. Probably the statue was carved in the thirteenth century. In many ways its physiognomy recalls the "Commaille" Buddha, which could hardly be much earlier than this wood figure. There are other less fine Buddhas from the same school of sculpture, but they are all damaged.

A much later Buddha is in the National Museum of Phnom-Penh. The curls on his head are flattened into lozenges and the flame crowning the *uṣnīṣa* is replaced by a slim polished spindle. The arch of the brows is much more mechanical and the nose is slightly aquiline with large, flaring nostrils. The costume is scarcely altered. The workmanship is rather dry and the modelling casual. The piece, which may date from the late thirteenth or early fourteenth century is proof of the gradual deterioration of the Bayon tradition.

*Pl. XXI

NEW DEVELOPMENTS

Apparently the figures of the Royal Buddha disappeared from the iconography of the reign of Jayavarman VII. It was natural that no immediate renaissance occurred after the introduction of the puritanical Theravādic school. With the exception of a few diademed images prolonging the Angkor Vat tradition, many decades – more than a century in fact – were to pass before the Buddha appeared once more adorned in his royal finery. The question of the date when Theravādic Buddhism adopted the Buddha in royal attire is a vexed one, and we can only notice the existence of the two iconographies side by side during the sixteenth century. From that date the ornate Buddha once more took his place in the sanctuaries, in fewer numbers than those in monk's robe at first, but multiplying over the centuries. Thereafter the two schools went their separate ways and it is only on very rare occasions that the school specializing in ascetic Buddhas would condescend to add chiselled ornament to the monastic figure.

Pl. XXII Standing Buddha. Angkor Vat. Dépôt archéologique de la Conservation d'Angkor. Height: 177 cm.

BUDDHA – THE MONK

Many of the unadorned Buddhas are so different in workmanship, expression and the handling of the figure and clothing that they are impossible to classify, but on close examination an increasing Thai influence is discernible. The faces grow longer, less oval, the eyebrows have a deeper curve while the clothing is simplified and the thin arms become stiff and shapeless. The hair is curled with great artifice and finished either with a skull-cap bristling with spines or with engraved chequer-work. Nevertheless there are about a dozen definitely homogeneous pieces, proving the existence of a school among the infinitely variable techniques applied to the monastic Buddha.

All the Buddhas of this type are standing with hands held forward in the gesture which "banishes fear" *(abhaya mudrā)*. The arched chest is very stylized beneath the monk's robe, which is handled with great sobriety, falling unpleated, austere and rigid. The monastic robe and *antaravāsaka* are exactly the same length, cut off, as it were, above the ankles. There are no curls on the head and the top and bulbous base of the *uṣṇīṣa* are covered with small engraved checks. This chequer-design was always upright on the early pieces, but is slanting on the later ones. The *uṣṇīṣa* is crowned with a conical flame jutting from a lotus flower. But it is the face rather than the clothing and hair style which creates a sense of unity in the Buddhas of this school. The eyeball is prominent beneath finely-drawn eyebrows, joined and curving gently upwards on the temple, and the downward glance scarcely filters through the slit in the eyelid. The nose is straight, barely modelled at all and is cut short above the upper lip. This stylized face, dominated by

Pl. XXIII Decorated arhat. Angkor Vat. National Museum of Phnom-Penh. Overall-height: 92 cm. 16th century (cf. Pl. 98).

a horizontal shadow below the eyes and nose, has a young expression, sometimes childish, often almost sulky.

A Buddha, number 1812 in the Dépôt de la Conservation at Angkor, is evidently a product of the same school; the face is characteristic, the lines of the costumes are exactly the same, but though the head is uncrowned the pectoral and *antaravāsaka* are ornamented. The leafy, snail-like spiral *motifs* which decorate it seem to me no earlier than the eighteenth century, which leads to the suggestion that this school could have flourished in the seventeenth century. To my knowledge the type of Buddha which I have just described has no equivalent in Thai art and it seems to me to be the most original of post-Angkor monastic Buddhas.

Bayon, four-headed tower

BUDDHA ADORNED

Forced to suppress their taste for fantasy and finery in the carving of the monkish and austere Buddha, post-Angkor artists were able to give their passion for decoration free rein when they were carving Buddha in his princely aspect. Consequently among all the Cambodian artists who were engaged in the carving of Buddhas, it was the schools making the decorated versions that produced the most lively images. Among these schools some sought inspiration in Angkor art, others adopted aesthetic changes which followed the last burst of glory in the Bayon. The dating of these images is a thorny problem even though parts of the decoration do give some clues. They are comparable with late Khmer bas-reliefs and even the painting of Thailand. The first well-defined school of ornate Buddhas arises from the Angkor tradition of the twelfth century, and probably the two wood Buddhas discussed with the style of Angkor Vat

inspired the whole school. Certainly venerable images of this kind were copied and recopied. It is interesting to see the successive deviations from the original which appeared on the various statues during the centuries following the beginning of Angkor Vat. These statues, formerly crowded together in the Angkor Vat galleries, are now in the Dépôt de la Conservation at Angkor.

Like the two statues of Angkor Vat the Buddha is represented standing with raised hands. The monk's robe is restrained and rarely has any decoration on the belt and front panel. All the Buddhas of this school are crowned with a diadem and conical chignon-cap and they wear a finely chiselled pectoral. Nervetheless the rather slick workmanship has lost its freedom and in order to overcome the deficiencies of these feeble reliefs the artists resorted to incrustation of mother-of-pearl and coloured glass. The face, square-jawed in the Angkor Vat tradition, grows softer and smiling while the cheeks puff out slightly giving a rather doll-like appearance. Eyes, as at Angkor Vat, are open and a small sliver of mother-of pearl is inserted in the white of the eye to give the figure a more lively look. Even the first copies are taller than the sturdy figures of Angkor Vat and the last images are excessively long and thin.

The other schools did not try to copy the earlier models systematically. They nevertheless got their inspiration from the Khmer of the Angkor period but filtered through the thirteenth and fifteenth centuries; sometimes they accepted foreign ideas and often enriched inherited traditions with innovations. At first the ornate decoration was chiselled in the wood but this was soon followed by incrustation in the design and, later still, arabesques and scrolls were enhanced with lacquer.

The finest Buddhas adorned with carved decoration are at present in the Dépôt de la Conservation at Angkor after receiving the prayers of the faithful for centuries at Preah Pean or in the galleries of Angkor Vat. Angkor-period temples and modern sanctuaries such as Banon near Battambang have several rare examples. Hands, held forward in the gesture of reassurance, are nearly always broken. A few statues of Buddha (considered to be among the very best) have the right arm falling beside the body, while the left is held across the breast in the gesture of peace.

The coiffure of the ornate Buddhas is very original. It consists of a high tiara constructed in tiers; the diadem, fused with the neck-cover, encloses the whole head framing the ear. The terminal *motif* crowns the broad diadem and is a degeneration of the Angkor-period chignon-cover. It usually comprises two tiers; a row of petals supports the crown in the shape of a bishop's mitre and the diadem often has a flower in its design – a kind of cruciferous plant in which the side petals take on the shape of a flame.

The monk's robe covers both shoulders but allows the rich chiselling to show – the pectoral, arm-bands, bracelets and richly woven *antaravāsaka*. The pectoral edged with broad scallops covers the shoulders and falls in a point on the chest. It is handled in the same spirit as the tiara; the same leafy scrolls and the same flower on the breast with flame-like petals. On the *antaravāsaka* the artists often carved the belt, the front panel and two *motifs* with the appearance of wings, hiding the hips. The decoration is founded on plant scrolls. On the front panel there is a long sinuous branch or spiral twisted backwards.

We do not know exactly when this school of sculpture developed. The tiered tiara is worn by several figures in the

Pl. 98 Decorated arhat. Angkor Vat. National Museum of Phnom-Penh. Height: 92 cm.
Pl. 99 Fragment of a carved partition. Babaur (Kompong Chnang). National Museum of Phnom-Penh. Height: 160 cm. 17th century.

north-east gallery of Angkor Vat, carved in the sixteenth century. Nevertheless, although these leafy scrolls appear here and there at Angkor Vat in the border of a sampot, the decoration of a howdah, or in the earrings of a *garuḍa*, at that period they do not attain the decorative freedom which they were to exhibit in the carved ornament of the Buddhas. The flame-like flowers only appear on the pectoral, where one would expect to find them, since they are an adaptation of the cruciferous flower to the curving shape of the neck ornament. Generally the decoration of the bas-reliefs at Angkor Vat still preserves the characteristics of the Angkor period, which no longer appear on the Buddhas crowned with a tiara. This suggests a slightly later date. Perhaps the earliest ones could have been carved at the end of the sixteenth century.

One of the finest Buddhas of this school (number 5533 in Pl. 97
the Dépôt de la Conservation) is almost life-size, but the feet have rotted away. The rich ornament lends it a very hieratic appearance. The plant decoration of the robes and jewellery shows very vigorous relief and freedom of design, and no stiffness mars the workmanship. The face is particularly interesting. The Angkor square chin gives an authoritative expression while the nose is long with broad nostrils. The thick, outlined mouth is self-willed, almost disillusioned. The way the incrusted eyes glitter beneath lowered lids increases the realism of the face, a realism which even at a distance of several centuries preserves the Bayon style and bears witness to the survival of Khmer tradition.

Other schools of ornate Buddhas add lacquer-painting to the wood-carving, a technique which was also used in Burma. Two Buddhas in the Dépôt de la Conservation and another in the National Museum of Phnom-Penh wear an

Pl. XXIV Devatā. Babaur (Kompong Chnang). National Museum of Phnom-Penh. Height: 234 cm. 17th century.

unusual ornament, partly carved and partly painted-in with lacquer fillets. The first of these has a carved tiara while on the second only the rows of water-lily petals decorating the chignon were cut out in relief. On the diadem and necklace of this second Buddha a lacquer filigree design is developed from the scrolls and stylized flowers. It is noticeable on these two pieces that the diadem and neck-cover, although firmly joined, have a different decoration. Lacquer fillets decorate the pectoral and then run, like lace, round the belt, the panel, the border and the hip decoration of the *antaravāsaka*. The fillets are in groups outlining the principal curves and they roll up to form small croziers. The lacquer design which is rich and free on these pieces becomes stiff and mechanical on the later ones.

Two Buddhas in the Dépôt de la Conservation exhibit a braided decoration in lacquer which is handled less freely. Thai influence is very noticeable on these two statues. The diadem, fitted close to the temples, supports a tapering conical crown. The pectoral is extended to form a necklace and belt decorated with butterfly wings. This *motif*, and their physiognomy generally, lead to a rather later attribution for these Buddhas, perhaps early eighteenth century. The Conservation also has a Buddha fragment which is much more Siamese in influence with partly carved and partly lacquered decoration. In this case the lacquer is not simply painted on but applied thickly and carved with the design. The fragment is unfortunately in too poor a condition for detailed study. It is, however, interesting to observe that the artist made an attempt on this piece to adapt to wood and lacquer a specifically bronze *motif* from Thai art of the first period Bangkok style.

THE ARHATS

In principle Theravādic iconography allowed the image of Buddha alone to appear on the altar but sometimes one sees praying disciples kneeling before the Sage. The Cambodians call them *Tep Pranam* (Divinities in adoration). Three of these are noteworthy; one was brought to Angkor Vat a very long time ago and the others came from a monastery at Babaur in the province of Kompong Chnang. All three are in the National Museum of Phnom-Penh.

No other free-standing figure of the post-Angkor period is comparable with the ornate *arhat* of Angkor Vat. It would Pl. xxiii, Pl. 98
be difficult to imagine a more beautiful figure. It is of a very young person, adolescent, kneeling with hands joined and legs turned under in the graceful position still adopted by *Pl. xxii
the Cambodians during religious ceremonies. He wears a tiara and his sampot, folded over the trousers, is fastened to the waist by a belt decorated with chiselled scrolls. Denticulations and leafy scrolls decorate the pectoral hanging in large festoons over the chest. On the back the pectoral is the same as the headdress. The tiara itself is of outstanding richness and beauty. The crown, unfortunately broken, springs from rows of pearls and denticulations and the diadem, clearing the forehead, comes to a point on the temple to frame the ear and completely cover the nape of the neck. The whole surface is filled with plant decoration; flowers with flame-like petals proliferate among scrolls, rosettes and lotus-buds over the headdress. The richness of this delicate and nervous modelling contrasts sharply with the simplicity of gesture and restrained workmanship on the face and body. The face is a pure oval with delicate chin and full cheeks. Beneath softly-joined arching eyebrows the slanting eyes are

Pl. 100 Fragment of a carved partition. Babaur (Kompong Chnang). National Museum of Phnom-Penh. Height: 93 cm. 17th century.

open but downcast. The thin nose is broken at the end. A slight smile flits across the mouth; the lips are asymmetrical and open as if about to speak. The movement of arms and legs is realistic and eloquent, but it is clear that the artist was more concerned with the intensely spiritual expression of the face and praying hands than with anatomical details. Hieratic in pose the figure is still intensely human, perhaps because it was venerated less than the statues of Buddha. It is after all a very original piece differing from other free-standing figures in its handling, costume and unusual tiara. It is not easy to date exactly. It could have been made towards the middle of the sixteenth century. Slight touches of gold enhance the brown face, and the fine carving of the tiara is pointed with traces of lacquer.

The two *arhats* of Babaur are not really comparable with such an exceptionally beautiful statue. Both are rather damaged, having been eaten away by insects. The torso of the latest one is intact, the hands holding out a chalice as if in offering. Both have tiered crowns and wear a sampot with the "tail" enhanced by flying panels forming a basque behind. The faces are long with thick, arched and joined eyebrows. The style of the earliest *arhat* is distinguished by its gentleness and supple workmanship, whereas the other suffers from a distinct stiffness, which is accentuated by the stylization of the face. In the first one the sculptor has tried to suggest the movement of the drapery. A decoration of engraved flowers within leafy scrolls brightens the sampot of these two *arhats*. The tiaras are reminiscent of the decorated Buddhas.

Although these figures are not apparently earlier than the seventeenth century it would be unwise to try to date them more precisely.

THE RELIEFS

For long decades the monastery of Babaur preserved the carved panels which are the oldest wood-reliefs we know. They formed a kind of interior court to the monastery. About twenty fragments have been saved; some are pieces of façades, but mostly parts of screens pierced with balustered windows and surmounted by a seated divinity beneath a nimbus of *nāga*-heads. Below the window another god was seated in the same position. Humans and animals surrounded them. We have not been able to reconstitute a single panel. Often the figures stretch towards the god above; a woman with lotus-buds in her hand walks along, followed by a rider cavorting in the clouds and by *apsaras*; above this group cockerels fight among flowery branches. Elsewhere monkeys bring their offerings to the central divinity; all the animals turn towards the god, bearing an oriflamme, a casket or simply with their hands joined in *añjali*, the attitude of adoration. On one or two fragments scenes can be discerned – grimacing creatures threaten a figure no longer there. They hurl arrows which are transformed at once into flowering branches. This may be a representation of the famous story in which armies of demons sent by Māra attacked the meditating Buddha. Or monkeys struggle with snakes despatched no doubt by the magic arrows of Indrajit. We recognize again scenes from the Buddha's former lives.

It is impossible to try to assess the value of these reliefs as compositions because none is complete. However, on the few fragments we possess it can be seen that the groups of humans and animals and the masses of scrolling plants are well-balanced. The movements are executed with vitality and vigour.

Elephant terrace, elephant struggling with a lion

Four of the Babaur fragments are taken up with a big
Pl. xxiv standing *devatā*, above which are carved rosettes and kneeling *arhats* supported apparently by the scrolling tendrils of foliage. The *devatā* is full face; one hand holds the stems of two lotus buds in front of her breast. The head is crowned with a tiara decorated on the rolled diadem with a four-petalled flower; the chignon-cap is made of lacy lotus petals from which springs a flower. Richly-wrought wings rise up behind the ears and all the figures, princely and divine, have this type of coiffure; the terminal flower sometimes rests directly on the lotus-petals, at other times it is on a short stem. The costume is made of soft material. The breast is exposed, although a gauzy scarf drapes one shoulder and floats over the back and the skirt is shaped on the hips with a double or triple flying panel. It is fastened at the waist by a basque belt encircling the hips. Belts of this type are elaborately decorated with stylized foliage like embroidery.

The artist was at great pains to carve the *devatā*-heads. The fashioning of the oval face and determined chin is faultless. The forehead is broadly handled; beneath the lifted arch of the brows downcast eyes give a serious and withdrawn expression to these female figures.

All these images are vividly reminiscent of the *devatās* of the Angkor period – the same fine silhouette and feet carved in profile; the same slim body with matured breasts and even the same gesture, seen so often at Angkor Vat, of the hand drawn across the breast and holding the stem of a flower. The smile is more serious, the hieratic pose more pronounced, yet the figure is still supple and freely modelled.

Moreover one of the Babaur *devatās*, the face of which has unluckily been eaten away, has a winged diadem with three branches of flowers like those adorning some of the Angkor Vat *devatās*.

In the small temple of Prasat Phum Prasat, built in the style of Kompong Preah, are preserved some doors from the post-Angkor period. One of these is carved with a male person standing on a lion; the other has a large female figure on a small pedestal. The male figure, doubtless a *dvārapāla*, brandishes a sword in one hand and an open flower in the other; the female is a *devatā* with the hand against her breast holding a lotus-bud. On his trousers the man wears a sampot with floating panels tied in a loop. The female skirt has two floating panels on each side and broad bias-draped pleats on the hip. Both wear a leafy tiara close to the forehead without diadem; a necklace of leaves hangs down in a point on the chest. This type of tiara and draped costume with floating panels adorns the *arhat* painted on a frieze of Wat Yai Suvannaram at Phetburi in Thailand. It has been attributed to the early seventeenth century. The folding doors of Prasat Phum Prasat cannot be so exactly dated, though they were certainly made in the seventeenth century.

The reliefs of Babaur seem to be of an earlier school of sculpture. The tiaras on the figures are less developed and the draping of their clothing more restrained. On these reliefs the male costumes are arranged in the same way as the sampots on some of the late bas-reliefs of Angkor Vat. Finally, although the Prasat Phum Prasat faces seem more Siamese because of their simple modelling and slanting eyes beneath high arched brows, the Babaur *devatās* have a more naturalistic face and serene expression. I am inclined to attribute them to a date later by several decades than the later reliefs of Angkor Vat, possibly the sixteenth or early seventeenth century. It must be remembered that the sixteenth century was the finest period of Babaur, when King Ang Chan had his capital there.

Carved panels, doors and screens are very rare, though there are not a few pediments and remains of ruined temples. They are all much later than the Babaur of Prasat Phum Prasat reliefs. None can be dated before the early nineteenth century. The gilded wood-carvings stand out against a ground inlaid with glass. On the earliest pediments both gilding and ground have disappeared, the wood has been worn into channels by the rain and perished in many places. Foliage twists and turns, spreading like a flame to surround a god, or comes to the rescue of a prince fighting a giant demon, and sometimes it encircles the royal emblems. In richly-embroidered costume and high, winged tiara, gods and heroes fight, or turn and twist in the harmonious, measured movements characteristic of the modern Cambodian dance.

It would be incomplete to finish this survey of Khmer wood-carving without mentioning the large number of everyday objects – weather-vanes with fantastic animals, parts of looms, spoons and many kinds of boxes. All these decorations depict animals. On the looms monkeys form the spool, birds perch on pulleys and butterflies alight on the corners. Many of the boxes are in the shape of an animal; a bird, elephant or frog. Often they are naturalistic, sometimes stylized. They are always handled sympathetically, even with humour. But the proportions and lines are always pleasant, whatever their form. These minor arts should not be underestimated, though of course they are not comparable with the sculpture or bas-reliefs of the sixteenth and seventeenth centuries, of which the finest is the adorned *arhat* of Angkor Vat.

CONCLUSION

The art of the Khmer appears as a unified whole over a long period in which materials, technique and inspiration varied widely. The sculptors followed their instincts – love of plastic beauty, of balance, proportion and form, respect for tradition and a profound understanding of the human mind.

We have seen that Khmer artists perfectly understood the rules governing a work of art. While never losing sight of their personal vision they tried to give every piece of sculpture its proper decorative value. The proportions and shape of a statue had to harmonize with the sanctuary in which it was placed. The composition of a bas-relief had to fit into the shape of a wall or gallery or the wing of a building. And embroidered or jewelled decoration on a statue was carefully chiselled to contrast with the polished surface of the body. Sometimes the face was stylized so as to become a decorative element in itself, for instance in the head of Yakṣa from Koh Ker, in which striated, arched eyebrows over large, round eyes are joined by a kind of chiselled rosette on the forehead; on this face everything is subject to the decorative effect, the large mouth with its fangs quite as much as the beard and the moustache. This attraction for the interplay of decoration and flat surface occupied the artists even when they were faced with the austere iconography of Theravādic Buddhism; the richly adorned Buddhas multiplied and the Sage's severe monastic robe was tempered with the embroideries and jewels of a prince.

Respect for tradition undoubtedly assured continuity but it did not take the form of blind imitation. True the artists drew on the artistic products of their ancestors for inspiration but far from clinging to a more or less stiff, archaic style they extracted the elements which suited their purpose. An archaizing style does, however, appear in some statues, one of which, an unusual head of Śiva, is in the Dépôt de la Conservation at Angkor. The cylindrical chignon and diadem imitate a style from Preah Ko, while the slightly smiling face resembles the early Angkor Vat style; that is to say it is gentle and serene in the manner of the art of the Baphuon. There is no doubt that the piece was carved at the very beginning of the twelfth century. The head is reminiscent of those Egyptian statues of the Ptolemaic period in which the headdress alone retains the early traditional style, whereas the workmanship, and the expression of the face and body bear the stamp of Hellenism. One can only guess at the origin of such a copy. Could it be the replica of a venerable, even miraculous image, or perhaps the repetition of a celebrated idol destroyed in some catastrophe? It is impossible to decide. The most interesting thing is the archaization of detail on the figure in contrast to the style of the face, where the sculptor has followed the normal ideas of his own period without any attempt to render the physical features of the style which he was copying. In Khmer art the artist nearly always allowed his own personality and the style of his period to colour his work, perhaps subconsciously.

Despite the rules of a fixed iconography and the respect for religion and tradition Khmer sculpture has a profoundly human aspect, which never ceased to break through even when the piece was in the most hieratic style. Every aspect of human life was described by the artists, not only the physical, but the moral, emotional and intellectual. A lively scene could be set on the bas-reliefs disguised as a mythological or historic tale. These spontaneous carvings appear on the bas-reliefs of Bakong at a time when the idols were at their most rigid and impersonal. At Banteai Srei in the Baphuon the walls and pediments are filled with people in pavilions: a woman suckles her infant, a man prepares for war, and sorrow and joy are seen on the face of the people. Nor are animals neglected, in their role as man's friend, or free in the jungle. Clearly they had a great interest for the artists, introducing a humorous, sometimes even a poetic note. And at Angkor Vat the king, his court and army fill the walls beside the heroes and the gods. Tender and sorrowful scenes are slipped in beside epic combats and legendary adventures, but of all the bas-reliefs the Bayon illustrates most eloquently the life of the Khmer people. The activity of the village goes on calmly between the scenes of battle and palace life. Games are played on the royal terraces while the peasants walk along beside a file of elephants; the suffering of a warrior wounded by an elephant is poignantly described, and a poor man is depicted fervently praying beside a horse with five heads.

But the figures recall far more than the simple, material facts of existence; they express the aspirations, emotions and the character of men. Some images seem to have been drawn from a gallery of portraits. The "Noble Lady of Koh Krieng", authoritarian and majestic, receives her due homage, while the proud and graceful Lakṣmī of Prasat Thleay is radiantly youthful. In the Kulen the Viṣṇus of Prasat Damrei Krap are self-confident and proud of their healing power; the Śiva of Banteai Srei is a happy man holding his docile little wife to his bosom; the Lakṣmī of Prasat Trapeang Totung Thngay raises her delicate hand in a friendly gesture; Sūryavarman II, the magnificent king glorying in his power, sits upon the throne or moves into battle on his elephant. With pensive face Queen Jayarājadevī awaits the return of her husband. Jayavarman VII is an imposing figure of powerful will, but the expression of dominion and ambition on his face is transfigured by compassion as he meditates everlastingly upon the laws of Buddha. The ornate *arhat* of Angkor Vat carved with perfect simplicity in wood is itself a symbol of the spirit of Khmer art, which seems to realize all its aspirations in this figure. Smiling, serene and withdrawn, he appears to listen to a distant music which only he can apprehend.

CATALOGUE

Cat. 1 Sūryavarman II. The earliest portrait of Sūryavarman II appears on the so-called historical bas-relief of Angkor Vat. The king is portrayed idealistically, seated in regal splendour. He is wearing the traditional jewels of a Khmer king described by Ch'ou Ta-k'uan: "He wears a golden crown and a necklace of pearls weighing more than three pounds." Bracelets and gold rings adorn his wrists, fingers and ankles.
Angkor Vat, Southern gallery of the third court. Angkor Vat style. First half of the 12th century.

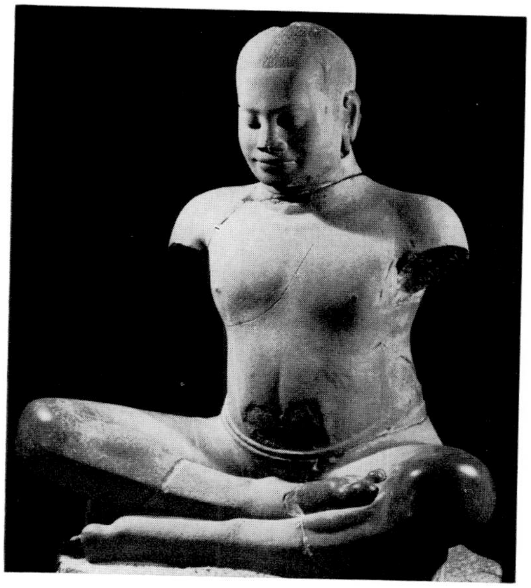

Cat. 2 Jayavarman VII. This is evidently a realistic portrait of Jayavarman VII. There is a striking resemblance between this figure and the silhouette on the bas-relief of the Bayon which commemorates the naval victory over the Cham. Several other statues have been discovered scattered over the former Khmer empire. One of the finest is undoubtedly the head found at Preah Khan in Kompong Svay (Pl.IX). The king is portrayed here without any of his royal attributes and insignia, seated in the position of the Buddha in meditation.
Krol Romeas, Angkor. National Museum of Phnom-Penh. Bayon style. Late 12th / early 13th century.

Cat. 3 Jayarajādevī. Images of Jayarajādevī, Jayavarman VIIth's first wife, were erected by her sister Indradevī, who became queen after her death. Indradevī wrote a long tribute in praise of her sister, describing the pious works done in the name of her husband who was fighting in Champa. "Grateful to the gods for the safe return of her husband she (poured forth) a rain of magnificent gifts... in her charity she gave all her possessions to the gods and to the poor." But Jayarajādevī barely survived the triumphal return of Jayavarman VII, "and she entered Nirvana soon after his coronation."
Preah Khan, Angkor. Musée Guimet, Paris. Height: 110 cm. Bayon style. Late 12th / early 13th century.

Cat. 4 The "Lady of Koh Krieng". This is the figure of a mature woman of Cambodia, probably an aristocrat.
Koh Krieng (Kratie). National Museum of Phnom-Penh. Height: 127 cm. Sambor style. Early 7th century.

Cat. 5 Umā (?). This is a young and sturdy figure with fine, high breasts underlined by a ripple of skin. Her transparent skirt barely veils the spreading hips.
Kompong Khleang (Siem Reap). National Museum of Phnom-Penh. Height: 62 cm. Prei Kmeng style. End of the 7th / early 8th century.

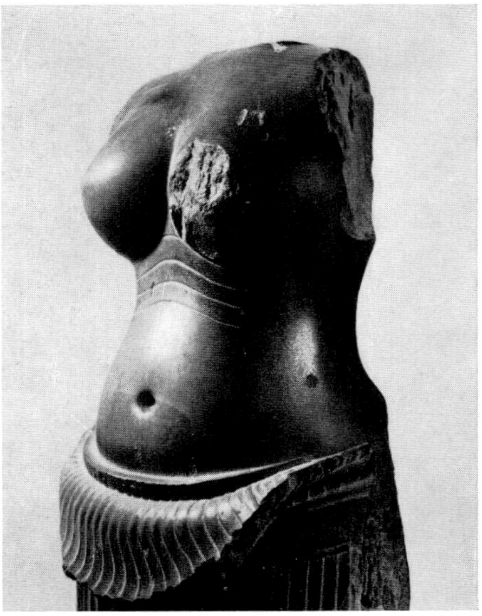

Cat. 6 The "Dark Lady". The goddess, carved in a dark stone with green highlights, is exceptionally fine despite severe damage. She has high, firm breasts and well-rounded hips. The stiffness which is usually a feature of the early 10th century has not affected this supple figure.
Prasat Neang Khmau (Ta Keo). National Museum of Phnom-Penh. Height: 108 cm. Koh Ker style. Second quarter of the 10th century.

Cat. 7 Female goddess. At the end of the 11th century figures are often slender with a large head; this one, however, is sturdy with fine hips beneath a pleated skirt. The statue is gentle and serene.
Khum Samlanh (Kampot). National Museum of Phnom-Penh. Height: 133 cm. Baphuon style. Second half of the 11th century.

Cat. 8 Female figure. This darkly polished figure is among the most beautiful of all 12th-century Khmer pieces. The square shoulders are a dominant feature of the Angkor Vat style. The hips are quite hidden by the stiff skirt, but the breasts are moulded with grace and charm.
Angkor region. National Museum of Phnom-Penh. Height: 82 cm. Angkor Vat style. First half of the 12th century.

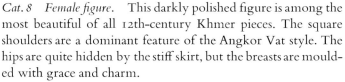

Cat. 9 Female figure. The Bayon statues are often carved in a coarser sandstone than those of earlier periods and are usually left unpolished. But the artists knew how to use the grain of the stone and the finest figures are proof of their anatomical knowledge.
Provenance unknown. Dépôt archéologique de la Conservation d'Angkor. Height: 60 cm. Bayon style. Late 12th/early 13th century.

Cat. 10 Coiffure of the "Lady of Koh Krieng". This remarkable headdress consists of a chignon poised like a tiara. The plaited hair has been laid over the top in strips and looped round the chignon at the back and sides.
Koh Krieng (Kratie). National Museum of Phnom-Penh. Height of the statue: 127 cm. Sambor style. Early 7th century.

Cat. 11 Woman's head. The face of this piece is crudely done, but the long, twisted plait has been broadly sketched in. This unfinished piece gave the artist no opportunity to express the fashions of his period in minutely chiselled detail. Tightly woven plaits and flower wreaths are absent; only a few flowers have been roughly cut into the chignon.
Vat Barai (Ta Keo). National Museum of Phnom-Penh. Height: 21 cm. Banteai Srei style. Second half of the 10th century.

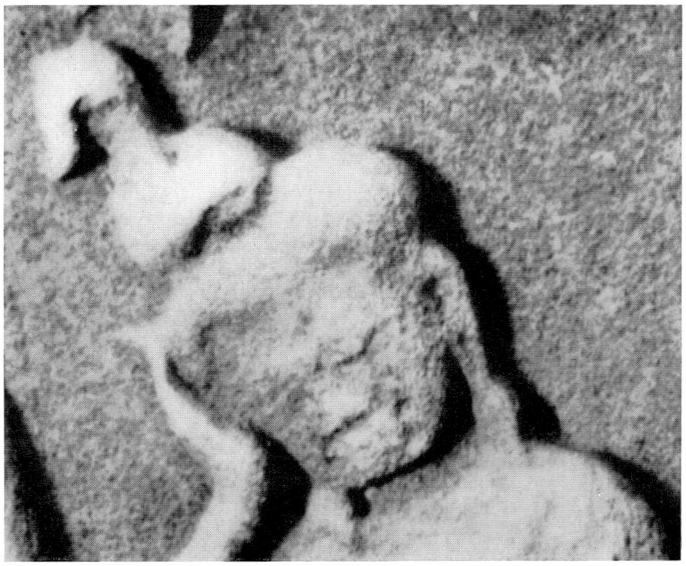

Cat. 12 Female coiffure of the 11th century. Some of the statues in the Baphuon style retain the complicated headdress with diadem and chignon-cap, but others, including figures on bas-reliefs, both goddesses and humans, wear their hair on the top of the head coiled into a bun, or knotted in a simple way leaving the long ends free.
Detail of a bas-relief on the Baphuon relating the childhood of Krishna, Angkor. Baphuon style. Second half of the 11th century.

Cat. 13 Devatā headdress at Angkor Vat. Female coiffures are at their most elaborate at Angkor Vat and attain a rich variety unknown elsewhere. This *devatā* wears a minutely-carved edifice of jewellery above her tiara: rosettes, garlands and flowery branches. This sumptuous headdress was never surpassed.
Angkor Vat. Angkor Vat style. First half of the 12th century.

Cat. 14 Devatā headdress at Angkor Vat. Sometimes the hair is dressed without jewels. This type of *devatā* has a lotus bud knotted into her hair as on the Baphuon, or wears a short, smooth style framing her face combined with long plaits, stiffly braided, and probably reinforced, in fantastic shapes on the top of the head.
Angkor Vat. Angkor Vat style. First half of the 12th century.

Cat. 15 Apsaras coiffure on the Bayon. The jewelled headdress of the Angkor Vat *devatās* gradually evolved into an elaborate crown which was used both for *devatās* and *apsaras* in the Bayon. The rosettes, flower-branches and finely-carved plumes multiplied, as exemplified by the graceful tiara of this little *apsaras* dancing on a pillar of the Bayon.
Bayon, Angkor. Bayon style. End of the 12th / early 13th century.

Cat. 16 Śiva profile of the Harihara. The ascetic chignon has been treated in a peculiar way on this head. It is the same size as the Viṣṇu mitre, but the hair is very stylized and a narrow band of leaves on the forehead is the herald of the diadems of the 9th century.
Prasat Andet (Kompong Thom). National Museum of Phnom-Penh. Height of the statue: 194 cm. Prasat Andet style. End of the 7th / early 8th century.

Cat. 17 Head of a god. This headdress consists of the octagonal Viṣṇu tiara, reduced in height and surmounted by an octagonal *motif* in the form of a rosette and adorned with a tiara on the forehead.
Thma Dap, Phnom Kulen (Siem Reap). National Museum of Phnom-Penh. Height: 25 cm. End of the Kulen style. Middle of the 9th century.

Cat. 18 Dvārapāla head. The fearsome *dvārapālas* have a headdress covered with spiky curls, whereas the amiable ones wear their hair in a cylindrical chignon, done all over with little loops which hang in regular rows. A jewelled diadem with rosettes on the temples fits close to the forehead.
Preah Ko (Siem Reap). Preah Ko style. Second half of the 10th century.

Cat. 19 Head of Lokeśvara. The hair is gathered up in finely plaited loops and threaded with pearls into a chignon which is fastened with a jewelled clasp. Amitābha is carved in the front of the chignon.
Prasat Kdak. Dépôt archéologique de la Conservation d'Angkor. Height: 24 cm. Baphuon style. Second half of the 10th century.

Cat. 20 Head of Harihara. The iconography of this bronze differs from that usually associated with Harihara, for the head is of Śiva, while the attributes are those of Viṣṇu. The hair is combed up high on the head and the roots are concealed by a band of piping. The diadem is simply decorated with pearls and denticulation.
Pursat. National Museum of Phnom-Penh. Height of the statue: 29 cm. Second half of the 12th century.

Cat. 21 Head of Viṣṇu. The diadem has disappeared and the plaited hair is gathered into a high chignon fastened with a jewelled band. The plaited loops of hair are stylized into the shape of small crescents bound with braid.
Bakong (Siem Reap). Bayon style. End of the 12th / early 13th century.

Cat. 22 Female statuette from Phnom Da. This is the earliest figure to have been found in Cambodia. She wears a simple skirt arranged in pleats in front and held by a broad, loosely-folded belt round the hips.
Phnom Da, Angkor Borei (Ta Keo). National Museum of Phnom-Penh. Height: 50 cm. 6th century.

Cat. 23 Female goddess from Prasat Thleay. The folds of the skirt are incised in the stone, while the material is draped on the hips and gathered in a loosely knotted bow held by a plain, flat belt.
Prasat Thleay (Ta Keo). National Museum of Phnom-Penh. Height of the statue: 48 cm. Prei Kmeng style. End of the 7th / early 8th century.

Cat. 24 Female figure. The skirt is a plain sheath following the flexed pose of the hips. The soft bow which was used on skirts in the 7th century has been handled here like a crozier.
Prasat Prei Prasat, Roluoh (Siem Reap). Dépôt archéologique de la Conservation d'Angkor. Height: 36 cm. Kompong Preah style. 8th century.

Cat. 25 Devatā of Preah Ko. The opulent figures of 9th-century *devatās* are draped in a skirt with a floating panel and flowing pleats in front. The hips are adorned with a richly jewelled belt.
Preah Ko, Roluoh (Siem Reap). Preah Ko style. Second half of the 9th century.

Cat. 26 Devatā of Banteai Srei. The skirt is made of flimsy material which is knotted in a large bow and falls in pleats. The belt is very broad with luxuriant pendants and garlands of pearls.
Banteai Srei (Siem Reap). Banteai Srei style. Second half of the 10th century.

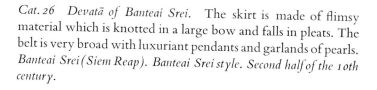

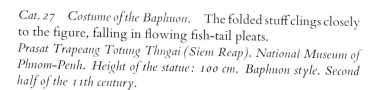

Cat. 27 Costume of the Baphuon. The folded stuff clings closely to the figure, falling in flowing fish-tail pleats.
Prasat Trapeang Totung Thngai (Siem Reap). National Museum of Phnom-Penh. Height of the statue: 100 cm. Baphuon style. Second half of the 11th century.

Cat. 28 Female figure. The supple costume fashionable in the 9th century has gone and has been replaced by a rigid stiff skirt, with almost no flare and a deep fold at the top. The material is incised in a way which seems to represent stripes rather than pleats and the front panel is richly decorated.
Provenance unknown. Vat Po Veal Museum at Battambang. Height: 44 cm. Angkor Vat style. First half of the 12th century.

Cat. 29 Back of a female figure. The back of the skirt, in contrast to the embroidered front panel, is soberly pleated and its only decoration, a fine one it is true, is a broad jewelled belt adorned with pendants.
Neak Ta Noreay. Dépôt archéologique de la Conservation d'Angkor. Height: 59 cm. Angkor Vat style. First half of the 12th century.

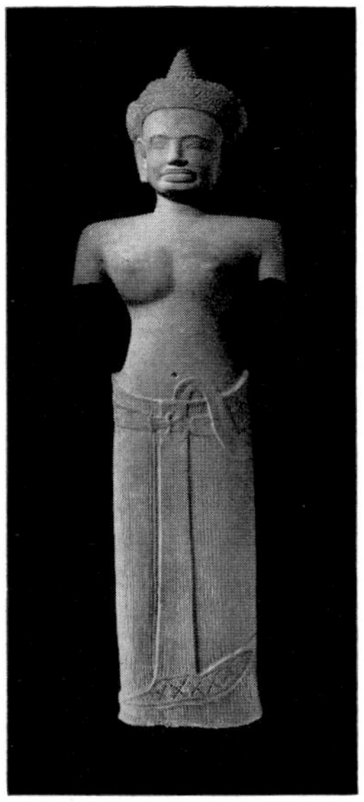

Cat. 30 Female statue. This rigidly sheathed figure has a very stylized front panel and a bow knotted at the waist in the style inherited from the 11th century. The plain costume confers a certain dignity on this female figure which is the product of a provincial artist still swayed by the influence of the preceding century.
Phum Chamkar Svay (Battambang). Vat Po Veal Museum, Battambang. Height: 117 cm. Angkor Vat style. First half of the 12th century.

Cat. 31 Devatā. Fine cloth is draped round the body and the material falls in a folded triangular panel over the right hip, and in a long piece down the left side, which the young goddess is sometimes shown lifting coquettishly.
Angkor Vat. Angkor Vat style. First half of the 10th century.

Cat. 32 Devatā on the Bayon. The skirt is broader here with a triangular front panel. Apart from an incised floral decoration the material of the costume is plain.
Bayon, Angkor. Bayon style. End of the 12th / early 13th century.

Cat. 33 Lower part of a female figure. The finely-pleated skirt is decorated in front with a long triangular panel and two shorter ones in a fan shape. A heavily jewelled belt girds the hips.
Unknown provenance. Dépôt archéologique de la Conservation d'Angkor. Height: 51 cm. Bayon style. End of the 12th / early 13th century.

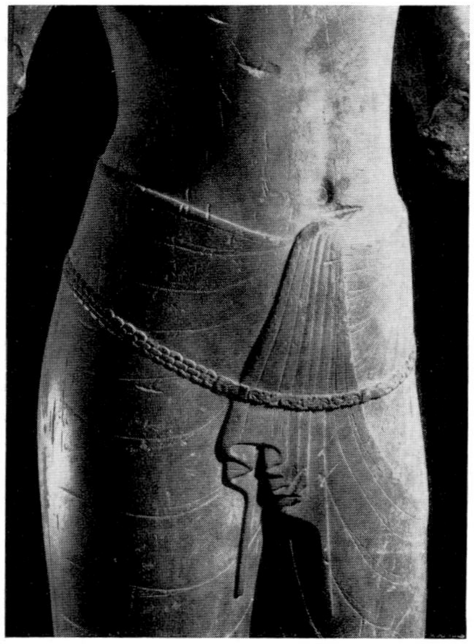

Cat. 34 Harihara of Prasat Andet. The short sampot knotted on the hips has carefully-arranged pleats and a particularly well-handled panel falling from the waist.
Prasat Andet (Kompong Thom). National Museum of Phnom-Penh. Height of the statue: 194 cm. Prasat Andet style. End of the 7th / early 8th century.

Cat. 35 Śiva. Fine pleating and a flat belt decorate the sampot of Śiva, whose limbs are "entwined by the arms of Umā and Ganga". They each hold a hand on his thigh.
Bakong. Roluoh (Siem Reap). Preah Ko style. Second half of the 9th century.

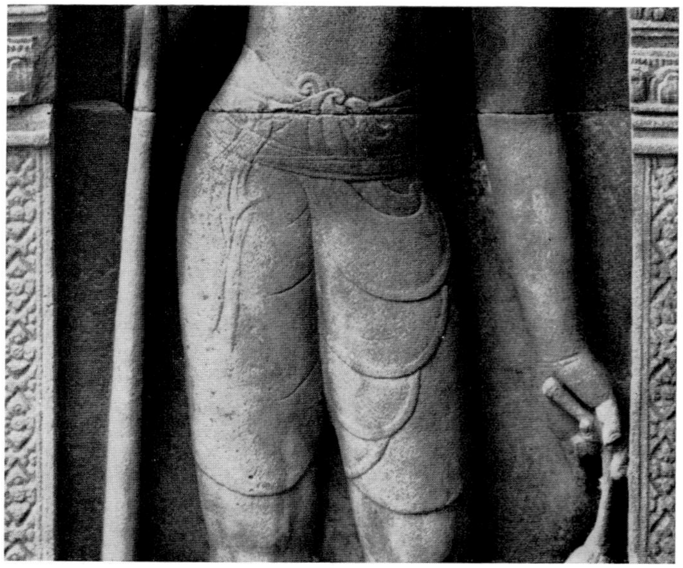

Cat. 36 Dvārapāla. The *dvārapālas* of Banteai Srei represent a break with the tradition of carving corpulent and aggressive guardians for the temples. They are full of graceful youth and the sampot clings closely to the hips with a simple decoration on the left thigh.
The central sanctuary of Banteai Srei (Siem Reap). Banteai Srei style. Second half of the 10th century.

Cat. 37 Warrior. The butterfly-bow which decorates the back of male costumes in the late 9th century is generally in the form of an appliqué; on this bas-relief the bow is seen in profile and floating free behind.
Baphuon, Angkor. Baphuon style. Second half of the 11th century.

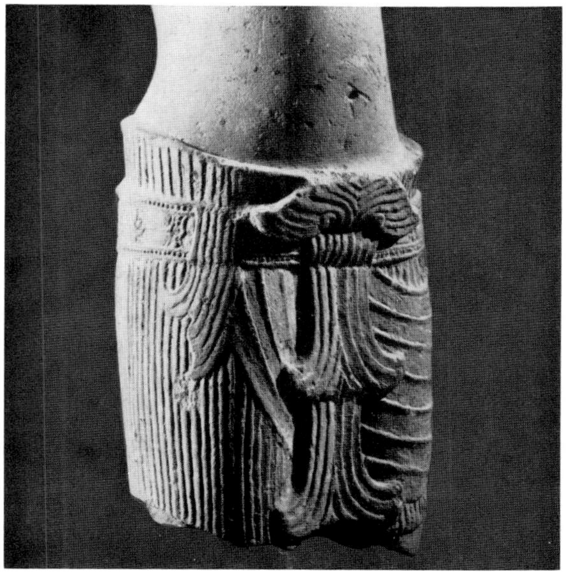

Cat. 38 Male torso. The draped and pleated sampot is held by a broad belt on the hips; the double-anchor fold forms a stylized pocket covering the front.
Preah Pithu, Angkor. Dépôt archéologique de la Conservation d'Angkor. Height: 47 cm. Angkor Vat style. First half of the 12th century.

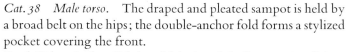

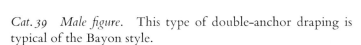

Cat. 39 Male figure. This type of double-anchor draping is typical of the Bayon style.
Ta Keo, Angkor. Dépôt archéologique de la Conservation d'Angkor. Height: 69 cm. Bayon style. End of the 12th/early 13th century.

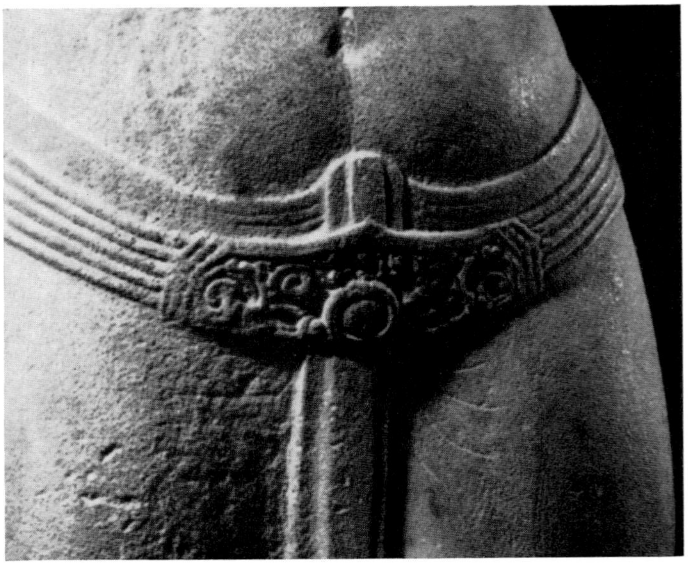

Cat. 40 Belt on the "Lady of Koh Krieng". Belt-buckles of the pre-Angkor period show a surprising skill and richness in metal work which no later period was able to surpass or even equal. The "Lady of Koh Krieng" wears a belt made of five galloons within the clasp and decorated with stylized leaf-scrolls.
Koh Krieng (Kratie). National Museum of Phnom-Penh. Length of the clasp: 14 cm. Sambor style. Early 7th century.

Cat. 41 Necklace and earrings on a devatā. The breast of this *devatā* is richly apparelled with a necklace of rosettes and scrolled leaves in the Khmer tradition; but from the lobes of the elongated ears two florid rings rest on the shoulders.
Banteai Srei (Siem Reap). Banteai Srei style. Second half of the 10th century.

Cat. 42 Necklace on a devatā. Female ornament attained its greatest variety and richness at Angkor Vat where floral *motifs* were very popular. Rosettes and garlands of jasmine decorate the three-pointed tiaras, and lotus flowers the earrings. This fine necklace with petal-shaped pendants has flower-*motifs* all over.
Angkor Vat. Angkor Vat style. First half of the 12th century.

Cat. 43 Necklace. Only a few of the Angkor Vat *devatās* have this curious decoration. The traditional jewelled pectoral has a heavy ring attached by a chain which falls between the breasts.
Angkor Vat. Angkor Vat style. First half of the 12th century.

Cat. 44 Pectoral on an apsaras. By the end of the 12th century *devatās, apsaras* and princesses wear a necklace and belt combined. This type of pectoral, which passes between the breasts and is fastened at the back, is formed of long strings of pearls.
Pillar of the Bayon, Angkor. Bayon style. End of the 12th / early 13th century.

Cat. 45 Female jewellery of the late Bayon. Chiselled metalwork has given place to heavy strings of pearls in this elaborate decoration.
Terrace of the Leper King, Angkor. Dépôt archéologique de la Conservation d'Angkor. Height: 33 cm. End of the Bayon style. Early 13th century.

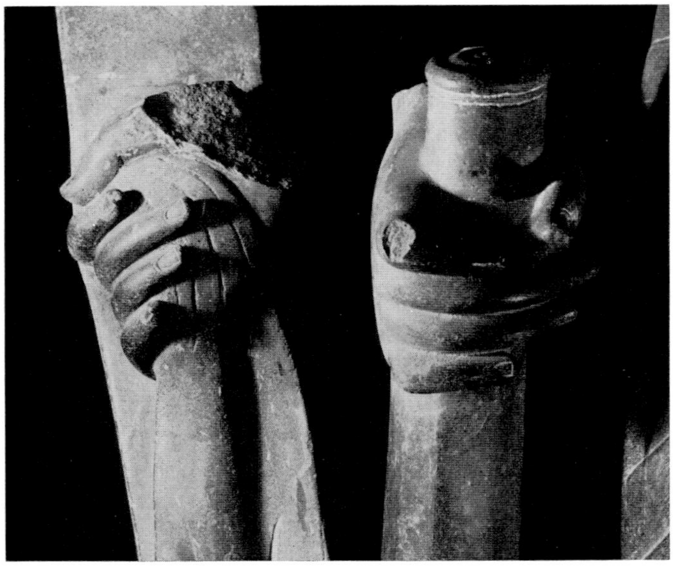

Cat. 46 Viṣṇu. Two hands from the eight-armed god of Phnom Da. Although the wrists are clumsy the long tapering fingers, slightly lifted at the tips, are extremely elegant. One hand holds an attribute which is difficult to define and the other an antelope hide.
Phnom Da, Angkor Borei (Ta Keo). National Museum of Phnom-Penh. Height of the statue: 270 cm. Phnom Da style. 6th century.

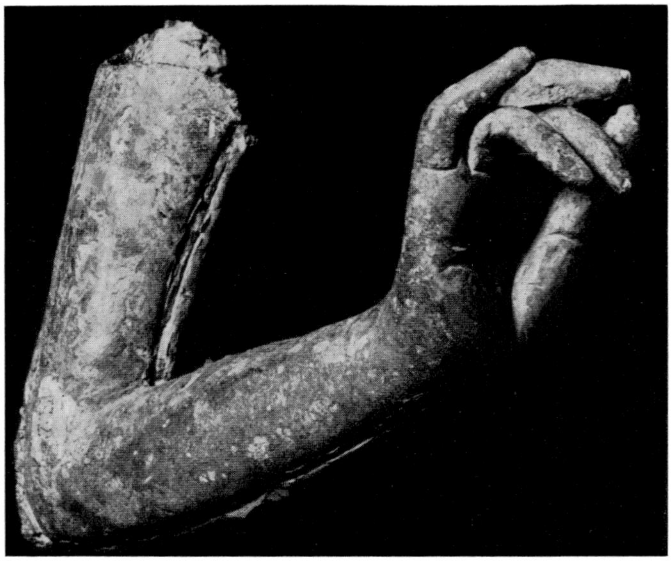

Cat. 47 Bronze hand. The second and third fingers join the thumb while the other two are raised. This is the gesture known as *kaṭakahasta*. It well reveals the fine carving of the fingers.
Group at Angkor. National Museum of Phnom-Penh. Width: 10 cm. 11th / 12th century.

Cat. 48 Hands on a devatā. The hands are shown holding flowers and the artist has been at great pains to model the delicate fingers.
Angkor Vat. Angkor Vat style. First half of the 12th century.

Cat. 49 *Sakra.* The disc, *sakra*, is one of the four attributes of Viṣṇu. This was the weapon which Viṣṇu used to kill the *asura*, Rahu, when he tried to drink the water of immortality which he had stolen.
Ta Set (Siem Reap). Dépôt archéologique de la Conservation d'Angkor. Height: 16 cm. 12th/13th century.

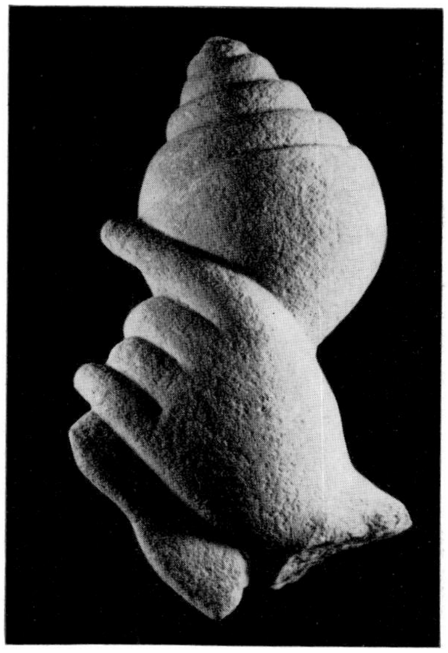

Cat. 50 *Conch.* The conch-shell, which was used either for holy water or as a musical instrument is also one of Viṣṇu's attributes.
Preah Pithu, Angkor. Dépôt archéologique de la Conservation d'Angkor. 12th/13th century.

Cat. 51 *Triśula.* The trident of Śiva. The prongs are ornamented in varying designs.
Prasat Kuk. Dépôt archéologique de la Conservation d'Angkor. Height: 30 cm. 12th/13th century.

Cat. 52 *Yama.* The God of Death mounted on a buffalo. Yama is depicted here as the terrible god described in the Mahābhārata: "crowned with a diadem, but dark and fearful with flaming eyes."
Angkor Vat, South gallery III. Angkor Vat style. First half of the 12th century.

Cat. 53 *The Terrors of the Damned.* Those finally damned by Yama for sins which are set forth on inscriptions suffer the most frightful tortures.
Angkor Vat, South gallery III. Angkor Vat style. First half of the 12th century.

Cat. 54 *Paradise.* Those elected to paradise spend their time in flying palaces supported by *garuḍa.* Dressed in the robes of royalty, they seem to be enjoying a rather monotonous happiness.
Angkor Vat, South gallery III. Angkor Vat style. First half of the 12th century.

Cat. 55 Kneeling ascetic. This carving may be a representation of Śiva. He wears the ascetic headdress in which the hair is drawn upwards and fastened in a cylindrical chignon held in place by beads, perhaps a rosary. His bracelets and long necklace are also made of beads. The face is smiling and serene.
Prasat Thom, Koh Ker (Siem Reap). National Museum of Phnom-Penh. Height: 123 cm. Koh Ker style. Second quarter of the 10th century.

Cat. 56 Ascetics at the feet of Śiva. Ascetics were meditating on Mount Kailāsa at the feet of Śiva, when Rāvaṇa came and shook the mountain. All the creatures on Mount Kailāsa are panic-stricken and flee in all directions. Even the ascetics are disturbed and turn for protection to Śiva, who remains smiling and unconcerned.
Southern Library of Banteai Srei (Siem Reap). Banteai Srei style. Second half of the 10th century.

Cat. 57 Meditating ascetic. The ascetic, with his hands joined and his legs crossed, is absorbed in meditation. He wears a chignon and a pointed beard.
Banteai Chmar (Battambang). Bayon style. End of the 12th / beginning of the 13th century.

Cat. 58 An ascetic fighting a boar. There is a series of pictures placed one above the other on a wall of the Baphuon, with scenes showing the lives of ascetics in the jungle. Generally the monkish figures meditate beneath a tree; but sometimes, as here, they struggle with the wild beasts of the forest.
Baphuon, Angkor. Baphuon style. Second half of the 11th century.

Cat. 59 The bird hunt. A squirrel is climbing up the tree-trunk towards the birds perched on the branches. Two hunters wait below; one is trying to reach the birds with a blow-pipe, while the other picks up the game as it falls, clutching the feet of three birds in the other hand.
Baphuon, Angkor. Baphuon style. Second half of the 11th century.

Cat. 60 Rāma hunting the deer. Responding to Sītā's whim, Rāma chases a golden-hued hind, which in fact is an enchanted beast sent by Rāvaṇa. The legend has been depicted by the artist at the moment when Rāma draws back his bow.
South-west pavilion of Angkor Vat. Angkor Vat style. First half of the 12th century.

Cat. 61 The palace of Kaṃsa. The artist has chosen the moment when Krishna enters the palace of his uncle Kaṃsa, whom he attacks. Desolation reigns in the whole building, in the galleries below as well as in the throne-room.
North Library of Banteai Srei (Siem Reap). Banteai Srei style. Second half of the 10th century.

Cat. 62 Royal pavilions. A prince, princess and their children giving alms to the monks. They are seated under arched window-frames. The tiled roof of the palace is supported by pillars.
Angkor Vat, Western Gate. National Museum of Phnom-Penh. Height: 40 cm. Bayon style. End of the 12th / beginning of the 13th century.

Cat. 63 The throne of Sūryavarman II. The throne is a low chair, a shape which can still be seen in modern monasteries. A narrow balustrade encircles the throne which is supported on *nāga*-heads.
Angkor Vat, South gallery III. Angkor Vat style. First half of the 12th century.

Cat. 64 Palace women. A young woman is attended here by her women who hold parasols and fans.
Angkor Vat. Pavilion at the North-west corner. Angkor Vat style. First half of the 12th century.

Cat. 65 Seated princess. This princess wears the tiara of a *devatā* and many necklaces. She is receiving the homage of two kneeling women who are offering gifts from cups.
Banteai Chmar (Battambang). Bayon style. End of the 12th / beginning of the 13th century.

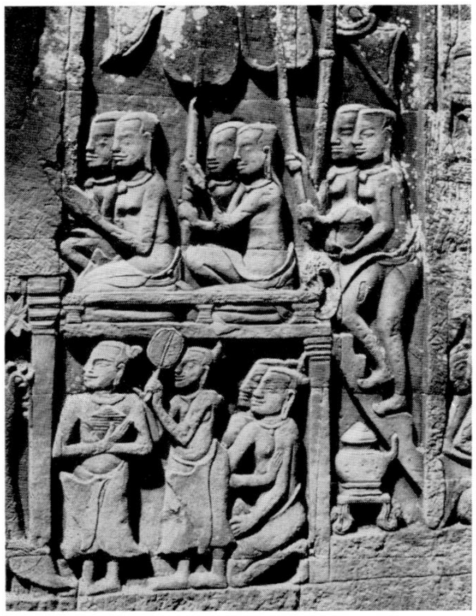

Cat. 66 Women on a stair. Two women are climbing the staircase of a house in which the attendants of a noble lady are seated. A kettle on a tripod can be seen beneath the stair.
Bayon, East exterior gallery, Angkor. Bayon style. End of the 12th / beginning of the 13th century.

Cat. 67 Archers. A troop of archers stringing their bows. The precision of their gestures, muscled bodies and facial expressions show the artist's painstaking observation.
Bayon, West exterior gallery, Angkor. Bayon style. End of the 12th / beginning of the 13th century.

Cat. 68 Ballistas. Several of the bas-reliefs on the Bayon show these machines, which are either drawn on a chariot or mounted on an elephant.
Bayon, South exterior gallery, Angkor. Bayon style. End of the 12th / beginning of the 13th century.

Cat. 69 Foot-soldiers. "The infantry wears no armour and goes barefoot. They bear a lance and shield" (Ch'ou Ta-k'uan).
Bayon, exterior gallery, Angkor. Bayon style. End of the 12th / beginning of the 13th century.

Cat. 70 War elephants. While the army is marching, the commander remains seated on his saddle. When the battle is engaged he stands upright. The mahout on the elephant's neck carries a round shield and the elephant hook in his right hand.
Bayon, exterior gallery, Angkor. Bayon style. End of the 12th/beginning of the 13th century.

Cat. 71 Khmer and Cham fighting. The Khmer wear no headgear, while the Cham have helmets in the shape of an upturned flower. This is one of the battles which preceded Jayavarman VII's triumph over his enemies.
Banteai Chmar (Battambang). Bayon style. End of the 12th/beginning of the 13th century.

Cat. 72 Battle of Kurukṣetra. Mythological battles were no less violent than real ones: here the Pandava fight to the death with the Kaurava.
Angkor Vat, South gallery III. Angkor Vat style. First half of the 12th century.

Cat. 73 Prince on his war-chariot. The commander is a prince, recognizable by the diadem adorning his forehead. He is riding on his war-chariot behind rearing horses, with one foot on the pole. His javelin is poised for flight, and his shield is held high above his head.
Angkor Vat, South gallery III. Angkor Vat style. First half of the 12th century.

Cat. 74 The soldiers' farewell. This scene of soldiers bidding farewell to their families is carved at one end of a Bayon bas-relief. One or two soldiers linger with their families although their comrades have already gone.
Bayon, West exterior gallery, Angkor. Bayon style. End of the 12th/beginning of the 13th century.

Cat. 75 Soldier drinking from his gourd. The foot-soldiers march solemnly along, but one of them has tucked his shield under his arm and is drinking greedily from his bottle.
Bayon, Angkor. Bayon style. End of the 12th/beginning of the 13th century.

Cat. 76 Scene from the childhood of Krishna. In the 11th century artists began to depict children. The legend of the exchange which saved Krishna from the fate threatened by Kaṃsa, his uncle, has been interpreted here with charm and freedom.
Baphuon, South Gopura II, Angkor. Baphuon style. Second half of the 11th century.

Cat. 77 Women and children. A few family scenes are carved at Angkor. On one bas-relief parents are playing with their children. Here a group of women stand idly with their children beside them. One of them is bending over a little girl.
Angkor Vat, South-west pavilion. Angkor Vat style. Second half of the 12th century.

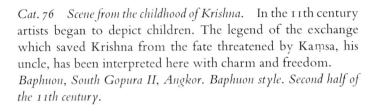

Cat. 78 Family following a cart. The father is carrying his little daughter on his shoulders, while his wife walks behind, touching his shoulder as though to attract his attention. The son walks ahead, playing with a dog.
Bayon, East exterior gallery, Angkor. Bayon style. End of the 12th/beginning of the 13th century.

Cat. 79 Market scene. A man is bringing supplies in baskets, while a young woman approaches a bench where an old woman is squatting beside her fish. This scene, at least 800 years old, is still enacted almost daily in all the markets of the Far East.
Bayon, South exterior gallery, Angkor. Bayon style. End of the 12th/ beginning of the 13th century.

Cat. 80 Carpenters. This is a scene in which carpenters are cutting wood with axes, and carrying planks and beams. Ch'ou Ta-k'uan must have seen them working: "The workers have no saws and can obtain planks only by using their axes."
Bayon, South exterior gallery, Angkor. Bayon style. End of the 12th/ beginning of the 13th century.

Cat. 81 Stewing the pig. Everyone watches as the whole pig is plunged into the pot boiling over the fire.
Bayon, South exterior gallery, Angkor. Bayon style. End of the 12th/ beginning of the 13th century.

Cat. 82 Ox-cart. The oxen trudge slowly along, while the driver, with one foot on the shaft, holds the reins. This simple cart, with cradle-shaped roof and sober decoration, is a type which can still be seen in Cambodia.
Bayon, East exterior gallery, Angkor. Bayon style. End of the 12th/ beginning of the 13th century.

Cat. 83 Palanquin. "Palanquins are made from a single piece of wood bent in the middle, the two ends of which are straight; these are carved with floral *motifs* and covered with silver and gold. About a foot from each end a hook is sunk into the wood, to which a piece of pleated material is attached. Here the passenger sits, and the palanquin is borne by two men" (Ch'ou Ta-k'uan).
Angkor Vat, South gallery III. Angkor Vat style. First half of the 12th century.

Cat. 84 Bearers' chair. This is a parade chair borne on shafts, and forming a kind of throne for royal persons. This is a scene of the elect entering the gates of paradise.
Angkor Vat, South gallery. Angkor Vat style. First half of the 12th century.

Cat. 85. Canoes and boats. The upper part shows the sides of a junk made of planks, and a fisherman in a canoe casting a net. Below, a man sitting beneath a parasol in a canoe hewn out of a single tree-trunk points his hand as though giving orders; other people dance and sing.
Bayon, South exterior gallery, Angkor. Bayon style. End of the 12th/beginning of the 13th century.

Cat. 86 Boat with warriors. This boat is carrying Cham soldiers who are preparing to go aboard the enemy. The heads of the rowers can be seen above the sides. It seems as though this boat was carved out of a single trunk. Ch'ou Ta-k'uan described them as "hewn from a huge tree in the shape of an ear of corn; it was softened in the fire and enlarged by adding pieces of wood, so that they were broad in the centre and pointed at both ends".
Bayon, South exterior gallery, Angkor. Bayon style. End of the 12th/beginning of the 13th century.

Cat. 87 Prow and poop of two boats. On the right of the picture, the richly decorated prow has a *garuḍa* on a *makara* mask. The poop of the other is less elaborate, boasting only a *nāga*-head; the pilot is holding the rudder.
Bayon, South exterior gallery, Angkor. Bayon style. End of the 12th/beginning of the 13th century.

Cat. 88 Sugar-palm. This seems to be a stylized attempt to reproduce the big palm-leaves and branches of fruit of the sugar-palm. This tree, *borassus*, grows everywhere in Cambodia.
Bayon, East exterior gallery, Angkor. Bayon style. End of the 12th/beginning of the 13th century.

Cat. 89 Coconut-palm. This tree, growing on a river bank, is undoubtedly a coconut-palm with its long, frond-like leaves. A man is climbing the stem to gather coconuts.
Angkor Vat, pavilion at the South-west corner. Angkor Vat style. First half of the 12th century.

Cat. 90 Forest tree. It is difficult to put a name to this fine-leaved tree under which some young women are dancing.
Angkor Vat, pavilion at the North-east corner. Angkor Vat style. First half of the 12th century.

Cat. 91 Elephants. The massive silhouettes of elephants move forward with unceasing and unimpeded progress. But a bearer walks undeterred between their huge feet, his yoke over his shoulders.
Terrace of the Elephants, Angkor. Bayon style. End of the 12th/ beginning of the 13th century.

Cat. 92 A horse. This rearing horse is ridden by an *asura* and is carved in the stylized manner of all the horses on the frieze of the western portal at Angkor Vat. Each leaping animal-rider has an arch of foliage overhead.
Angkor Vat, Western Portal. Angkor Vat style. First half of the 12th century.

Cat. 93 A rhinoceros. This animal has actually disappeared from Cambodia, but it is often mentioned in early texts. Here it serves as Agni's mount.
Banteai Samre (Siem Reap). Angkor Vat style. First half of the 12th century.

Cat. 94 Cow suckling its young. This simple group is full of tenderness and charm.
Trapeang Phong (Siem Reap). Dépôt archéologique de la Conservation d'Angkor. Height: 11 cm. Bayon style. End of the 12th/beginning of the 13th century.

Cat. 95 Monkeys fighting. The two monkey kings, Sugrīva and Vālin, are fighting furiously, tearing at each other with their teeth. Although they seem almost human in their anger they fight like animals.
Banteai Srei. Central Sanctuary (Siem Reap). Banteai Srei style. Second half of the 10th century.

Cat. 96 Geese. These three geese are supporting a pedestal with a *devatā*. The detail of the carving is typical of Banteai Srei.
Banteai Srei (Siem Reap). Banteai Srei style. Second half of the 10th century.

Cat. 97 *A crocodile.* The waters stirred up by the boats are full of aquatic animals. Crocodiles wait for corpses to fall into the water. Here the crocodile contents itself with a fish.
Bayon, South exterior gallery, Angkor. Bayon style. End of the 12th/beginning of the 13th century.

Cat. 98 *A tortoise.* The tortoise was carved either in the round as a support, or in bas-relief. The beasts which figure in the incarnation of Viṣṇu at the "Churning of the Sea of Milk" are often very beautiful, as at Angkor. This tortoise has been handled with a primitive naturalism.
Causeway of the North Gate, Angkor Thom. Dépôt archéologique de la Conservation d'Angkor. Height: 14 cm. 12th/13th century.

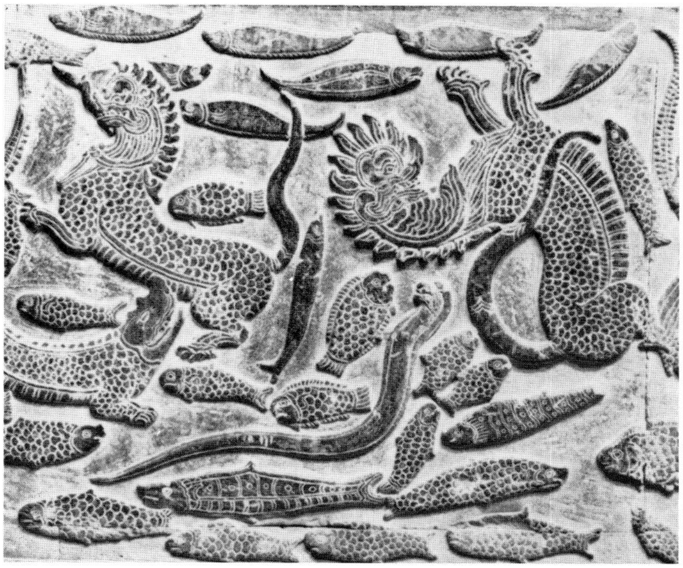

Cat. 99 *Fish.* Fish and marine creatures populate the sea stirred up by Deva and Asura. The force of the water in the centre of the whirlpool tears them apart.
Ankgor Vat, East gallery III. Angkor Vat style. End of the 12th/beginning of the 13th century.

Cat. 100 Balustrade of nāga-heads. At Preah Vihear, the undecorated *nāga*-heads on the balustrade rear up aggressively.
Preah Vihear (Phnom Thbeng). Khleang style. First half of the 11th century.

Cat. 101 Crest of a façade. At the edge of this façade the *nāga* emerges from a *kāla* and spreads his five flower-decorated heads.
Banteai Srei (Siem Reap). National Museum of Phnom-Penh. Banteai Srei style. Second half of the 10th century.

Cat. 102 Bronze motif. The *nāga*-heads stand erect beside a wide-open blue lotus flower, almost like a folded leaf. A single open-work diadem, the restrained diadem of Beng Meala, makes a background for the five heads.
Danrun (Battambang). National Museum of Phnom-Penh. Height of the lotus: 24.5 cm. 11th century.

Cat. 103 A lion. The lion has never been a native of Cambodia, and it became a fantastic beast in Khmer art. Although this one has suffered considerable damage, it preserves the features of the Angkor Vat style.
Angkor Vat. Angkor Vat style. Beginning of the 12th century.

Cat. 104 Guardian lion. This lion is a temple guardian. Its wide-open mouth and drawn-back lips, curly-crest and rigid attitude give a stylized effect.
Bayon, Angkor. Bayon style. End of the 12th/beginning of the 13th century.

Cat. 105 Lion-mask. This crowned lion-mask does not seem to have belonged to a lion on a stairway, but is more likely to have been part of a statue of Viṣṇu in his incarnation of man-lion.
Preah Khan of Angkor. Dépôt archéologique de la Conservation d'Angkor. Height: 23 cm. Bayon style. End of the 12th/beginning of the 13th century.

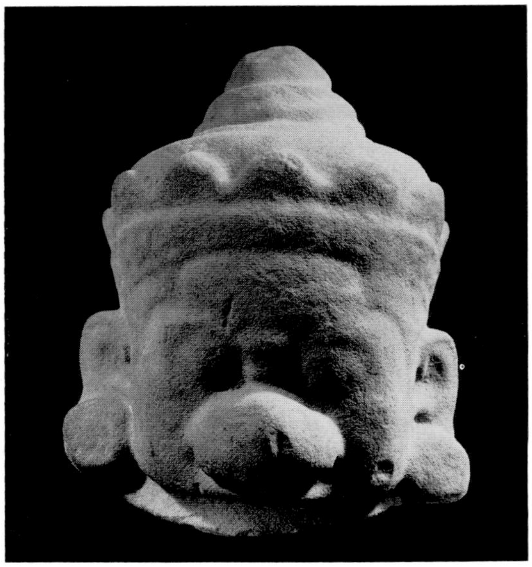

Cat. 106 Garuḍa head. Although it is very worn, this *garuḍa*-head still keeps its malicious expression under the festooned diadem and chignon-cap. The bird of Viṣṇu is rarely seen in such a caricature.
Thma Dap, Phnom Kulen (Siem Reap). National Museum of Phnom-Penh. Height: 22 cm. Kulen style. First half of the 9th century.

Cat. 107 Garuḍa – part of a balustrade. In the late 11th century the tops of walls were decorated with small, standing *garuḍa*, without arms and with their wings spread like leaves.
Baphuon, Angkor. Dépôt archéologique de la Conservation d'Angkor. Baphuon style. Second half of the 11th century.

Cat. 108 Garuḍa (atlas-figure). Joined by flower garlands, many small *garuḍas* support the celestial palaces with their arms.
Angkor Vat, South gallery III. Angkor Vat style. First half of the 12th century.

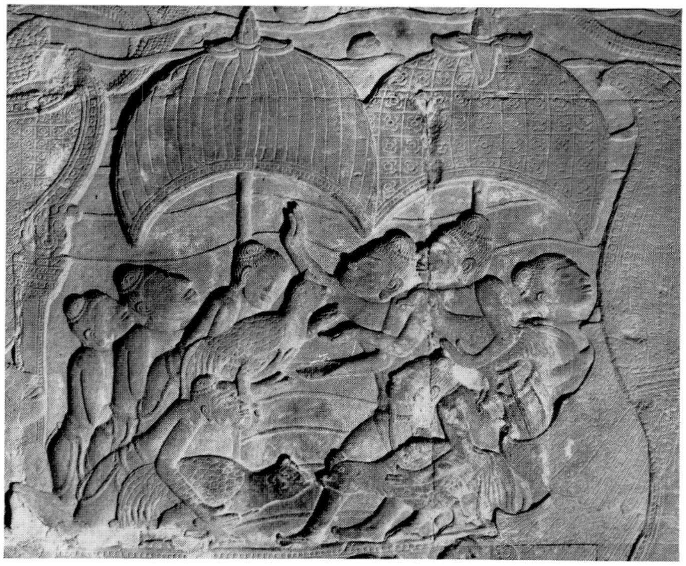

Cat. 109 Cock-fighting. The Chinese tell us that, after the Funan period, the favourite pastime of the Khmer was cock-fighting. This fight is taking place on a boat and is accompanied by vigorous argument.
Angkor Vat, South-west pavilion. Angkor Vat style. First half of the 12th century.

Cat. 110 Drinking. This man is drinking an intoxicating drink from a jar. This custom no longer exists among the Cambodians, but is still common among the mountain-people of Indo-China at their festivals.
Angkor Vat, South-west pavilion. Angkor Vat style. First half of the 12th century.

Cat. 111 Chess-players. Leaning over the chess-board, the player contemplates his move. Apparently the game was common in the Angkor period and has survived till the present day.
Angkor Vat, South-west pavilion. Angkor Vat style. First half of the 12th century.

Cat. 112 *Menagerie.* Spectators on a high stand watch the animals, indigenous and foreign, go past. The Khmer probably received gifts of animals from foreign rulers, just as they sent typical Cambodian beasts to neighbouring kings. For instance, in the Fu-nan period they despatched elephants to the Chinese emperors.
Bayon, North exterior gallery, Angkor. Bayon style. End of the 12th/beginning of the 13th century.

Cat. 113 *Acrobats.* Jugglers and other acrobats act out a scene to the music of two orchestras.
Bayon, North exterior gallery, Angkor. Bayon style. End of the 12th/beginning of the 13th century.

Cat. 114 *Wrestlers.* The Cambodian people enjoyed wrestling, and several games are depicted on the Bayon bas-reliefs.
Bayon, North exterior gallery, Angkor. Bayon style. End of the 12th/beginning of the 13th century.

Cat. 115 *Woman playing the harp.* This woman harp-player is part of an orchestra accompanying dancers.
Banteai Samre (Siem Reap). Angkor Vat style. First half of the 12th century.

Cat. 116 *Military band.* This band marches ahead of the soldiers. The gong-player is often a dancer, and here he beats time for the march. A trumpet and drums complete the orchestra.
Bayon, East exterior gallery, Angkor. Bayon style. End of the 12th/beginning of the 13th century.

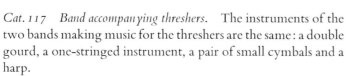

Cat. 117 *Band accompanying threshers.* The instruments of the two bands making music for the threshers are the same: a double gourd, a one-stringed instrument, a pair of small cymbals and a harp.
Bayon, North exterior gallery, Angkor. Bayon style. End of the 12th/beginning of the 13th century.

Cat. 118 Dancer. Among the few fragments of bas-relief which have been preserved on the Bakong, these small dancers twist and turn, half-dancing, half-flying.
Bakong Roluoh (Siem Reap). Preah Ko style. Second half of the 9th century.

Cat. 119 Flying figures. This aerial ballet retains some of the classical features of the Cambodian dance.
Banteai Srei (Siem Reap). National Museum of Phnom-Penh. Height of the figures: 20 cm. Banteai Srei style. Second half of the 10th century.

Cat. 120 Dancer and musicians. A young woman is dancing beneath an arch while two cymbalists beat the rhythm.
Banteai Srei (Siem Reap). Banteai Srei style. Second half of the 10th century.

Cat. 121 Apsaras. Dancing *apsaras* are carved on the base of a façade. Here the sculptor has not been content to keep on repeating the same image; each *apsaras* has been modelled separately with an unusually free and youthful effect.
Chau Say Tevoda, Angkor. Angkor Vat style. First half of the 12th century.

Cat. 122 Two apsaras dancing. These two *apsaras*, loaded with jewels, stand with one foot on a lotus blossom. Their movements are rigidly symmetrical.
Decoration on a pillar, Bayon, Angkor. Bayon style. End of the 12th/ beginning of the 13th century.

Cat. 123 Apsaras. Slim and graceful, this *apsaras* has a certain religious gravity.
Bayon, Angkor. Bayon style. End of the 12th / beginning of the 13th century.

Cat. 124 Women lamenting the death of Kaṃsa. As Krishna prepares to kill Kaṃsa the whole palace is in panic and the women begin to mourn.
Banteai Srei. Detail of a façade of the North Library (Siem Reap). Banteai Srei style. Second half of the 10th century.

Cat. 125 Soldiers weeping over their dead comrade. The wounded man lies on the ground and is probably dead. Two of his friends help him, one weeping as he lifts the head. Their grief makes them oblivious of the battle raging round.
Angkor Vat, West gallery III. Angkor Vat style. First half of the 12th century.

Cat. 126 The supplicant. This figure, kneeling on a lotus, turns his face towards a merciful god – now lost – and prays with intense anxiety.
Royal Terrace, relief of the five-headed horse, Angkor Thom. End of the Bayon style. Beginning of the 13th century.

Cat. 127 Śiva and Umā. Umā runs to Śiva for protection from the earthquake of Kailāsa and the god holds her gently in his arm.
Banteai Srei, detail of a façade of the South Library (Siem Reap). Banteai Srei style. Second half of the 10th century.

Cat. 128 The groom and the horse of Buddha. On the upper portion of the façade the future Buddha is cutting his hair in preparation for the life of a monk. The horse and groom, now separated from their master, try to console one another.
Façade found near Preah Palilay (Angkor). 15th / 16th century.

Cat. 129 Women dancing. Beneath a representation of Viṣṇu, these women are dancing with joy among the trees.
Angkor Vat, North-west pavilion. Angkor Vat style. First half of the 12th century.

Cat. 130 *Head of Buddha.* This fine head smiles with meditative serenity.
Tuol Chan, Angkor Borei (Ta Keo). National Museum of Phnom-Penh. Height: 15 cm. 7th century.

Cat. 131 *Lokeśvara.* The Bodhisattva is covered with a beautiful green patina, and smiles benevolently on all who seek his help.
Ak Yom (Siem Reap). National Museum of Phnom-Penh. Height of the statuette: 35 cm. 7th century.

Cat. 132 *Female Divinity.* The goddess of Prasat Thleay wears a subtly charming smile.
Prasat Thleay (Ta Keo). National Museum of Phnom-Penh. Height of the statuette: 48 cm. Prei Kmeng style. End of the 7th / beginning of the 8th century.

Cat. 133 Devatā. The goddess has a full face with almond-shaped eyes and fleshy lips. Her smile is young, almost childlike.
Banteai Srei (Siem Reap). Banteai Srei style. Second half of the 10th century.

Cat. 134 Devatā. This *devatā* is carved on a background of flowers. Conscious of her beauty, she wears an almost imperceptible smile.
Angkor Vat, Western Gate. Angkor Vat style. First half of the 12th century.

Cat. 135 Face on a Bayon tower. All the faces on the Bayon towers, but especially this one which is probably the most beautiful, have a smile expressing the deep joy of Buddhist meditation.
Bayon, Angkor. Bayon style. End of the 12th / beginning of the 13th century.

The photographs other than those of Hans Hinz were taken by Cécile Beurdeley, Paris: Fig. 19, Cat. 100. – Brunet, Phnom-Penh: Fig. 65. – Jean Hirschen, Fribourg: Pl. VIII, Fig. 54, Cat. 103. – Ecole Française d'Extrême-Orient, Phnom-Penh: Cat. 9, 24, 27, 29, 33, 38, 39, 45, 49, 50, 51, 52, 53, 54, 60, 64, 67, 68, 74, 80, 81, 83, 84, 88, 89, 90, 94, 98, 99, 105, 107, 108, 110, 111, 112, 113, 114, 117, 129.

The reproductions on the following pages have been taken from L. Delaporte: Monuments du Cambodge, Etudes d'architecture khmère (Presses Universitaires de France, Paris): 16, 46, 55, 56, 70, 102, 126, 132, 138, 148, 154, 162, 175, 176, 182, 193.

For the most part it has proved impossible to measure pieces of sculpture at the site; measurements are, therefore, given only for objects in museums or collections.

The publisher wishes to thank the Ecole Française d'Extrême-Orient for the assistance so willingly given to the photographer.

The publisher acknowledges with gratitude the help and advice given with the Sanskrit transliterations for the English edition by Mr. Emmerick of the School of Oriental and African Studies, University of London, and by Mr. Barrett, Assistant Keeper in the Department of Oriental Antiquities, British Museum, London.

APPENDIX

GLOSSARY

Abbreviations:

Skt. – Sanskrit
Kh. – Khmer

ACYUTA
Skt. "The Steadfast One", Viṣṇu.

AGNI
Skt. The sacrificial flame. Brahman god of fire.

AMARĀVATI
Skt. Place in the north-east Deccan in the valley of the Krishna, where a school of Buddhist art developed after the 2nd century A.D.

AMITĀBHA
Skt. "Infinite Light", a Buddha of the Mahāyāna doctrine. He appears on the headdress of Avalokiteśvara.

AÑJALI
Skt. Gesture of homage with the hands joined in prayer.

ANTARAVĀSAKA
Skt. An undergarment worn by Buddhist monks, tied at the waist with a girdle, the lappets of which hang down between the legs or on the right thigh.

APSARAS
Skt. Female divinities; celestial dancers.

ASURA
Skt. Demon king, enemy of the gods.

AVALOKITEŚVARA
Skt. "The Merciful Lord who looks down from above". He rescues mankind from the recurring cycles of life and the dangers of this world. This Bodhisattva is the object of deep devotion in the Mahāyāna sect. Also called Lokeśvara.

AVATAR
Skt. Incarnation, animal or human, of Viṣṇu, who descends as a saviour of the world.

AYUDHYĀ
Skt. Capital of the Thai kingdom founded in 1350.

BALARĀMA
Skt. Krishna's elder brother.

BĀNA
Skt. An *asura* vanquished by Krishna, but released by Śiva's prayer.

BARAI
Kh. Sacred, artificial lake in Cambodia.

BHAGAVANT
Skt. "The Blessed One", a name often given to Viṣṇu.

BHĀGAVATA-PURĀNA
Skt. Indian epic poem in praise of Viṣṇu.

BHĪMA
Skt. "The Terrible One", an epic hero.

BODHISATTVA
Skt. A being on the way to enlightenment. In the Mahāyāna creed, one who delays his own admission so as to help others on the way.

BRAHMA
Skt. The Supreme Principle, god of the Hindu Trimūrti.

DAITYA
Skt. Demon, enemy of the gods.

DEVARĀJA
Skt. Śiva ritual. The foundation of the Khmer monarchy after the 9th century.

DEVATĀ
Skt. Female divinity. The name given to female figures carved on the temples.

DHOTI
Draped Indian undergarment

DURGĀ
Skt. "The Inaccessible One". One of the names given to Śiva's wife, daughter of the Himālaya.

DURYODHANA
Skt. "The Invincible", the first of the Kaurava tribe and the commander of their army.

DVĀRAPĀLA
Skt. Temple guardian.

DVĀRAVATĪ
Skt. Pre-Thai kingdom of the lower Menam.

GANGĀ
Skt. Goddess personifying the Ganges, daughter of the Himālaya. When this river, which formerly flowed only in heaven, came to earth Śiva held out his hair to break its fall.

GARUḌA
Skt. Mythical bird, enemy of snakes and Viṣṇu's mount.

GOPURA
Skt. Entrance pavilion to an Indian temple.

GUPTA
Skt. Indian Buddhist dynasty. The Gupta kingdom was one of the greatest centres of civilization and Indian art. It was defeated early in the 6th century.

GURU
Skt. Religious teacher.

HAṂSA
Skt. Wild bird, perhaps a swan. Brahma's mount.

HANUMAN
Skt. Captain of the monkey army. Rāma's helper.

HARA
Skt. Incarnation of Śiva.

HARIHARA
Skt. Idol combining Śiva and Viṣṇu in one.

HASTA
Skt. A hand or position of the hands.

HEVAJRA
Skt. Mahāyāna Buddhist divinity represented with eight heads and sixteen arms dancing on a demon.

HĪNAYĀNA
Skt. "The Small Vehicle". Name given to the philosophical system in contrast with the Mahāyāna – "The Great Vehicle" (on the way to salvation).

IŚVARA
Skt. Lord. Śiva.

INDRA
Skt. Name of the God of the Tempest. King of the gods.

INDRAJIT
Skt. Magician, son of Rāvana.

JATĀ
Skt. Braided chignon worn by ascetics.

KAIKEYĪ
Skt. One of the wives of Dasaratha, father of Rāma. She plotted the exile of Rāma.

KAILĀSA
Skt. Mountain in the Himālayas. Śiva's palace.

KĀLA
Skt. Time, death. Kāla is represented by a monstrous head.

KAṂSA
Skt. Prince of Mathurā and Krishna's uncle. A prophecy that he would be killed by one of his sister's sons caused him to slay all his nephews at birth. Krishna escaped and when he became a man slew Kaṃsa.

KAṬAKAHASTA
Skt. Gesture. The first two fingers join the thumb forming a ring to hold a flower or an attribute.

KAURAVA
Skt. Descendants of Kuru. Their struggle with their cousins, the Pandava, are recounted in the Mahābhārata.

KRISHNA
Skt. "The Black One", the name of a hero, the incarnation of Viṣṇu.

KURUKṢETRA
Skt. Battlefield where the last struggle between the Pandava and the Karauva took place.

KUT
Funerary stele in Champa.

LAKṢMAṆA
Skt. Younger brother and companion of Rāma.

LAKṢMĪ
Skt. Goddess of Beauty, wife of Viṣṇu. She is also identified with the Goddess of Prosperity who arose from the "Churning of the sea of milk".

LINGA
Skt. Idol representing the phallus of Śiva.

LOKAPĀLA
Skt. Guardian of the points of the compass.

LOKEŚVARA
Skt. "The Lord of all the worlds", a Bodhisattva, also called Avalokiteśvara.

MAITREYA
Skt. "The Friendly One", name of a Bodhisattva who is the future Buddha.

MAHĀBHĀRATA
Skt. Epic poem about the rivalry between the five Pandava and their fifty Kaurava cousins. The Pandava were helped by Krishna in their battles.

MAHĀYĀNA
Skt. The Great Vehicle. A Buddhist philosophical system.

MAKARA
Skt. A sea-monster with fangs and a trunk, sometimes identified as a crocodile.

MĀRA
Skt. Personification of death and the passions. Māra is identified in Buddhist law with the spirit of evil, the enemy of Buddha.

MERU
Skt. Legendary mountain of gold and precious stones. Home of the gods.

MON
Race of people related to the Khmer, who established themselves in Burma and the north-east of Thailand.

MUDRĀ
Skt. Symbolic gesture of the hands and fingers.

MUKHALINGA
Skt. *Linga* with the head of Śiva.

NANG THORANI
Kh. Cambodian name for the earth goddess (Skt. Dharaṇī), who was called to witness by Buddha in his victory over Māra.

NĀGA
Skt. Snakes, water-gods, usually polycephalic. In pre-Angkor art, as in India, they may appear with a human body in a halo of cobra-hoods. *Nāga-rāja* – king of the serpents.

NANDIN
Skt. "The Delightful One", name of the bull on which Śiva rides.

PĀLI
Language of the holy texts, partially Indian. The Buddhist canon is written in Pāli.

PALLAVA
Kingdom of the Dravidian Indians, situated in the east of the Dekkan. It was at its height in the 7th century. Pallava culture had a marked influence on the Indianized states of Indo-China.

PANDAVA
Skt. Descendants of Pandu. Their struggle with their cousins the Kaurava are recounted in the Mahābhārata (q.v.).

POPIL
Kh. Metal candle-holder in the form of a banyan leaf.

PREAH PEAN
Kh. Group of Buddhas in the Southern Gallery of the cruciform court at Angkor Vat.

PRAJÑĀPĀRAMITĀ
Skt. "Perfect Wisdom". Mahāyāna Buddhist female divinity.

RĀKṢASAS
Skt. Demons. The *rākṣasas* of Laṇkā (Ceylon) commanded by Ravāna were crushed by Rāma.

RĀMA
Skt. "The Charming One." Rāma, or Rāmachandra, is one of the *avatars* or reincarnations of Viṣṇu and the hero of the Rāmāyana. Son of Dasaratha, king of Ayudhyā, he was exiled on the demand of his stepmother, Kaikeyī. With the aid of an army of monkeys he crushed the followers of Rāvaṇa, king of the *rākṣasas* on the island of Laṅkā (Ceylon) who had abducted Sītā, his wife. He was crowned king at Ayudhyā after this victory.

RĀMĀYANA
Skt. The Adventures of Rāma. An epic poem by Valmiki.

RĀVAṆA
Skt. A demon king of Ceylon who was vanquished by Rāma (q.v.).

RUDRA
Skt. God of the Tempest and Destruction, identified with Śiva.

ŚAKA
Skt. Indian calendar measurement which starts in 78 A.D.

SAKRA
Skt. Disc. One of the attributes of Viṣṇu in the Brahman iconography. The symbolic wheel of the law.

ŚĀKYA
Skt. Royal line of Kapilavastu whence Buddha arose.

ŚĀKYAMUNI
The ascetic of the Śakya people, the Buddha.

ŚAMBHU
Skt. He who brings joy. "The Benevolent One" – Śiva.

SAMPOT
Kh. Undergarment worn by the Cambodians draped round the hips and knotted in front; the ends are passed between the legs and attached to a belt behind.

SANSKRIT
Skt. Sacred language deriving from Indo-European. It is the language of the religious texts of Aryan India.

ŚILPAŚĀSTRA
Skt. Indian didactic treatise on art.

SĪMĀ
Skt. Boundary marking the sanctuary in a Buddhist temple.

SĪTĀ
Skt. "Furrow", daughter of Janaka, king of Mithila in the Ganges basin. She was called Sītā because she appeared in a furrow while Janaka was ploughing. She became Rāma's wife.

ŚIVA
Skt. One of the gods of the Trimūrti. A destructive god given the euphemistic name of the Propitiator.

ŚRĪVIJAYA
Skt. Name of an Indonesian kingdom which grew up in Sumatra during the 8th century.

STŪPA
Skt. Dome-shaped Buddhist monument for the preservation of relics, or built to commemorate a religious festival.

SUGRĪVA
Skt. "The Stiff-necked One", king of the monkeys, who was overthrown by his brother Vālin, but re-established on the

throne by his ally Rāma. His army of monkeys helped Rāma to vanquish Rāvaṇa.

SUKHODAYA
Skt. Capital of a Thai kingdom founded on the middle reaches of the Menam, which won its independence from the Khmer kingdom towards the middle of the 18 th century.

TANGTOK
Kh. An exhibition in the royal palace celebrating the king's birthday.

THERAVĀDA
Skt. "The Wisdom of the Ancients": Buddhist doctrine expounded in the Pāli canon.

TILOTTAMA
Skt. An *apsaras* sent by the gods to sow seeds of discord between the two *asura* brothers Sunda and Upasunda.

TRIBHANGA
Skt. "Thrice bent": cf. Trans. notes (p. 257).

TRIŚŪLA
Skt. Śiva's trident.

UGRA
Skt. "The Impetuous, the Terrible One" – Śiva.

UMĀ
Skt. Goddess, daughter of the Himālaya, wife of Śiva, sometimes called Parvatī and Durgā.

UṢNĪṢA
Skt. In late Buddhist texts and iconography a cranial bump; but not its original meaning. In the older lists of auspicious signs by which a great man or universal king may be recognized, the word *uṣṇīṣa* means simply a turban, symbol of kingship in ancient India.

VAJRA
Skt. Symbol of lightning, comprising a very short stick with either three or five points.

VAJRAPĀṆI
Skt. He who bears the lightning symbol, a *yakṣa* converted by the Buddha and now a Bodhisattva.

VĀLIN
Skt. A monkey who usurped his brother Sugrīva's throne and was killed by an arrow shot by Rāma while struggling with Sugrīva.

VIṢṆU
Skt. One of the *trimūrti*, god of the sun. He descends to earth in the form of *avatars* (q. v.) to save it from danger.

YAKṢA
Skt. Supernatural beings which were probably plant spirits originally. Although they are usually beneficent guardians of cities and kingdoms, they sometimes take on the aspect of demons.

YOGIN
Skt. Ascetic who follows the rules of the philosophical system known as *yoga*.

BIBLIOGRAPHY

Abbreviations:

A.A.	Arts Asiatiques, Musée Guimet, Paris
Ar. As.	Artibus Asiae, Ascona
B.C.A.I.	Bulletin de la Commission archéologique de l'Indochine, Paris
B.E.F.E.O.	Bulletin de l'Ecole Française d'Extrême-Orient, Hanoï, Saïgon et Paris
B.S.E.I.	Bulletin de la Société des Etudes Indochinoises, Saïgon
J.A.	Journal Asiatique, Paris
R.A.A.	Revue des Arts Asiatiques, Musée Guimet, Paris

BELLUGUE, P.: *L'Anatomie des formes et la statuaire Khmère ancienne.* Paris 1926. (Art et Archéologie Khmers, II.)

BOISSELIER, J.: *La statuaire khmère et son évolution.* Paris et Saïgon 1955.

BOISSELIER, J.: *Tendances de l'art khmer.* Paris 1965. (Annales du Musée Guimet.)

BOISSELIER, J.: «Évolution du diadème dans la statuaire khmère», in: *B.S.E.I.*, XXV, 2, 1950.

BOISSELIER, J.: «Note sur deux Buddhas parés des galeries d'Angkor Vat», in: *B.S.E.I.*, XXV, 3, 1950.

BOISSELIER, J.: «Beng Mealea et la chronologie des monuments du style d'Angkor Vat», in: *B.E.F.E.O.*, XLVI, 1, 1952.

BOISSELIER, J.: «Le Harihara de Bakong», in: *B.E.F.E.O.*, XLVI, 1, 1952.

BOISSELIER, J.: «Précisions sur la statuaire de style d'Angkor Vat», in: *B.E.F.E.O.*, XLVI, 1, 1952.

BOISSELIER, J.: «Réflexions sur l'art de Jayavarman VII», in: *B.S.E.I.* XXVII, 3, 1952.

COEDÈS, G.: *Catalogue des pièces originales de sculpture khmère conservées au Musée Indochinois du Trocadéro et au Musée Guimet.* Paris 1910.

COEDÈS, G.: «Les bas-reliefs d'Angkor Vat», in: *B.C.A.I.*, 1911.

COEDÈS, G.: *Bronzes khmers.* Paris et Bruxelles 1923. (Ars Asiatica, 5.)

COEDÈS, G.: *Les Collections archéologiques du Musée National de Bangkok.* Paris et Bruxelles 1924. (Ars Asiatica, 12.)

COEDÈS, G.: *Pour mieux comprendre Angkor.* 2nd ed. Paris 1947.

COEDÈS, G.: *Les États hindouisés d'Indochine et d'Indonésie.* Paris 1948. (Histoire du Monde, VIII.)

COEDÈS, G.: *Inscriptions du Cambodge.* 7 vols. Hanoï puis Paris 1937–1964.

CORAL RÈMUSAT, G. de: *L'Art khmer. Les grandes étapes de son évolution.* Paris 1940. (Etudes d'Art et d'Ethnologie asiatiques, I.)

DUFOUR, H., ET G. CARPEAUX: *Le Bayon d'Angkor Thom.* Paris 1910.

DUPONT, P.: *La statuaire préangkorienne.* Ascona 1955.

DUPONT, P.: «Art de Dvâravatî et Art khmer. Le buddha debout de l'époque du Bayon», in: *R.A.A.*, IX, 1935.

DUPONT, P.: «La statuaire en ronde bosse dans l'Asie du Sud-Est», in: *R.A.A.*, X, 1936.

DUPONT, P.: «L'art du Kulen et les débuts de la statuaire angkorienne», in: *B.E.F.E.O.*, XXXVI, 2, 1936.

DUPONT, P.: «Vishnu mitré de l'Indochine Occidentale», in: *B.E.F.E.O.* XLI, 2, 1941.

DUPONT, P.: «Les Buddha sur nâga dans l'art khmer», in: *Ar. As.* XIII, 1/2, 1950.

DUPONT, P.: «Les premières images brahmaniques de l'Indochine», in: *B.S.E.I.*, XXVI, 2, 1951.

GITEAU, M.: *Guide du Musée National de Phnom-Penh. I: Sculpture.* Phnom-Penh 1960.

GITEAU, M.: «L'Expression de la sensibilité dans l'art khmer», in: *A.A.*, *III*, 1955.

GITEAU, M.: «Note sur un Garuda récemment entré au Musée National de Phnom-Penh», in: *A.A.*, VIII, 3, 1961.

GLAIZE, M.: *Les Monuments du groupe d'Angkor. Guide.* 2nd ed. Saïgon 1948.

GROSLIER, B.-PH.: *Angkor: Hommes et pierres.* Paris 1956. – German edition: *Angkor. Eine versunkene Kultur im indochinesischen Dschungel.* Köln 1956.
GROSLIER, B.-PH.: *Indochine. Carrefour des Arts.* Paris 1961. – German edition: *Hinterindien. Kunst im Schmelztiegel der Rassen.* Baden-Baden 1960.
GROSLIER, G.: *Recherches sur les Cambodgiens.* Paris 1921.
GROSLIER, G.: «Notes sur la sculpture khmère», in: *Etudes Asiatiques, B.E.F.E.O., 1.* – Publiées à l'occasion du 25e anniversaire de l'Ecole Française d'Extrême-Orient.
GROSLIER, G.: *Les Collections khmères du Musée Albert Sarraut à Phnom-Penh.* Paris 1931. (Ars Asiatica, XVI.)
LUNET DE LA JONQUIÈRE, E.-ED.: *Inventaire descriptif des monuments du Cambodge.* 3 vols. Paris 1902–1911.
MALLERET, L.: *Catalogue du Musée Blanchard de la Brosse. I: Arts de la famille indienne.* Saïgon 1937.
MARCHAL, H.: *La collection khmère. Musée Louis Finot.* Hanoï 1939.
MARCHAL, H.: *Le décor et la sculpture khmers.* Paris 1951. (Etudes d'Art et d'Ethnologie asiatiques, 3.)
MARTINI, F.: «En marge de Râmâyana cambodgien», in: *B.E.F.E.O.*, XXXVIII, 1938, and in: *J.A.*, CCXXXVIII, 1950.
PARMENTIER, H.: «Catalogue du Musée Khmer de Phnom-Penh», in: *B.E.F.E.O.*, XII, 3, 1912.
PARMENTIER, H.: *Art khmer primitif.* Paris 1927.
PARMENTIER, H.: *Art khmer classique.* 2 vols. Paris 1939. (Publications de l'École Française d'Extrême-Orient.)
STERN, PH.: *Le Bayon d'Angkor et l'évolution de l'art khmer.* Paris 1927.
STERN, PH.: «Esquisse d'une évolution de la statuaire», in: *Musée Guimet, Catalogue des collections indochinoises,* Paris 1934.
STERN, PH.: *La transition de l'art préangkorien à l'art angkorien et Jayavarman II.* Paris 1932. (Etudes d'orientalisme à la mémoire de Raymonde Linossier, II.)
STERN, PH.: «Le style du Kulen», in: *B.E.F.E.O.*, XXXVIII, 1, 1938.

TRANSLATOR'S NOTES

1 The French word *hanchement* for the Sanskrit *tribhanga* has been translated as "oblique" or "oblique position". "*Tribhanga* means 'thrice bent'. The weight rests on one leg, the other knee is bent with the foot slightly advanced. Thus the line of the hips is oblique and that of the shoulders slopes in the other direction." William Willetts, Chinese Art, volume I.

2 Buddha Commaille. (Albert Sarraut Museum, Phnom-Penh) Sandstone: H. 0.93 m. cf. Boisselier, *La Statuaire Khmère et son évolution*, plate 100. *Buddha on a nāga. Ars Asiatica XVI. Art du Xe au XIe siècle*. Paris, Brussels, 1931.

"The Sage, although he seems to be naked, is actually wrapped in his monk's robe which is conventionally shown in statues of the period by a thickening of the stone between the torso and the left arm, a formula inherited from pre-Khmer art. The sakra is engraved on the palm and the sole of the foot. The hooded *nāga*-heads have not been recovered.

The troubled fate of the Bayon and the discussions and differences of opinion about the date of its construction make it very difficult to date this statue. However it is known that Jayavarman VII collected figures from many places to put in this monument and it is possible that some of them may be considerably older than the temple itself. It could be regarded as the masterpiece of a period when Khmer art achieved a classic purity, by an unbiassed observer, though allowances must be made for the absence of works for comparison..."

3 Koki wood. *Hopea Species*. Either Mengarawan, Odorata, Lowii, Sangal or Pierrei.

PLAN OF THE GREAT SQUARE OF ANGKOR THOM

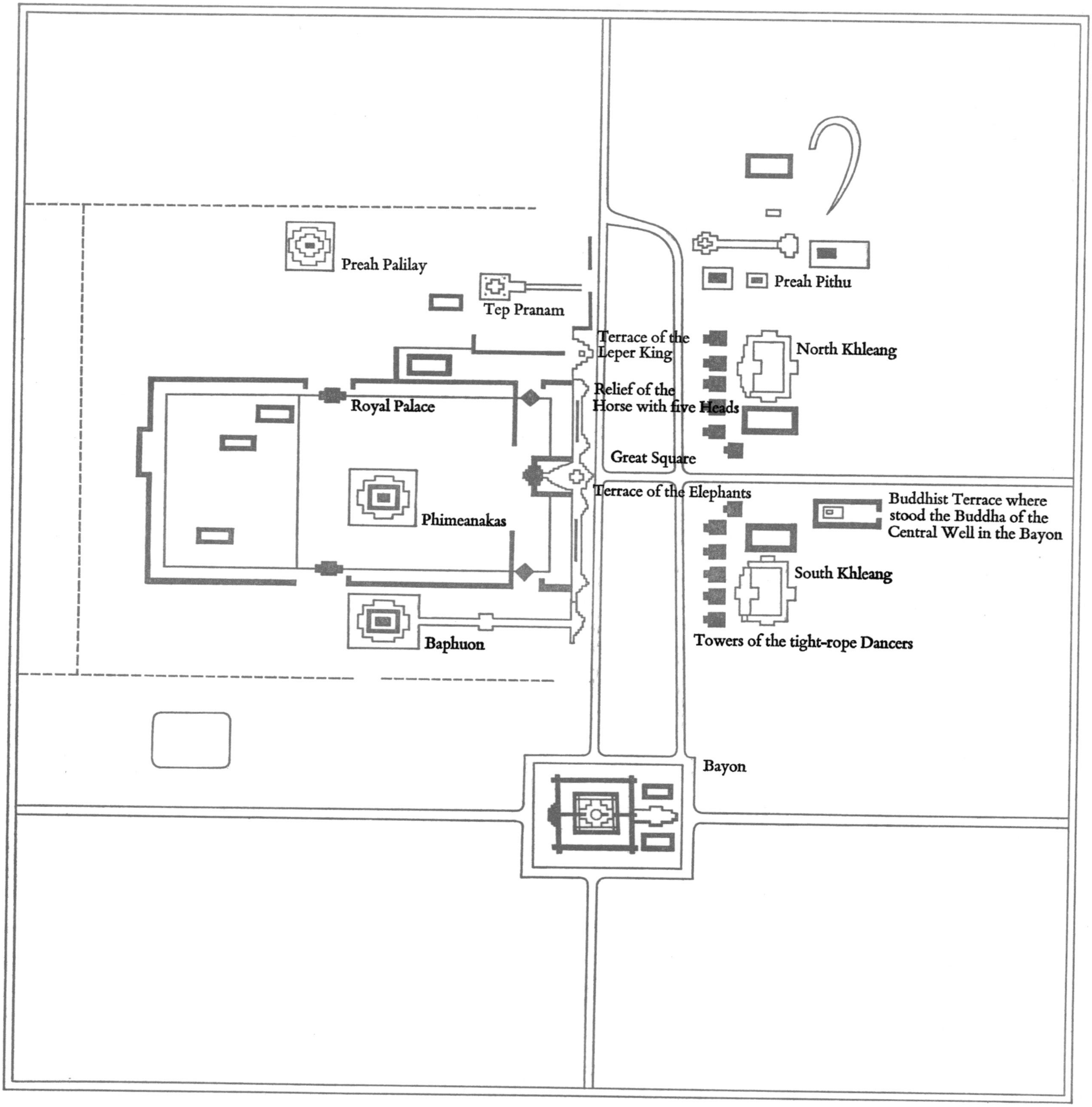

MAP OF CAMBODIA

△ = monuments sited on a hill or mountain (= phnom)
○ = modern city
+ = ancient site

PLAN OF THE GREAT SQUARE OF ANGKOR THOM

MAP OF CAMBODIA

PLAN OF THE MONUMENTS AT ANGKOR

263–266

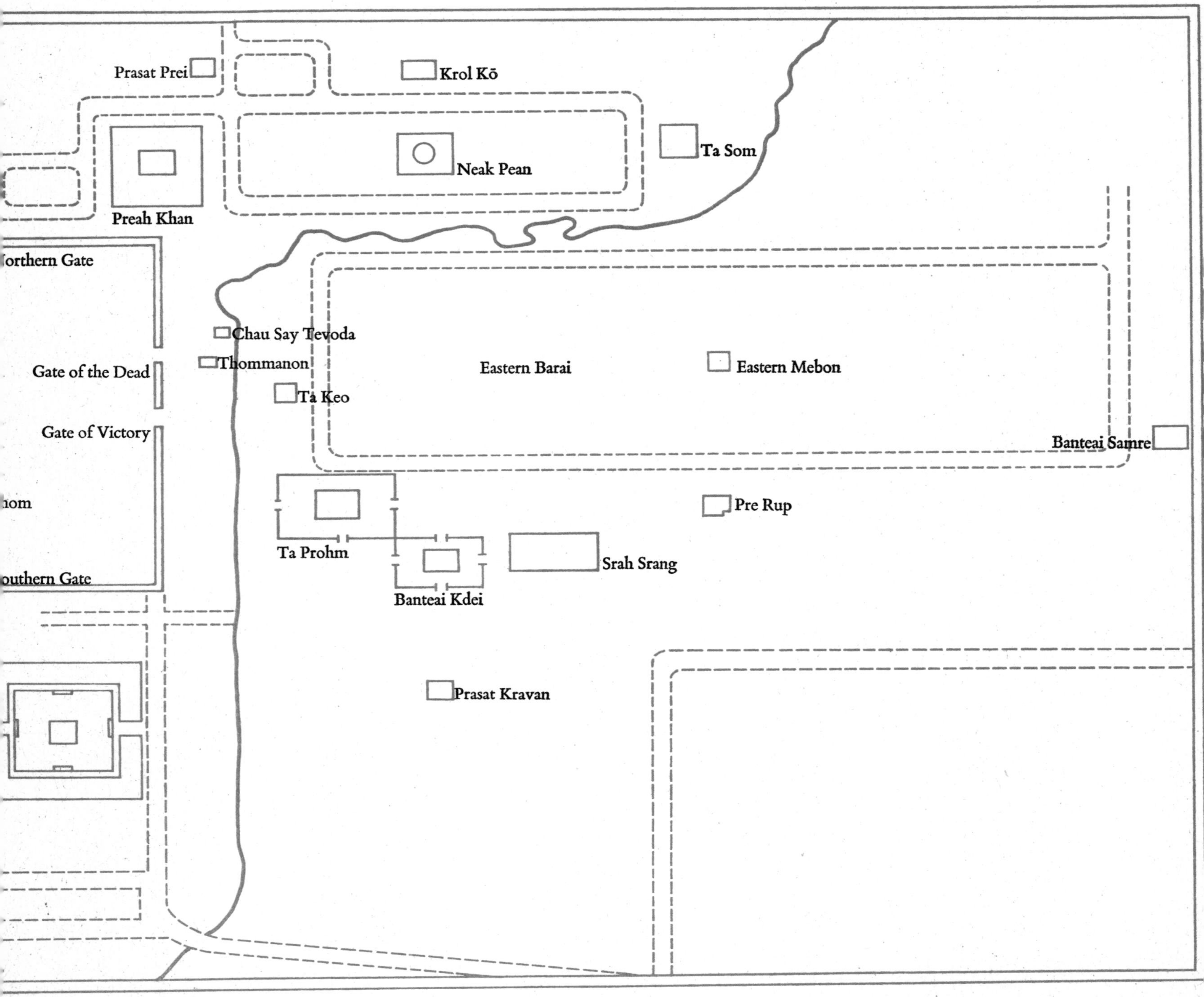
Prasat Prei
Krol Kō
Neak Pean
Ta Som
Preah Khan
orthern Gate
Chau Say Tevoda
Thommanon
Gate of the Dead
Eastern Barai
Eastern Mebon
Ta Keo
Gate of Victory
Banteai Samre
om
Pre Rup
Ta Prohm
Srah Srang
outhern Gate
Banteai Kdei
Prasat Kravan

PLAN OF THE MONUMENTS AT ANGKOR

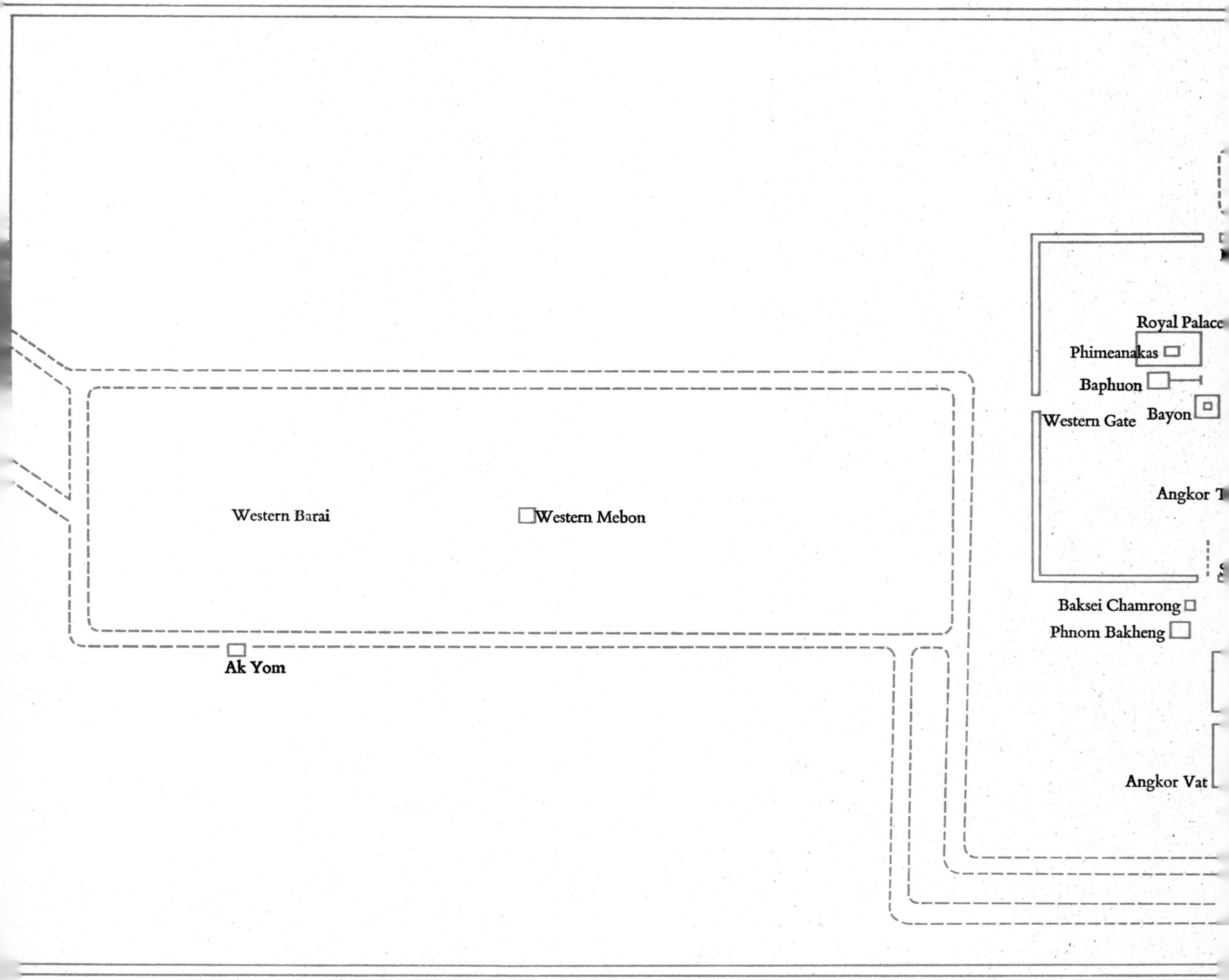

MAP OF CAMBODIA

△ = monuments sited on a hill or mountain (= phnom)
○ = modern city
\+ = ancient site

PLAN OF THE GREAT SQUARE
OF ANGKOR THOM

MAP OF CAMBODIA

	CAMBODIA			SOUTH EAST ASIA
	KINGS	HISTORICAL EVENTS	ARTISTIC STYLES	
1				
		Indian expansion		
100				
200	200 Fan cho-nan			200 Formation of Lin-yi, the first state of Champa
				250 Pyu kingdom of the Irrawady, Burma
300				
	357 Tchan-t'an	Visit of Chinese ambassador Second Hindu expansion in Fu-nan		
400	400 Regin of Kauṇḍinya Jayavarman			
		484 Kauṇḍinya Jayavarman dispatches the monk Nāgasena to China		
500	514 Death of Kauṇḍinya Jayavarman 514–39 Rudravarman		Phnom Da. Style A.	500 Champa. Foundation of Mi-son E_1
600				600 Buddhism

	INDIA	CHINA AND THE FAR EAST	THE WEST	THE MIDDLE EAST
1	1 Sāñchī stūpa 78 Śaka period 85 Separation of the two religious schools Mahāyāna and Hīnayāna	8 End of the Western Han dynasty 73 General Pan Ch'ao conquers Central Asia	Birth of Christ 14 Death of Augustus 80 Construction of the Coliseum 96 Accession of the Antonines	70 Destruction of the Temple at Jerusalem
100	Begram ivories Amarāvatī stūpa 144 Kanishka Greco-Buddhist art Mathura school of sculpture	160 The first Buddhist monks in China	123 Ptolemy's *Geography*	138-61 Baalbek
200	200 Composition of the Mahābhārata Pallava dynasty appears in the Kanchi region	220 Division of China: the Three Kingdoms	211 Baths of Caracalla Establishment of the Franks on the Rhine 293 Diocletian organises the Tetrarchy	225 Beginning of the Sassanian dynasty Palace of Ctesiphon
300	300 Beginning of the Gupta dynasty	300 Nomad invasions of North China 336 Tun-huang – The Cave of the Thousand Buddhas 386–535 Period of the Northern Wei. Wei style 397 Lung-mên	311 Edict of Milan 330 Foundation of Constantinople 393 Last Olympic games	
400	400 Huns established at Gandhara Wall-paintings in caves XVI and XVII at Ajanta Ceylon. Wall-paintings of Sīgirya	Ku K'ai-chih: *Admonitions of the Instructress*	451 Defeat of Attila at Châlons 475 Deposition of the last Western Emperor 481–511 Clovis	
500	500 Temple of Deogarh Fall of the Gupta Empire Temple of Aiholi Caves of Ellura and Aurengabad 526 Temple of Mahābodhi at Bodh Goyā	557 Hsieh Ho: *The Six Canons of Painting* 593–645 Japan: Suiko period	525 St. Benedict founds a monastery on Monte Cassino 532 Constantinople: Santa Sophia 536 Ravenna: St. Vitale 590–604 Gregory the Great	531–79 Chosroes I, King of Persia
600				

COMPARATIVE CHRONOLOGY I

267–270

COMPARATIVE CHRONOLOGY II

71–274

	INDIA	CHINA AND THE FAR EAST	THE WEST	THE MIDDLE EAST
600	606–47 Harsha Temples of Māmallapuram		600–50 Invasions of Bulgars and Slavs in the Balkans	
	629–664 Voyage of Hsüang-tsang	618 Beginning of the T'ang dynasty 627–50 Reign of Li Shih-min as emperor T'ai-tsung		622 The Hijra 640 Fall of the Sassanian Empire
650				661 Beginning of the Umayyad dynasty at Damascus
	Temple of the bank of Māmallapuram	669 The Chinese in Korea 673–710 Wall-paintings on the kondō of Horyu-ji 682 Li Ssŭ-hsün – father of Chinese landscape painting The Empress Wu usurps the throne		688 Mosque of 'Umar at Jerusalem
700	700 Rāshtrakuta Pala dynasty in Bengal 712 Muslim penetration of India 725 Temple of Vijayeśvara at Pattadakal	713 Ming Huang. Painter, Wu Tao-tzŭ: landscape and Buddhist subjects Wang Wei of the Southern school of painting	711 The Arabs in Spain 714–68 Pepin the Short, king of France 722 St. Boniface first bishop of the Germans 732 Charles Martel halts the Arab invasion at Poitiers	
750		749 Erection of the Daibutsu of Todaiji at Nara in bronze, 53 ft. high c. 750 Death of Li T'ai-po	750 Umayyad Caliphate at Cordova	750 Beginning of the 'Abbasid dynasty 763–809 Reign of Harun ar-Rashid
800	800 Temple of Kailasa at Ellura	794 Japan: Jōgan, early Heian period. Capital moved to Kyōtō		c. 790 Works of Euclid translated into Arabic

	CAMBODIA			SOUTH EAST ASIA
	KINGS	HISTORICAL EVENTS	ARTISTIC STYLES	
600	600 Mahendravarman Iśanavarman I			
		Iśanavarman's first embassy to China	Temples of Sambor Prei Kuk	
650	650 Accession of Jayavarman I	Return of the capital to Angkor Borei		
				658 Burma: Kingdom of Sriksetra
			Style of Prei Kmeng	On the lower Menam: Dvāravatī Kingdom c. 680 Malaya: Empire of Srivijaya
	681 Death of Jayavarman I			Burma: Prome Foundation of the kingdom of Nan-ch'ao by the Thai
700			Prasat Andet	686 Prakasadharma. Style of Mi-son E_1
	Puskaraksa, King of Sambhupura	Cambodia divided into Ch'en-la of earth and Ch'en-la of water		
750			Kompong Preah	750 Java: foundation of the Śailendra dynasty
		Java conquers part of Ch'en-la		Java: Borobudur
800				800 Javanese raids on the Indo-Chinese coasts

COMPARATIVE CHRONOLOGY III

	INDIA	CHINA AND THE FAR EAST	THE WEST	THE MIDDLE EAST
800		800 Uighur Turks occupy Turfan Frescoes and miniatures of Turfan	800 Charlemagne, Emperor of the West Carolingian Renaissance	
		816 Japan: Foundation of the monastery of Kōyosan		
			Beginning of the Norman invasions	
				842 Great Mosque at Samarra
			843 Partition of Verdun	
850	850 Pratihara dynasty at its height	850 Fall of the T'ang dynasty		
		860–86 Huang Chao's rebellion in eastern China 868 Earliest known printed books. Found at Tun-huang	864 Foundation of Kiev	
	Restoration of the Chalukya dynasty at Mahārāshtra			
	Temple of Mukteśvara			
				879 Mosque of Ibn Tulun at Cairo
			885 Siege of Paris by the Normans	
900	900 Fall of the Pallava dynasty			

	CAMBODIA			SOUTH EAST ASIA
	KINGS	HISTORICAL EVENTS	ARTISTIC STYLES	
800	802 Accession of Jayavarman II at Indrapura			
		Coronation of Jayavarman II at Mt. Mahendra (Phnom Kulen)	Style of Phnom Kulen	
		Return of Jayavarman II to Hariharālaya (Roluoh)		
850	850 Death of Jayavarman II 850–77 Jayavarman III			850 Prasat Damrei Krap constructed on the Phnom Kulen in Cambodia
	877–89 Indravarman	Construction of the Barai of Hariharālaya	879 Preah Ko 881 Bakong	880 Burma: foundation of Pegu Champa: Hoa-lai style Java: Sewu, Prambanam, Borobudur 890 Champa: dynasty of Indrapura
900	889–900 Yaśovarman	Transfer of the capital to Yaśodharapura (Angkor) Construction of the Eastern Barai at Angkor	893 Lolei, Phnom Krom, Phnom Bakheng, Phnom Bok	Champa: Style of Dwong-Dzuong

COMPARATIVE CHRONOLOGY IV

279–282

	INDIA	CHINA AND THE FAR EAST	THE WEST	THE MIDDLE EAST
900	900–1170 Chola Empire		901 Arab conquest of Sicily	
		907–960 The Five Dynasties		
			910 Founding of Cluny Abbey 911 Treaty of St. Clair-sur-Epte	912 First Fatimid attack on Egypt
			936 Hungarian invasion halted at the battle of Lechfeld (955)	
		947 The Ch'i-tan established at Peking		
950	949 Battle of Takkolam			
	954 Temple of Lakṣmaṇa at Khajurāho			
		960 Beginning of the Sung dynasty 960–1125 Northern Sung	961 Otto the Great founds the Holy Roman Empire	
				969 Fatimid conquest of Egypt and invasion of Syria 970–79 Al-Azhar mosque, Cairo
	973 Mahārāshtra: the Rāshtrakuta overthrown by the Chalukya of Kalyāni			
	986–1014 Emperor Chola Rājarāja		987 Beginning of the Capetian dynasty 991 The Danes in England	
1000	998–1030 Mahmud of Ghazna			

	CAMBODIA			SOUTH EAST ASIA
	KINGS	HISTORICAL EVENTS	ARTISTIC STYLES	
900	900 Accession of Harshavarman I			Java: first appearance of the Matāram dynasty 900 Champa: style of Mi-son A_1
			Baksei Chamkrong	
	Iśanavarman II			
	928–41 Jayavarman IV	921 Usurpation by Jayavarman IV Capital at Koh Ker		Java: Matāram dynasty moves its capital to the west Java: Composition of the Javanese Rāmāyana
	941–44 Harshavarman II	Return of the capital to Angkor		
	944–68 Rājendravarman	945–6 Campaign against the Cham		946 Champa: the Khmer capture the golden statue of Pō Nagar of Nhatrang
950				
			952 Eastern Mebon	
			961 Pre Rup	
			967 Banteai Srei	
	968–1001 Jayavarman V			
				971 Jaya Indravarman restores the Pō Nagar
			Ta Keo	980–1009 Vietnam: Earlier Lê dynasty Struggles between Champa and Vietnam The Javanese attack on Srīvijaya
1000				

COMPARATIVE CHRONOLOGY V

283–286

	INDIA	CHINA AND THE FAR EAST	THE WEST	THE MIDDLE EAST
1000	1000 Khajurahe: Bhuranśvar (Lingarāja)			1000 Seljuk Turks invade Transoxania
	1005 Mohammedan occupation of the Punjab Chola invasion of Ceylon		1010 Conquest of Sicily by the knights of Normandy	
			1015 Hildesheim Cathedral: bronze doors	
	Mahmud invades the eastern delta of the Ganges Temple of Tanjore		1023 Frescoes at St. Savin-sur-Gartempe	
			1030 Speyer Cathedral	
	1033 The Ghaznavids take Benares		1033 Death of Canute the Great	1037 Death of Avicenna (Ibn Sina)
		1040–1100 Li Lung-mien	1042–85 St. Mark's, Venice	
1050				
		1051–1107 Mi Fu. Embodiment of the *wên jên* ideal		
			1054 The Great Schism	
	1055–1113 Rāmanuja			1055 The Turks at Baghdad
	Chola – Chalukya		1065 *Chanson de Roland*	
	Chola overthrown in Ceylon	1068 Social Reform party of Wang An-shih (1019–85) which took steps to secure a balanced economy. Almost a Sung welfare state	1066 Norman Conquest of England 1075 Investiture disputes	
			1079 Foundation of Winchester Cathedral	1078 Capture of Jerusalem by the Turks
	Fall of the Ghaznavids		1096 Foundation of Durham Cathedral	
1100				1099 Capture of Jerusalem by the Crusaders

	CAMBODIA			SOUTH EAST ASIA
	KINGS	HISTORICAL EVENTS	ARTISTIC STYLE	
)0	1001–2 Udayādityavarman I 1002–50 Sūryavarman I	1003–11 War of Succession		
			Khleang style at Angkor, Phimeanakas, the Gopura of the Royal Palace	
		1011 Sūryavarman controls the throne	Provincial Khleang: Preah Vihear, Phnom Chisor, Vat Ek, part of Vat Ph'u	
				1025 The Chola overthrow Sumatra
				1035 Airlanga unifies Java
				1044 Champa: Vijaya capital 1044–77 Burma: reign of Anoratha
o	1050–66 Udayādityavarman II	1051 Revolt quelled by Sangrama	Baphuon style At Angkor: Baphuon, Western Mebon	c. 1050 Burma: conversion to Theravādic Buddhism
			Provinces: Prasat Khna Sen Keo	
		1065 Two revolts quelled by Sangrama		
			Preah Vihear Vat Ph'u	1074–81 Champa: Harivarman IV
		Unsuccessful battle against the Cham		
	1080–1107 Jayavarman VI			
				1084–1112 Burma: Kyanzittha Burma: Temple of Ananda at Pagan
)				

COMPARATIVE CHRONOLOGY VI

287–290

	INDIA	CHINA AND THE FAR EAST	THE WEST	THE MIDDLE EAST
1100		1101 Hui-tsung. Emperor. Founder of the Academy of Painting	1100 Monastery of Moissac	
	Hoysala		1120–1178 Autun Cathedral	
		1122–1215 Peking occupied by the Northern Liao, called Chin 1127–1276 Southern Sung dynasty. Capital: Hang Chou		1128 Zengi, Atabeg of Mosul
			1130 Abelard's *Ethics* 1130–95 Chrétien de Troyes 1132–44 Abbey of St. Denis	
			1145 Chartres: Royal Portal	
	Reform of Singhalese Buddhism			
1150			1150 University of Paris 1155–70 *Tristan and Iseult* 1160 *Das Nibelungenlied* 1163–1235 Notre-Dame de Paris 1167 Oxford University 1170 Murder of Thomas à Becket	
	1171 Temple of Kāśīvisveśvara			1171 Salah ad-Din ends the Fatimid Caliphate of Cairo
			1182–1226 Saint Francis of Assisi	
	1186 Mahmud of Ghor	1185 Japan: Shōgunate government established 1185–1333 Japan: Kamakura period		1187 Capture of Jerusalem by Salah ad-Din
1200	1192–1196 Conquest of Northern India by the Mongols 1193 Sultanate of Delhi 1193–1239 Kutub Minar, Delhi 1202 Taking of Benares by the Mohammedans	c. 1200 Ma Yüan. Sung Academician Mu Ch'i and Liang K'ai (c. 1140–1210) 1215 Occupation of Peking by the Mongols. Genghiz Khan	1198–1216 Innocent III 1209–29 The Albigensian Crusade 1214 Battle of Bouvines 1215 Magna Carta 1216 Foundation of the Dominican Order	1204 Capture of Constantinople by the Fourth Crusade

CAMBODIA			SOUTH EAST ASIA
KINGS	HISTORICAL EVENTS	ARTISTIC STYLES	
1107–13 Dharanīndravarman I			
1113–c. 50 Sūryavarman II	Revolt of the future Sūryavarman II. Civil War	Angkor Vat style at: Angkor, Angkor Vat, Preah Pithu, Preah Palilay, Thommanon, Chau Say Tevoda, Banteai Samre	1113 Champa: death of Jaya Indravarman II
	1128 First Cambodian expedition against the Dai Viet	Provinces: Centre of Preah Khan of Kompong Svay, Beng Mealea, part of Vat Ph'u, Phimai	
	1138 Second expedition against the Dai Viet		1141 Pagan: Temple of Shwegu
	1145 Invasion of Champa by the Khmer. Seizure of Vijaya Failure of expedition against the Dai Viet		1145 Champa: Annexation by the Khmer 1149 Champa: Jaya Harivarman throws off the Khmer yoke
Dharanīndravarman II Yaśovarman II			Thailand: Adityarāja
1165–77 Tribhuvanādityavarman	1165 Yaśovarman is overthrown by Tribhu-vanādityavarman		1164 Singhalese raid on Pegu Burma: building of the Dhammayan at Pagan
	1177 Cham invasion		1177 The Cham seize the Khmer capital 1180 Singhalese raid on Burma
1181 Coronation of Jayavarman VII		Bayon style At Angkor: Banteai Kdei, Ta Prohm (1186), Preah Khan (1191), Neak Pean, Bayon, Courts of Angkor	
	1203 Champa becomes a Khmer province	Provinces: Banteai Chmar, part of Preah Khan of Kompong Svay, Vat Nokor, Ta Prohm of Bati	1200 Thailand: Wat Kukut
1219 Death of Jayavarman VII			

COMPARATIVE CHRONOLOGY VII

	INDIA	CHINA AND THE FAR EAST	THE WEST	THE MIDDLE EAST
1220				
			1226–70 Saint Louis c. 1230 Bamberg Cathedral sculptures	
	Temple of Kanarak		1236–c. 1307 Cimabue	
			1243–47 La Sainte Chapelle 1245–1380 Siena Cathedral	
	Pandya art	1254–1322 Chao Mêng-fu: painter of horses	1250–73 The Great Interregnum 1265–1321 Dante 1266–1337 Giotto 1266–74 Saint Thomas Aquinas: *Summa Theologica*	1258 Capture of Baghdad by the Mongols. Fall of the 'Abbasid Caliphate 1261 End of the Latin Empire of Constantinople
		1270–1368 Yüan dynasty 1271–95 Marco Polo's visit to the court of Kublai Khan 1279 Kublai Khan completes the conquest of China	1275–1524 Ratisbon Cathedral	
	1290 Firuz seizes Delhi		1285–1314 Philip the Fair 1291 Formation of the Swiss Confederation	1291 Loss of St. John of Acre
1300	1306–1326 Mohammedan conquest of the Deccan 1320 Seizure of Delhi by the Tughluk dynasty Capital at Devagiri (Daulatabad)		1304–74 Petrarch 1316–91 The Popes at Avignon	1320–88 Persian poet, Hafiz
		1333 Japan: Restoration of Kenmu	1337 Start of the Hundred Years War	
			1340–1400 Geoffrey Chaucer	
1350	1350 Division of the Delhi sultanate		1347 The Black Death	

	CAMBODIA			SOUTH EAST ASIA
	KINGS	HISTORICAL EVENTS	ARTISTIC STYLES	
20	1220–43 Indravarman II	1220 Evacuation of Champa		1220 Pagan: Temple of the Mahābodhi Java: foundation of the kingdom of Tumapel 1225 Vietnam: rise of the Tran. Conflict with Champa Java: construction of Chandi Kidal Thai: Sukhotdaya and Lavo independent c. 1250 Introduction of Islam to Indonesia Rāma Kamheng, King of Sukhodaya 1283 Champa: Mongol invasion repulsed 1283 Invention of the Thai script 1287 Mongols seize Pagan 1296 Foundation of Ch'ieng Mai 1287 End of the Kingdom of Srīvijaya Champa: construction of Po Klaung Garai 1300 Thai: Sukhodaya style Thai: Uthong style
	1243(?) Accession of Jayavarman VIII			
	1295 Abdication of Jayavarman VIII	1282 Mongol invasion repulsed		
00	Accession of Srīndravarman 1300	1296 Ch'ou Ta-k'uan in Cambodia	Construction of the Mangalārtha	
	1307 Abdication of Srīndravarman in favour of Srīndrajayavarman 1327 Accession of Jayavarmādiparameśvara			1327 Thailand: foundation of Ch'ieng Sen
		Last Sanskrit inscriptions in Cambodia		
50				

OMPARATIVE CHRONOLOGY VIII

ᴋs

	INDIA	CHINA AND THE FAR EAST	THE WEST	THE MIDDLE EAST
1350				
		1368–1644 Ming dynasty	1378–1455 Ghiberti 1378 Church of the Transfiguration at Novgorod	
	1380–1420 Life of the poet Kabir	1380 Restoration of the Great Wall		
			1386–1466 Donatello 1387–1455 Fra Angelico	1386 Timur captures Isfahan, Shiraz and Baghdad
1400	1398 Timur	1397 Japan: Kinkakuji (The Golden Pavilion) 1398–1573 Muromachi period		
			1401–28 Masaccio 1415 Execution of John Huss	
		1421 Imperial Palace at Peking 1421 Peking. Construction of the Temple of Heaven	1420–34 Brunelleschi: Dome of Florence 1425–31 Jan Van Eyck: Retable of the Mystic Lamb c. 1425–80 Jean Fouquet	
		c. 1434–1525 Tosa School of painting. Three great painters: Jasoka, Sesshu and Soami	1429 Joan of Arc at the siege of Orléans 1431–c. 1470 François Villon 1431–1506 Mantegna 1434 Cosimo dei Medici, Duke of Florence 1436 Roger Van der Weyden: *Descent from the Cross* 1447–1510 Botticelli 1450 Beginning of the Wars of the Roses	
1450			1450 Gutenberg establishes a printing-press at Mainz 1452–1519 Leonardo da Vinci 1453 End of the Hundred Years War	1453 Capture of Constant-inople by the Ottoman Tur
		1483 Japan: Ginkakuji (The Silver Pavilion)		

	CAMBODIA			SOUTH EAST ASIA
	KINGS	HISTORICAL EVENTS	ARTISTIC STYLES	
50	1350 Nippean-bat. First king mentioned in the chronicles			1350 Thailand: foundation of Ayudhyā by Rāmādhipati
		1353 Angkor seized by the Thai		1353 Foundation of the Kingdom of Laos by Lan Ch'ang
			Schools of Buddhist sculpture	1364 Thai: kingdom of Ava
				Thai: Art of Ayudhyā
00				
				1402 Foundation of Malacca
				Thailand: Wat Rājapurana at Ayudhyā
	Ponhea Yat			
		1431 Recapture of Angkor by the Thai Ponhea Yat moves his capital from Angkor to Phnom-Penh		
				Thailand: end of the kingdom of Sukhodaya
0				

INDEX

This book was printed in the workshops of Benziger & Co., A. G., Einsiedeln. – The illustrations in four colour offset were executed by Imprimeries Réunies, S. A., Lausanne. – The heliogravure reproductions were executed by Braun & Cie S. A., Mulhouse-Dornach. – The halftone blocks were made by Process Engraver Schwitter, Ltd., Basel. – The binding is by Van Rijmenam N. V., 's-Gravenhage. – Lay-out by Irmgard Loeb, Basel, after a design by André Rosselet, Auvernier (Switzerland).

Printed in Switzerland

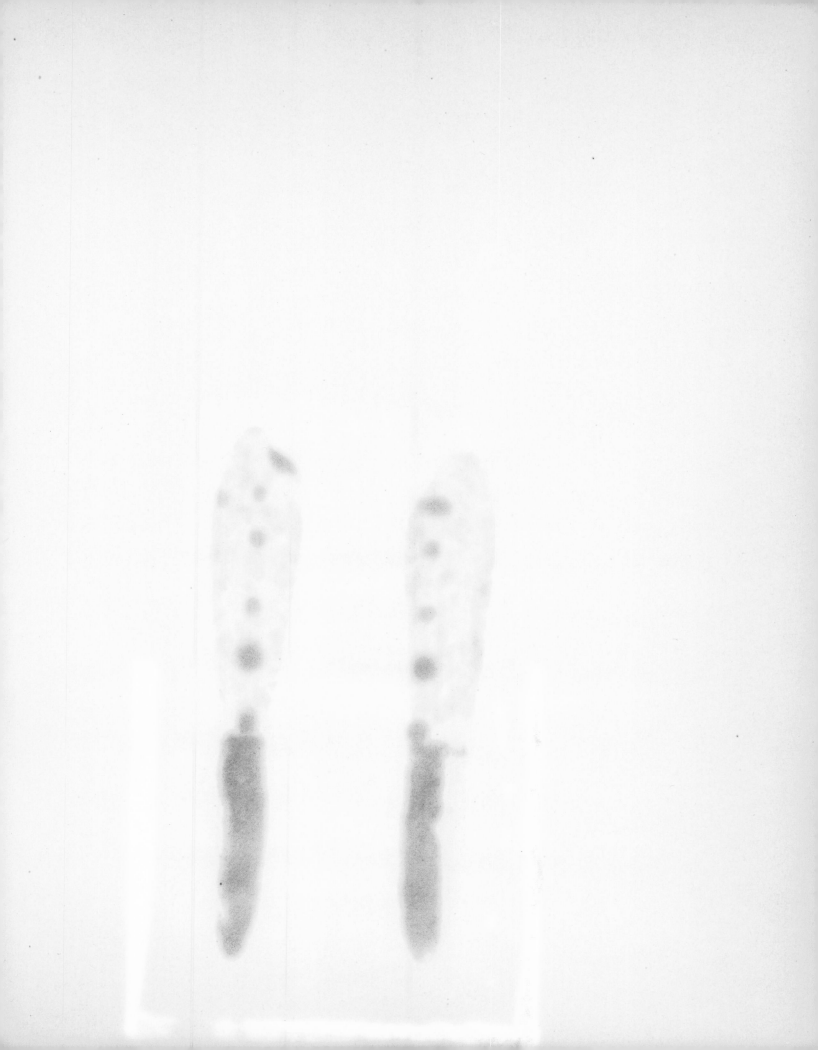

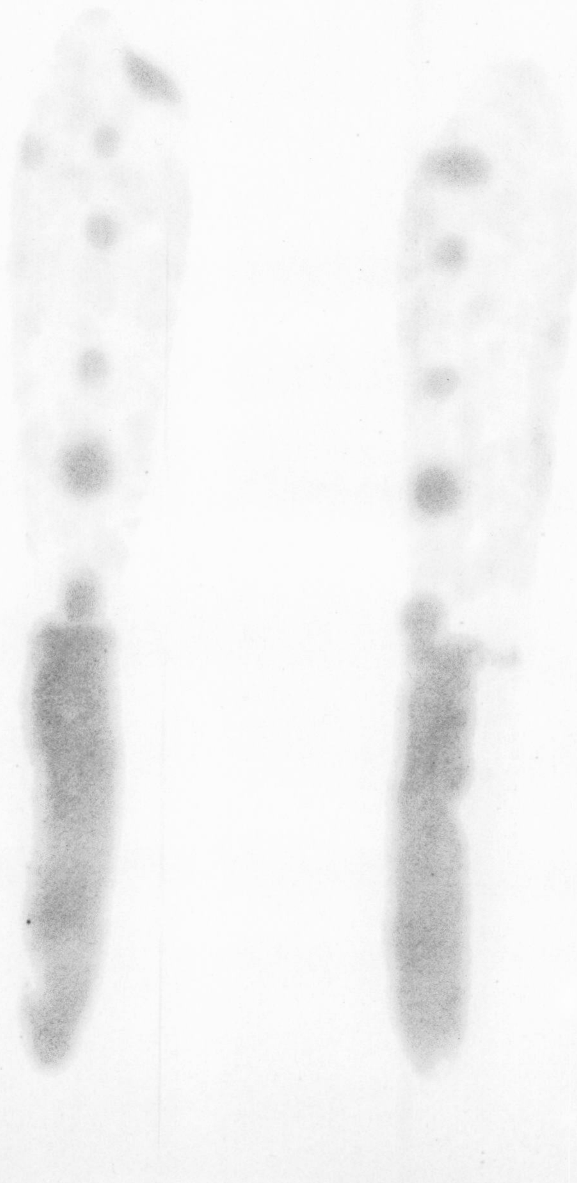